Cyber Security
in aid to
DISASTER MANAGEMENT

Cyber Security
in aid to
DISASTER MANAGEMENT

By

Col. (Dr.) Rajesh Kumar

Jharkhand Raksha Shakti University
Ranchi

KALPAZ

ISBN 978-93-5324-971-7

First Published, 2022

Published by

Kalpaz Publications
C-30, Satyawati Nagar,
Delhi – 110052
E-mail: kalpaz@hotmail.com
Ph.: 9212142040

Printed at: G. Print Process, Delhi

Distribution Network
gyanbooks.com
India, USA, Canada, UK, Australia, France

Contents

DEDICATION

I dedicate this book
CYBER SECURITY IN AID TO DISASTER MANAGEMENT
to
Captain Yashashvee Raj
(an Infantry Soldier & Aviator in Indian Army)
He motivated me by his choiced career-making and achieving the excellence alone by himself right from his RIMC days.
His total boycott & non-cooperation in my work affairs & duties has resulted adequacy to research this work.

Thank You Son...

Introduction

Cyber security is a global concern, reflecting the central importance of cyberspace for business, politics, and security. It has been an issue of concern for international security at least since 1998, when the Russian Federation first proposed a treaty in the United Nations General Assembly to reduce the risk of cyber conflict. At that time, only a few states had national programmes for cyber security[1] or cyber warfare in place. Now, more than half of all United Nations Member States have some kind of national effort to secure critical networks and to respond to cyber threats.

In the first chapter of part I, national cyber security efforts are divided into two general categories: those involving only domestic agencies[2] (usually communications ministries or law enforcement agencies) and those where the national military has a cyber-security role. The first section lists those states for which there is public information on a military role in cyber security including, in some instances, the development of offensive capabilities. The second section lists those states for which there is public information on cyber security as a civilian task.

The initial assessment undertaken in 2011 found that 68 of the 193 United Nations Member States had cyber security programmes. Of those, 32 states included cyber warfare in their military planning and organisations, while 36 states had civilian agencies charged with a domestic cyber security mission. This August 2012 assessment again surveyed publicly available information for the 193 states and found that the number of national cyber security programmes had grown to 114. Forty-seven states have cyber security programmes that give some role to the armed forces and 67 states have solely civilian programmes.

This assessment is based in publicly available sources from the states in question, from national media, published government sources, or, in some cases, government reports to multilateral organisations. It is important to note that transparency in cyber security efforts is limited, particularly

When it comes to the military use of cyber techniques, and much of the publicly available information is incomplete and uneven, reflecting the limited information that governments make available. Only six states have published military cyber strategies (with varying degrees of detail and specificity). Two other states plan to issue military cyber strategies. A further 30 identify cyber security[3] as a military concern or priority in policy documents (usually as part of national military strategies or national defence white papers).

These documents identify areas of military responsibility[4] and missions, but other information—on doctrine for use, command and control, budget, or cyber capabilities—is sparse or non-existent. A decision by governments to increase transparency in these areas could have been a stabilizing effect in the international community, or at least help to identify following issues that require greater attention.

1. Center for Strategic and International Studies, Cyber security and Cyberwarfare Preliminary Assessment of National Doctrine and Organisation, UNIDIR.

2. The three exceptions to this are Cuba, the Democratic People's Republic of Korea, and Myanmar.

States in all regions of the world now have cyber security initiatives, reflecting regional mandates (particularly in Europe), multilateral and bilateral discussions, or efforts at assistance in developing national programmes. Published information shows that 18 states in Africa have cyber security programmes, 16 states in the Americas, 39 states in Asia, 38 states in Europe, and 3 states in Oceania. Unsurprisingly, it is among the smaller and less-developed countries where no reference to national cyber security efforts could found.

The most dramatic increase since 2011 is in the number of states for which information was found showing the development of domestic cyber security programmes to protect networks and critical national infrastructures, with the number increasing from 36 to 67.

Many of these national programmes involved the most basic steps, such as passing cybercrime legislation, improving law enforcement capabilities, or creating a Computer emergency response team (CERT). States with more advanced cyber security programmes have developed strategies to protect critical infrastructure and have established dedicated organisations to carry out this responsibility.

3. Burundi, Cameroon, Egypt, Ethiopia, Ghana, Kenya, Madagascar, Mauritius, Morocco, Nigeria, Rwanda, South Africa, Sudan, Swaziland, Tunisia, Uganda, United Republic of Tanzania, and Zimbabwe.

In contrast to the growth in civilian programmes, only nine states have added military cyber programmes—41 states now have publicly acknowledged some military planning or specific military organisations for cyber activities. It appears that states are in a period of experimentation as they assess the risks and benefits of these new military capabilities, and as they develop strategies, doctrine, and organisations to best use them. The most advanced militaries are creating specific and dedicated military organisations for cyber warfare. The 2011 assessment identified 12 states that had established or planned to establish specific military cyber warfare entities.[5] By 2012, that number had grown to 27, and of these, media reports indicate that 17 are developing offensive cyber capabilities. It is likely that other states are pursuing similar organisational experiments on a covert basis.

The assessment indicates, unsurprisingly, that states with large defence budgets are most likely to invest in developing cyber warfare capabilities. The publicly available information suggests that 12 of the 15 largest military spenders have or are developing[6] dedicated cyber warfare units. Open-source information suggests that of these 12 states, 10 appear to possess or be developing offensive cyber capabilities. This growing military dimension makes cyber security an essential subject for discussion and negotiation on international security at both the regional and global level.

Cooperation on cybercrime, including cooperative efforts to develop effective national legislation, is also a major focus for national efforts, given cybercrime's transnational nature and the close relationship between crime and national security in cyberspace—the same tools used for crime can be used for espionage or attack, and often cybercriminals can be recruited to serve national purposes. The international community has recognised the importance of controlling cybercrime and has developed a number of multilateral instruments (sometimes cooperative, sometimes competing) to address it. Among the international agreements that could provide a foundation for cooperation on cybercrime, the Convention on Cybercrime has the greatest degree of support. Thirty-three states have ratified it, 11 are signatories, and another 10 have expressed their intention to sign, making the convention the de facto standard for cybercrime.

The elements of international cyber security—cooperation in building domestic security, the expansion of military capabilities, and law enforcement—present a robust agenda for multilateral work. Progress in building cooperation will take time and effort at many different levels of engagement. One encouraging development in recent years is the rapid growth of multilateral efforts, on the part of, among others, the Shanghai Cooperation Organisation, the Organisation of American States, the Asia–Pacific Economic Cooperation Forum, the Association of Southeast Asian Nations Regional Forum, the Economic Community of West African States, the

African Union, the European Union, the Organisation for Security and Co-operation in Europe, the Group of 20, the North Atlantic Treaty Organisation, and the Council of Europe. Capping these efforts, the work of the United Nations in the General Assembly, the committees and the Secretary General's Group of Governmental Experts provides a global underpinning to regional work. Chapter 2 of part I provides an overview of international and regional organisations and their activities.

The information found on cyber security programmes points to key issues at both the national and international level. These include a growing need for coordination, regionally and globally, among the many national programmes[7]. Given the degree and speed of interconnectivity among states in cyberspace, a purely national approach to cyber security could never be adequate for national defence or to meet existing obligations[8] under international law. Creating a CERT or a cybercrime unit, while a useful first step, is inadequate to protect infrastructure and information since CERTs and cyber police are often reactive rather than preventive. States cannot behave as if cyber security does not have a military dimension or that somehow it will be possible to eliminate or ban military and espionage cyber capabilities— recognition of this imposes new responsibilities upon individual states and the international community. As with others areas of cyber security, an immediate goal is to raise the level of discussion and decision-making from the technical to the political level.

Even with the limitations of publicly available data, this assessment confirms that cyber security and the military use of cyber techniques has become a central element for any discussion of national and international security. Stronger national policies and a cooperative framework of rules and understandings are needed to guide use and to reduce concern over cyber security. Current international understandings, structures, and institutions for cyber security are undeveloped and inadequate. As part II, chapter 2, of this study details, there are precedents from arms control negotiations and non-proliferation that may help to accelerate progress in making cyberspace more secure, but there are serious differences among states regarding political relations, human rights, trade, and warfare, and we are far from consensus. Part II, chapter 3, looks at some first steps towards international cooperation to secure cyberspace, specifically at embryonic efforts to create confidence- and security-building measures among states as a foundation for improved cooperation. As national programmes for both domestic security and military action continue to grow in number, resolving these issues will be a task that all states will share.

References

1. Alimo-Metcalfe B. (1993). Women in management: organisational socialisation and assessment practices that prevent career advancement. International Journal of Selection and Assessment 1, 2: 68-83.
2. Anastos D., Bedos A. and Seaman B. (1980). The development of modern management practices in Saudi Arabia. Columbia Journal of World Business, Summer 8: 1-92.
3. Argyris C. (1977). Double loop learning in organisations. H arvard Business Review, September-October 5: 9-72.
4. Adsit D.J., London M., Crom S. and Jones D. (1996). Relationships between employee attitudes, customer satisfaction and departmental performance. Journal of Management Development 15, 1: 62-75.
5. Alimo-Metcalfe B. (1993). Women in management: organisational socialisation and assessment practices that prevent career advancement. International Journal of Selection and Assessment 1, 2: 68-83.
6. Anastos D., Bedos A. and Seaman B. (1980). The development of modern management practices in Saudi Arabia. Columbia Journal of World Business, Summer 8: 1-92.
7. Argyris C. (1977). Double loop learning in organisations. H arvard Business Review, September-October 5: 9-72.
8. Arthur J. B. (1992).The link between business strategy and industrial relations systems in American Steel Minimi. Industrial and Labour Relations Review45: 488- 506.

The Emerging Cyber Security Agenda: Threats, Challenges and Responses

In the spring of 2007, Estonia was the target of politically motivated cyber-attacks which were unprecedented in scale, and were characterised by a sophisticated level of coordination. In addition to this first occasion in history where an entire country became the target of a large-scale cyber-attack, the past year witnessed also numerous other attacks and intrusions in the US, United Kingdom, France, Germany and elsewhere.[1] In 2008, well-coordinated cyber-attacks were launched to support the strategic objectives of an aggressor in a military conflict between Russia and Georgia. To add to the picture, recent years have witnessed a rapid increase of criminal activities in cyberspace, leading to the emergence of an organised cybercriminal industry, which works closely together with transnational organised crime and has some links with terrorist networks. With cyber-attacks against nation states and the rapid growth of cybercrime, the years 2007-2008 clearly mark the beginning of a new era in global security, where our dependence on Information technology can no longer be regarded as a mere technical matter, but has, instead, become a matter of survival for all modern societies.

An era of cyber security:

Cyber security[2] might sound as a catchword meaning something that "has to do with computers". In fact, the intuitive connotations attached to "cyber security" are right in a sense that they convey a notion of a core issue – our sense of vulnerability in an era of rapidly changing information technology. Advances in Information and Telecommunication Technologies (ICT) have yielded impressive rates of economic growth and innovation. However, these advances have been paralleled by an escalation in the mishandling of the same technological tools, arising from different motivations, starting with organised cybercrime and ending with mischievous behaviour by schoolchildren on Inter-net. This growth, in the use of technological tools for criminal or fraudulent purposes, points to a widening problem for the society-ties in general. The cyber-attack on Estonia, as well as subsequent serious cyber-attacks and intrusions against various other countries' governmental and commercial infrastructure, has led to the emergence of a new security agenda. National governments, as well as NATO, EU, and other international organisations have begun to consider cyber security as one of the most vital security issues.

Increasing dependence and decreasing awareness of information technology. An era of cyber security had already begun before the widespread production of PCs and other technological devices. Information security has been always a critical component of national security

Cyber security – national cyber security comprises all operations relating to electronic information, data media and information services that affect national security. Ensuring the security of a country's cyberspace includes various activities at different levels. The main objectives are to reduce the vulnerability[3] of cyberspace, prevent cyber-attacks and, in the event of an attacks, to recover the functioning of information systems as quickly as possible. In order to ensure cyber security, the following are necessary: assessing the vulnerability of the country's critical infrastructure;

establishing a system of countermeasures against cyber-attacks; determining the division of tasks between agencies and between the public and private sectors in combating cyber-attacks; improving international legislation and institutional cooperation; raising public awareness on cyber security and threats; and developing training and research programmes on cyber security.[4]

(Estonian Cyber Security Strategy) and defence, of internal security policies in large companies and of critical economic sectors (e.g. nuclear energy, air transport etc). In last two decades, the widespread use of Internet, the speed of development of information technologies, and lowering cost of ICT devices has brought about an IT revolution that has transformed our lifestyles, to an extent unimaginable a few decades ago. As the IT revolution transformed industrial societies into information societies, governmental regulations have unfortunately lagged behind the rapid developments in the ICT sector. Regulatory legislation is concentrated mostly on data protection, anti-trust policies in the ICT sector, and liberalisation of services. Up to now, the importance of information security, as a basis of a well-functioning information society, has gained relatively little attention from policy-makers and legislators, leaving the application of security measures largely to the owners of ICT systems or technical staff, with little supervision by the authorities.[5] Thus, a whole generation has grown up who have the necessary technical skills, but rather limited knowledge about the safe use of the in-formation and communication technology. General awareness of cyber threats remains quite limited, even as cyber crime has proliferated, war-like activities against nation states have occurred in cyberspace, and identity thefts and other types of computer crimes have mushroomed in every country. PC users in a majority of countries have not realised that their unprotected computer with a bandwidth connection can be part of a botnet[3] that is openly sold on the Internet by cybercriminals, and could be used to target other countries' critical infrastructure as a tool in cyber warfare. In contrast to the general unawareness about information security matters among wider public, there have always been professional communities who are well aware of the threats to national security by hostile IT penetration, most notably security analysts, military planners and people responsible for the protection of critical national infrastructures. Since the latest technology is often initially employed by de-fence systems, the cyber component in the offensive and defensive military operations has gained a central role in modern warfare. In addition to the military establishment, many Industrial countries have developed elaborate systems to protect the information technology component of critical infrastructures. Safeguarding of the governmental and military communication systems, as well as protection of critical national infrastructure and critical information infrastructure, rank highly among security concerns of nation states. While all the above mentioned issues are safeguarded by governmental procedures and control systems supervised by qualified experts, the broader public usually has limited access to information concerning the efforts and initiatives by governments focused on strengthening the state's resilience vis-à-vis cyber threats. Up to spring 2007 when the attacks on Estonia occurred, it was widely believed that protection of governmental communication systems and critical information infrastructure, provided sufficient defensive measures that ensured the IT aspect of national security. It had occurred only to a few that with the evolving interdependence between IT-services in our societies, none of the countries can guarantee the resilience of information systems in the case when they are attacked with coordinated Internet attacks using overloading data from millions of unprotected computers worldwide. Even if the critical infrastructure remains uncompromised by such attacks, a massive cyber assault carried out to disrupt the online services of the government and businesses, in order to manipulate the contents of governmental websites and to create information barriers, can create very serious disruptions for a society.

Estonian cyber-attacks and lessons for other information societies although the cyber-attacks and intrusions in cyberspace, for political and criminal motivations, had been witnessed on earlier occasions, Estonia was the first country to fall victim to Internet attacks on such a large scale. What makes the Estonian case different is the fact that attacks against Estonian governmental and private sector information infrastructure occurred simultaneously against thousands of targets, with the flood of data and coordination of the attacks being on an unprecedented scale. Although there is some dispute among the technical experts about the details concerning the attacks, the event marked a beginning of a new paradigm in international security. The Estonian case is still somewhat puzzling for leading security analysts, since the Estonian government has not revealed many of the details concerning the attacks to the public at large.

For those readers who are not familiar with the context of Estonian cyber-attacks, it should be stressed that these attacks were carried out in a larger context of politically motivated destabilising activities from within and outside the country. Cyber-attacks formed just one component of a larger information operation against the country in spring 2007. As the Estonian government started preparations for the relocation of the Soviet World War II monument from the center of Tallinn to the military cemetery, street riots and vandalism prompted the Estonian government to relocate the monument sooner than initially planned.

This move triggered many events in following weeks: a massive propaganda response, blockade of the Estonian embassy in Moscow, demonstration in streets as well as cyber hacktivism[4] and severe cyber attacks that required a professional response. From April 27 to May 18, Internet attacks occurred in several waves trying to disrupt or manipulate contents of governmental websites, to close down online services of news agencies, to disturb services of biggest banks and other private sector targets. Numerous attacking methods were used, most importantly distributed denial of service attacks, which involved sometimes very large botnets. Attacks took place at different levels simultaneously, involving hack activists, amateur hackers and professional attackers. Some of the attacks could have caused serious damage to the country's critical information infrastructure if the timely application of the rapid counter measures had failed.

To place the Estonian attacks in a larger context of similar operations, these types of attacks are usually launched in order to achieve dominance in the field of information distribution, to Hacktivism – use of computer systems by a hacker-activist for the purposes of propaganda and protest there is a detailed report issued on the Estonian attacks by the Swedish Emergency Management Agency, it includes also technical data and description of attack methods. The report "Large scale Internet attacks", SEMA Educational Series 2008:2, can be found at SEMA's website: www. krisberedskapsmyndigheten.se spread disinformation and disturb functioning of society with an aim to create chaos and panic.

In the Estonian case, the response by information security experts from the public and private sectors to the attacks was rapid and professional. The attacks there-fore could not dramatically disturb the country's information infrastructure, and the public noticed a few disruptions in online services, but did not panic.[6] Although the critical services in vital economic sectors and industrial control systems were not targeted, Estonian private sector experienced severe economic consequences, with some loss of revenues from disturbed online services.

The cyber-attacks on Estonia, and the defensive measures taken, provide other countries with an instructive lesson in how to cope with such an event. First, with the asymmetric cyber attacks originating from different networks, the response should follow the same logic and involve both domestic and international networks to assist the country under attack. The main lesson lies in the fact that asymmetry of threats in the Internet era requires new and different approaches in addressing risks in society. The Estonian reaction to the attacks was rapid and professional, facilitated by an informal small network of Internet security community, which assembled immediately for a coordinated response. Secondly, the major practical lesson, regarding the future handling of similar attacks, would be an improvement of the crises management procedures and critical infrastructure protection plans, with a special focus on regular compulsory tests and simulations. Simultaneously with fast advancing technology, vulnerabilities will develop at the same speed, and these need regular testing. Third, in this new era of threats ensuring the country's resilience should include some of the old strategies of total defence, and close public-private cooperation in society.

In defending the civilian networks against cyber threats, conventional hierarchical procedures are cumbersome, and governments need to find a way to build dialogue with the private sector, as well as with trust-based networks of IT security professionals. Fourth, in case of a serious cyber-attacks on one country, an efficient response requires international coordination. It is absolutely necessary to have supporting networks abroad that have the capacity to assist in a cyber-crisis.

In conclusion, the attacks against Estonia demonstrated to all developed information societies the vulnerability of civilian infrastructure when exposed to asymmetric threats. IT security analysts, policymakers and the general public in Estonia consider these attacks as a wake-up call, reminding all modern societies, heavily dependent on information and communication technology, of their vulnerability in the information age. As with many new events in the history of conflicts, the Estonian attacks are now widely being studied and used as a model for improving national cyber security response systems. Aware of growing threats in cyberspace, many countries dependent on information and communication technology are renewing domestic cyber security initiatives.

Cyber threats: types and levels of threats in cyberspace

There are some components of cyber threats that are similar to other systemic security threats like nuclear threats. Like nuclear radiation, activities in cyber-space are invisible to the human eye, cyber movements do not need physical efforts other than key strokes and cannot be controlled and caught by kinetic devices. What makes the "cyber" very challenging, is its absolute asymmetry compared with other national security threats. First, there is an asymmetry in terms of distance. Literally, a keystroke anywhere on the planet can reach the target in a few seconds. Secondly, there is also asymmetry in terms of resources and efforts to achieve the goals in cyber space. Terrorist groups or other malevolent actors need only a few professionals and can set the targets to be attacked from great distance with considerably lower cost compared to organizing physical attacks or using conventional warfare.[7] The third aspect of asymmetry lies in dual use of the medium used by cyber attackers, the Internet. Global network of networks, the Internet, serves humankind in a very positive way and is a motor of the global economy. At the same time, cyber criminals are using the deterritorialised world economy cleverly for their benefit and cyber-crime has become a serious problem for many industries. For instance, the globalisation of cybercrime was recently demonstrated by US and French authorities who caught an impressive network of cyber criminals, operating in a number of countries on the American, European and Asian continents.

Besides cybercrime, we have entered an era where terrorists, states and state-sponsored actors have begun to use Internet and cyber attacks for the purpose of attacking other countries. Techno-logically complex attacks and the total asymmetry of the networks allow them to carry out massive attacks without ever revealing the actors behind the operation. In this respect, the tools of cyber-crime can be used for cyber terrorism and cyber warfare. Unless some organisation or country publicly claims the responsibility for the attacks, the organizers who ordered and paid for the attack, can remain anonymous and unaccountable for their actions. IT security professionals can usually trace the "cultural" origins of attacks by analysing the methods used, but law enforcement needs more detailed and concrete evidence. In order to obtain a comprehensive appraisal of an attack, expertise on attack methods and forensics of attacks should be viewed in the context of a more strategic analysis. Because of the concomitant security issues, and the complexity of the analysis, only a handful of security analysts will see the true picture in the end, and the public will be informed about serious attacks only to limited extent and post-factum.

For reasons described above, analysis of cyber threats according to their origin and motivation can be very complicated. In order to reduce the complexity of cyber threats, it could be useful to analyse cyber security from the point of view of different threat levels, as well as different levels of vulnerabilities.

Threat levels

The cyber threats influence all levels in societies: individual, industrial, societal, national, and global. Each level has certain characteristics of threats and vulnerabilities that will have corresponding consequences. In this categorisation, origins of threats are not analysed, but rather the magnitude of the results if the ICT solutions are not exploited in an appropriate and purposeful way.

Global cyber threats

Global cyber threats include systemic technological failures in large interdependent information networks, which will bring about simultaneous disruption of the functioning of critical infrastructure in many countries and regions. Global IT collapses and catastrophy scenarios were popular before the turn of millennium, but fortunately the Y2K apprehensions about possible disasters were not realised, thanks to the successful coordination of many specialised agencies and efforts of experts. Since that time, the public's awareness about the misuse of technology has decreased, and the myth of all-mighty IT experts fixing every failure in the system has gained credence among the general pub-lic.[7] It might seem ironic, but the success of Y2K turned out to be counter productive for global cyber security, by creating the illusion of cyber threats as solely technical issues.

National and state level

The concept of national cyber security captures a wide spectrum of vulnerabilities that could be attributed to threats posed by cyberattacks. In the most serious cases, countries will have to face the possibility of cyberattacks against their critical military and civilian infrastructure by the hostile states, or state sponsored actors. These attacks could be carried out independently, i.e. using only cyberspace, or as part of a larger military or information operation. In either case, nation-states will have to build capabilities to prevent and to minimize the damage created by cyberattacks.

Apart from the possible physical damage created by cyberattacks, the attacks on e-services and government information[8] channels could also be used to inflict chaos and possibly destabilize a country. The latter was one of the strategic goals behind the attacks organised against Estonia in 2007.

Compared to conventional warfare or acts of sabotage, the asymmetric nature of cyber warfare allows the targeting of critical infrastructure and information infrastructure from great distances, with significantly smaller efforts, and less risk. The attacker has an additional advantage, in that the sources of attacks cannot be easily detected and the techno-logical innovations allow for a rapid renewal of assault methods. In view of the nature and the seriousness of the threats to national security inherent in cyberspace[9] conflicts, this issue should be addressed seriously by all nations.

Societal level

At the present time, our dependence on IT solutions has reached the point of no return, since all modern societies depend on social networks that are facilitated by the technological networks. With the increasing number of attacks and assaults against critical infrastructure, as well as the growth in global cybercrime,[10] we are at risk of losing the confidence necessary to use advanced IT solutions, and we are gradually instilling public apprehension about the trustworthiness of most of the means of information and communication technology. These trends would, in turn, prove very counter productive for economic growth and innovation. In democratic societies we realize that the rising number of security breaches and incidents should be addressed with balanced responses to ensure resilience of the information systems. However, the same excuses could serve the interests of the authoritarian governments to introduce further restrictions on the use of Internet, or to facilitate imposition of restrictions on individual rights and freedoms.

Sectoral and industry level

Economic interests are clearly the first ones hit by the growing number of the incidents in cyberspace. Large banks in the UK experienced massive attacks at the end of 2007, and many companies all over the world are regularly under attack. In some sectors, attacks take the forms of intrusions and economic espionage, in others, attacks towards companies fail and the end-users are at increasing risk. In any case, the frequent cyber-attacks are costly for the private sector, and this situation calls for more active involvement of the governments that must facilitate information sharing and assistance in incidence response. However, the extent of public-private cooperation varies widely across countries.[11] In some countries, the private sector has been painfully hit already, but is still in denial: they won't admit to having been attacked, for fear of losing their customers. In more successful cases, close cooperation has been established between various public and private stakeholders, an excellent CIIP (Critical Information Infrastructure Protection)[12] system has been set up, and the general public has a high level of awareness about cyber security concerns. In a few countries, large corporations and critical infrastructure operators are increasingly interested in joint efforts to fight cyber threats, but there is still distrust to-wards the close cooperation with the government.

Most of the advanced industrial countries have CIIP policies and systems, whereas many of the transition economies or new economic powers are struggling with getting their act together and establishing necessary defensive mechanisms. In many less advanced economies, where the regulations and standards of information security, as well as law enforcement practices, are very weak, companies would find it increasingly difficult to operate, if they had to face incidents of serious cybercrime. Such companies could establish joint CERTs (Computer Emergency Response Teams) there, or employ other technical measures, but they cannot enact or amend national laws, or ensure that police can deal effectively with cybercriminals. Thus, as in many other areas, the role of an efficient public service is a crucial component in the global fight against cybercrime.

Individual level

At the individual level cyber threats might emerge from a compromised PC at home that is used by somebody else as a part of botnet, or it could lead to the loss of personal data etc. Many small and medium sized businesses have no means to employ competent information security specialists, but might have sizeable non-professionally protected servers. For such businesses the real hazard arises when the company's server is hijacked for the purpose of an assault towards another company, or country. Of course, the Internet environment could be also used for intimidation or harassment of an individual. Such individual cases embody an important aspect of threat perceptions that have evolved with increasing exploitation of ICT.

These concerns about individual harassment could be addressed by more effective awareness programs for the general public, and by the imposition of stricter rules for the use of the Internet by children and teenagers.

An examination of the different levels of cyber threat demonstrates that the global cyberspace connects all these levels simultaneously, therefore, the threats at the individual level can quickly escalate to national level if the botnet of unprotected computers assaults a country, or if a server of a company is used to attack another company, or another country's governmental networks. Recognizing this interconnectedness between the levels, it becomes evident that addressing the challenges and organizing responses to cyber threats requires the concurrent involvement of all these levels.

Cyber-attacks carried out to support a military operation

Cyber-attacks have only been used in a few military conflicts so far, e.g. the Palestine-Israel conflict in 2000 and most recently, in the Russian war against Georgia in August 2008.

There have also been attempts to carry out cyber-attacks as supporting elements of the larger peace-making effort in Kosovo 1999. The recent conflicts demonstrate the trend of using cyber-attacks against critical civilian infrastructure and governmental communication infrastructure as a part of a military operation. As one reads reports about another successful cyber-attack against a country's websites and simultaneous attempts of rerouting and spreading disinformation, an inevitable question arises: to what extent will cyber-attacks be used in future military conflicts.

From the point of view of military planning, cyber-attacks could be used as any other offensive method to achieve strategic goals of a specific operation. If the goal was to destroy the country's civilian infrastructure, air raids or heavy artillery would be more effective than cyber-attacks to obtain this result. But if the goals were to create chaos and impair the functioning of civilian infrastructure, cyber-attacks could be easily used to achieve these[8] Although the clear evidence of attack organisers is hard to find in case of DDOS attacks, as millions of unprotected computers all over the world are used for attacking, a number of information security experts indicate the involvement of Russian criminal networks behind the Georgian cyber-attacks.

There are several categories of cyber-attacks that are likely to be included in military conflicts. The first category is based on the vulnerability of the Internet infrastructure, and includes attacks that aim to disrupt the adversary's public communication networks.[13] The methods used in these attacks include distributed denial of service attacks, defacements, rerouting etc. For destabilising the country and terrorising civilian population, the computer network operations that concentrate on mass media, disruption of online services and spreading propaganda will be used. For instance, in the Georgian case these methods were launched at the beginning of the conflict to prevent the Georgian government and the national media from communicating their messages inside the country as well as to the international audience. In the Estonian case, the attacks reached beyond the government infrastructure, and included the commercial banks as well as other targets, with an aim to disrupt financial services and civilian information infrastructure.

The second category includes attacks on critical civilian infrastructure such as power stations, transport systems, banks, water supplies etc. If the strategic goal prescribes disruption of the functioning of phone lines, mobile network, banking, food and water supply or transport and energy infrastructure, one can use cyber-attacks, electromagnetic pulse or cyber-attacks combined with physical attacks. Based on interdependencies between infrastructure objects, the cascading effect of such attacks, when combined with physical attacks, can achieve damage similar to that obtained in an attack by conventional weapons. If the tactic is to preserve the buildings, but damage information infrastructure only, one can successfully disrupt civilian infrastructure using electromagnetic interference or cyber-attacks. It could be organised also in a way that avoids substantial physical destruction of infrastructure.

Although the control systems of critical infrastructure are usually not connected to the public Internet, recent reports on security applications of SCADA systems show that there are serious security gaps in automated supervisory systems.[9] However, in order to inflict serious damage, using Internet-attacks focused on critical infrastructure, requires careful preparation and skilled hackers, only actors with vast resources can materialize these threats.[14]

The third application of cyber component in military operations includes offensive and defensive cyber activities on the battlefield, such as securing one's own and impairing the enemy's communication systems, misguiding one's adversary's weaponry, using electronic weapons etc. Unlike exploitation of criminal botnets in targeting governments' infrastructure, these activities should be covered by conventions of war, and the rule of proportional response should apply here.

One of the factors that will increase the likelihood of using cyber warfare elements in addition to conventional military weaponry is the relative cost-efficiency of cyber tools. Compared to the cost of modern equipment and military technology, cyber-attacks are a rather inexpensive option for gaining tactical advantage in warfare. For instance, in order to damage your enemy's public relations and disrupt communication with outside world, the easiest way to accomplish this would be to organise DDOS attacks in the beginning of the military conflick. One only needs to create or hire botnets from the criminal market and set them on the targets.[15] The cost of a decent botnet that could be hired from criminal networks is only between $200-400. It could cost more, depending on hiring time, capacity and complexity of targets, but the total cost would be well below that of using military equipment. If we consider the fact that most of conflicts since 1991 have been small regional wars, the skills and resources needed to impair Internet traffic and disrupt information infrastructure in these territories by cyber-attacks remain very modest.

Challenges in addressing threats and vulnerabilities in cyberspace

In addressing cyber security risks one has to be aware of threats and vulnerabilities, which serve as cornerstones of any threat assessment that forms an essential platform for developing a prevention and response system. Prevention activities should be spread across all levels described earlier, they should include all professional communities involved in safeguarding cyber security, as well as society at large. One of the first challenges that needs to be addressed is the prevalent misperception in most societies, that cyber security is only a technical problem that can be fixed by technical methods. Once that bridge is crossed, and the top policy-makers are aware of vulnerabilities in information age, new challenges arise. First is a need to raise nation-wide[16] awareness on cyber security, and the second is to create dialogue between different stakeholders interested in securing cyber space. Unless all concerned professional communities are involved in this effort, national cyber security response system cannot be functional. These communities include regulators of critical sectors, critical private sector operators, lawyers, law enforcement agencies, national security authorities and technical experts. To achieve a truly nation-wide response we have to add also research and development community, and leaders from higher education system, as well as people responsible for running public[17] awareness programs. All in all, it takes enormous effort to create a common knowledge base among people from so many different walks of life, in order to build a system that will work at the national level.

In addition to a comprehensive national response system, each country also needs up to date procedures for cyber crises management. The Estonian attacks provided a good example by revealing the importance of rapid response capability which can avoid most of the hierarchical decision-making procedures. There are many areas of importance in developing the national system for coping with cyber threats, but the following ones have proved most essential.

Building a dialogue with the private sector

Best practices for ensuring cyber security include improving the incidence response system, upgrading security measures and bolstering the resilience of critical information infrastructure.

All these activities need a comprehensive approach by government departments and specialised agencies in charge of supervision and regulation of the private sector. One of the challenges that most governments meet in implementation of security standards is how to include stakeholders in private sector and how to strike a balance between growing security concerns and the economic rationale of a private company. Depending on a country's history, and traditions of public-private partnership, the solutions could be very different. In most continental European countries, [18] laws and regulations have been enacted, with obligations and standards for critical operators. In the US, various joint programs and initiatives of public-private partnership have been launched by state authorities and the federal government in recent years. Since cyber security is of vital importance for both national and international security, it would be desirable to have a more active exchange of best practices and in-formation sharing on public-private cooperation in the various international security forums. Opeability of critical providers in times of crises, as well as how to coordinate an international cyber incidence response. Although mainstream approaches to cyber threats stress terrorist and criminal activities, risks can originate also from technological failures or human mistakes.

Recent analyses are so pre-occupied by the origin of attacks that the option of technological malfunction seems to get less attention. However, in all cases of severe disruptions of critical infrastructure sofar, i.e. electricity blackouts, explosions in chemical industry etc., the reasons were found in technological problems and negligence. According to private and public sector risk analysts, the majority of IT security incidents originated from mistakes of employees.[10] To minimize such risks, the governments could provide assistance to the private sector by sponsoring cyber risk awareness programs and sup-porting training programs for IT personnel of critical operators.

International response by governments and international organisations

The major lesson from the cyber-attacks in 2007 and 2008 confirms the acknowledgement that vulnerability of cyberspace is a serious asymmetrical security threat, which can affect all nations and which must be confronted on a global level. Unlike terrorism, nuclear weapons or land-mines, cyber security is something that concerns all of us and everyone can contribute to a more secure cyberspace. Securing global cyber space is possible only if there is a general international awareness of the potential threat, and condemnation of cyber-attacks that disrupt the normal functioning of society.

If actors at all levels of cyber threats and vulnerabilities take necessary security measures, it will be possible to shape a more secure global cyber space. In order to achieve this goal, every citizen, every company, every country and corporation must work towards this goal with a common understanding that if you do harmful acts in the cyber space, or do not secure your own information systems, you harm also yourself. In this respect, there is a clear analogy with anti-pollution and environmental issues. A presentation by William Pilgrim, Director of the New York State Office of Cyber Security and Critical Infrastructure Coordination (CSCIC), Cyber Warfare

2008, London, 31 March 2008 der to achieve a healthier environment, we have created numerous regimes and international laws. Similar regulatory regime is necessary, if we are to cope successfully with the growing threats in cyberspace. In order to create a less dangerous cyber environment, we have to find ways of cleaning it up and punishing the polluters. So far, the Council of Europe Convention on Cyber-crime is the only formal international agreement that addresses at least some of the threats in cyberspace. The convention, however, deals only with cybercrime, and does not apply to large-scale attacks, or attacks towards critical infrastructure or governmental information systems.[19] It might take few more years and many more incidents, but there will surely arise a shared understanding about the need for new international regulations in this field. In order to continue benefiting from a free global Internet, it is necessary to develop international norms, measures, and instruments aimed at strengthening global cyber security.

Astonishingly, so far the fight with global cybercrime has been managed very unevenly in many cases the IT security professionals have had to act as investigators, judges and police[20] at the same time, while watching criminal activities in the networks. This situation is rather odd, and sooner or later, the governments must intervene, and develop some sort of global incidence response system. The successful development of such a system will have to rely on the support of trust-based net-works of information security experts.

Towards an international regime in cyber security

A key challenge in achieving an international approach on Internet governance and adoption of international norms rests on the ability to reach political consensus among nation states. From the history of international relations, we know that the creation of international regimes has usually been spurred by tragic events in history, with the painful events providing the motivation for the countries to commit themselves to an international regime. The Bretton Woods institutions were created after World War II to stabilize the world economy, the International Atomic Agency was created after Hiroshima in order to avoid nuclear catastrophies etc. After the Estonian attacks many countries have realised the need for concerted international action, but as of now, consensus on the creation of a cyber-security regime has not yet emerged among the international community. International security organisations and governments aware[21] of cyber threats have a clear responsibility to pursue common action to prevent cybercrime, cyber terrorism and state sponsored cyber terrorism. The lack of such common action is the weakest link in the system and can prove costly in the global cyberspace. Criminals have realised this long ago, and in many cases, the countries with weak regulations and weak law enforcement are used as safe havens for cyber criminals and terrorists. The Estonian Cyber Security[22] Strategy therefore emphasizes the centrality of international awareness and cooperation in securing global cyberspace.

The Estonian Cyber Security Strategy

In order to enhance Estonian cyber security, the Estonian government adopted a Cyber Security Strategy in May 2008. The strategy stresses the importance of a high level of information security for both public and private sectors in Estonia, supported by information technology solutions. The Estonian Cyber Security Strategy sets strategic goals for the various organisations in order to reduce the vulnerability of cyberspace in the nation as a whole. This is accomplished through the implementation of domestic action plans, but also through active international co-operation, which supports the enhancement of cyber security in other nations as well. The Strategy is divided into five policy areas where specific objectives are raised for all public and private organisations in the country.

1. Bolstering security measures for critical information infrastructure and other information systems in Estonia

Activities under this policy area concentrate on critical information infrastructure protection and application of information security standards for all other information systems. The following measures will be taken by the government: strengthening the infrastructure of the Internet, enhancing the security of control systems of critical infrastructure, improving security solutions to meet new technologically complex attack methods and enhancing inter-agency cooperation and coordination, [23] with a special focus on public and private sector cooperation in protecting critical information infrastructure.

Increasing competence in cyber security

In order to enhance competence in the field of cyber security, the strategy stresses the centrality of providing a high quality of training in information security. It is necessary to increase competence both in the public and private sectors, and establish common requirements for the competence of IT staff in information security. The strategy also seeks to intensify research and development of cyber security and enhance international research cooperation.

- Improvement of the legal framework for ensuring cyber security. Legal framework in the field of cyber security needs to be improved, focusing on the protection of critical information infrastructure, as well as on initiatives to develop international legal instruments in the field of cyber security.
- Development of international cooperation. The strategy stresses the convention on cybercrime and EU legislation on cyber-attacks, and encourages the development of inter-national cyber security initiatives. A high level of political support should be given to the cooperative networks of information security professionals, CERT networks, international

efforts of law enforcement and the fight against cybercrime. Cyber-attacks should be morally condemned by the international community.

- Raising awareness in cyber security issues. The strategy aims to raise the level of awareness of information security among all computer users, with particular focus on individual users and small and medium enterprises. The goal is to inform the public about the threats in the cyber environment and to improve knowledge about safe use of computers.

Conclusion

The global cyberspace has formed a very complex network, with much of human activity and everyday life depending on the smooth and reliable operation of the systems in that environment. With societies increasingly dependent on cyber space, vulnerabilities and the likelihood of asymmetric attacks towards civilian infrastructure have grown. In order to address the cyber threats nothing short of a global response will suffice since the cyber threats are global and asymmetric. The idea behind inter-national cooperation is simple – more countries adopting the legal approach towards cyber criminals and terrorists,[24] will bring about a more secure cyberspace. In the current situation, only the USA, Japan, Canada, South Africa, and most EU countries have adopted the only existing international convention regulating this area,[25] and there is still no universal international instrument condemning cyber-attacks towards critical civilian infrastructure. One of the future tasks for international lawyers is to develop more comprehensive international rules that could, if adopted by a sufficient number of states, be applied in cases of cyber warfare. As more technically talented generations grow up, the number of technically skilled people with limited cyber security standards is increasing, a statistic which underlines the urgency for action by the governments to avoid a likely future catastrophe caused by cyber-attacks. With increasing insecurity that accompanies technological advancement, there are new research areas emerging also for social scientists, e.g. how dependency on technology influences human behaviour, how the social machinery in society can avoid or facilitate the threats related to cyberspace, how the frequent attacks will influence the confidence in reliance on ICT etc. Considering the degree of dependence of our societies on information technology, attention paid to comprehensive security policy analyses that also includes a cyber-security component, remains surprisingly modest. In view of the dependence of states on information security and growing cyber threats, it is surprising to find that the leading research on security studies and international relations have been quite detached from such issues.

In conclusion, threats mounting in global cyberspace can be met only by comprehensive approach by national and international actors alike. At the national level, an adequate response system should be developed that reaches beyond critical information infrastructure protection, and covers the whole society with information security education, cyber threat awareness campaigns and promotion of cyber security culture. At the international level, a greater degree of cooperation between states and international organisations, as well as launching new international instruments or regimes is desirable to attain more secure cyberspace. As it is unthinkable to close down the Internet for security risks, the threats in cyberspace could be addressed only by systematically reducing vulnerability of this cyberspace that is under one's control, be it one's country, company or home computer.

References

1. Amit R., Schoemakerp . J. (1993). Strategic assets and organisational rent. Strategic Management Journal 14: 3, 346.
2. Atkinson A. A., Waterhouse J. H., and Wells R. B. (1997). A stakeholder approach to strategic performance measurement. Sloan Management Review, Spring: 25-37.
3. Blasé, J. & Blasé, J. (2002). The micropolitics of instructional supervision: A call for research. Educational Administration Quarterly, 38 (1), 6-44.

4. Bredeson, P. V. (1985). An analysis of the metaphorical perspectives of the school principals. Educational Administration Quarterly, 21 (1). 29 – 50.
5. Baines A. (1997). Productivity improvement. Work Study 46, 2: 49-5 1.
6. Baird L. and Meshoulan 1. (1988). Managing two fits of strategic human resource management. Academy of Management Review 13, 1: 116-128.
7. Bae J., Chen S., and Lawler J. (1998). Variations in human resource management in Asian countries: MNC home-country and host-country effects. The International Journal of Human Resource Management 9, 4: 653-670.
8. Baird L. and Meshoulan 1. (1988). Managing two fits of strategic human resource management. Academy of Management Review 13, 1: 116-128.
9. Banker R., Datar S., and Kaplan R. S. (1989). Productivity measurement and management accounting. Journal of Accounting, Auditing, and Finance 4, 4: 528-554.
10. Barney J. (1991). Firm resources and the theory of competitive advantage. Journal of Management 17: 99-120.
11. Baruch Y. (1996). Evaluating quality and reputation of human resource management. Personnel Review 26, 5: 377-394.
12. Baruch Y. (1998). Walking the tightrope: strategic issues for human resources. Long Range Planning 31: 467-475.
13. Becker B. & Gerhart B. (1996). The impact of human resource management on organisational performance: progress and prospects. Academy of Management Journal 39: 779-801.
14. Borg M. (1989). Stress and job satisfaction among primary school teachers in Malta.Educational Review 41, 3: 271-279.
15. Boudreau J. W. (1991). Utility analysis in human resource management decisions. In M. D. Dunnette and L. M. Hough (Eds.), Handbook of industrial and organisational psychology (2nd ed.), Vol. 2: 621-745. Consulting Psychologists Press. Palo Alto, CA.
16. Bovaird T. & Davis P. (1999). Learning to manage with limited resources: coping strategies and learning breakthroughs in UK local government. International Journal of Public Sector Management 12, 3: 293-313.
17. Boxall P. (1992). Strategic HRM: a beginning, a new theoretical direction. Human Resource Management Journal 2, 3: 61-79.
18. Boxall P. (1996). The strategic HRM debate and the resource-based view of the firm. Human Resource Management Journal 6, 3: 59-75.

19. Boyle S. and Harrison A. J. (1995). Provider competition: Wheel and deal. Health Service Journal, 30 March: 24-26.

20. Brayfield A. H. & Rothe H. F. (1951). An index of job satisfaction. Journal of Applied Psychology35: 307-31 1.

21. Brignall T. J. (1993). Performance measurement and change in local government: a general case and childcare application. Public Money and Management, October-December: 23-30.

22. Carmer S. G. & Swanson M. R_ (1973). An evaluation of ten multiple comparison procedures by Monte Carlo methods. Journal of the American Statistical Association 68: 66-74.

23. Chambers R-J. (1965). Measurement in accounting. Journal of Accounting Research 3, 1: 32-62.

24. Charnes A., Cooper W., and RHOADES E. (1978). Measuring the efficiency of decision making units. European Journal of Operation Research 2: 429-444.

Cyber Security: The Strategic View

I'd like to start by giving everyone my own personal subjective assessment on the state of security capabilities of different enterprises around the globe. The good news is that the security capabilities of large enterprises relative to the growing sophistication of cyber-threats are growing steadily. However, the same cannot be said of small and medium enterprises, where over time, their relative capabilities are declining, and the gap between large and small medium enterprises is widening.[1] This is hardly surprising when you look at the figures IT Security spend per head. With economies of scale, large enterprises can hire the best and brightest security experts, purchase the best security tools, and put in place a truly robust security program that is able to operationalize the use of intelligence to detect threats.

In a number of countries, large enterprises have close collaboration with their security services in threat intelligence sharing. This leaves smaller enterprises lagging behind both at the level of technology as well as cyber-intelligence foresight, and furthermore, they cannot afford the required talent to manage the complexity of the multi-dimensional problems that cyber-attacks present.So what is the impact of these challenges on small businesses globally? As small and medium enterprises form the bedrock of most economies globally, this situation (lack of technology, talent and cyber-intelligence) is not sustainable in the long run. This holds true for such organisations as well as the relevant governments, which have such a high level of risk within their national GDP.

So what could be the solutions to this? I am inclined to believe that one key solution is for small and medium enterprises to outsource their security management to more capable organisations. Across the board, the use of cyber-insurance is going to be critical to lower their risk exposure and improve cash flow management. One could argue that there is a role of government in this arena as the "reinsurer of last resort" to provide some level of stability and certainty to the market place.

Let us explore this "role" for governments in greater detail, and I would argue that this is of vital importance. It is important to start with the premise that for most governments globally, the 1980s, 1990s and 2000s signalled an era of wide-scale deregulation and privatisation, with much of the nation's critical infrastructures – in sectors such as energy, transport, finance, medicine and so on – entrusted to the private sector.

Critical infrastructures are constantly targeted by cyber-adversaries, and we have seen security incidents exert both cascading and crippling effects regionally, nationally, and even internationally, due to the high degree of interconnectedness and interdependency that our global society now involves.[2] So when we look at the cost of a security incident it is not just the private cost of say replacing a power generator but essentially there is the social cost component as well. We call this a security externality but it is a negative one because it adversely affects everyone else.

Part of the reason why it can be difficult to secure critical infrastructures is due to the divergence of interests between the private and public sectors. The private sector's primary focus is corporate efficiency: in terms of security, it does what it believes is "enough", implementing the bare minimum level of security, since its main goal is profit-making. The government, in contrast, is principally concerned with achieving social order, national security and economic prosperity for its population.[3] In the EU for example, most citizens expect their governments to protect them from all hazards. Yet in this case, governments do not have supervisory and operational control over these critical infrastructures. Some people have argued that the role of government as the legitimate security provider has diminished and will continue to decline over time.

As I meet with different governing bodies around the world, I am of the opinion that this matter is not straight forward for them, and that they are indeed grappling with the challenge of determining what their role in cyber security could or should be, especially visa vies the private sector. I argue, however, that the changing global landscape should not imply that the role of governments, as the legitimate provider of security, be diminished, provided they are able to understand clearly how the world has changed and is changing, and what their role should be within this new environment of increasing interconnectedness. Furthermore, I argue that in order for governments to be successful in this new environment, their remit must transcend what their historical regulatory role has typically entailed. They now need to tackle the questions of how they can best assist the private sector to invest in security (facilitation), and how both the public and private sectors can improve the current state of security (collaboration). To formulate a viable approach, this is the framework through which governments must strategies, and they must be ready to draw upon analogous lessons learned from past preparedness efforts geared towards other areas of threat, such as pandemics and terrorism. With regard to law enforcement, the good news is that attribution is entirely possible. Law enforcement agencies are increasingly able to track down the bad guys, prosecute them in the court of law, and throw them behind bars. Why is this so? Firstly, bad guys make mistakes all the time, and these mistakes compromise their Operational Security (OPSEC). This, in turn, enables law enforcement personnel to track and monitor their varied activities closely. Furthermore, they sometimes fall prey to their own greed and inflated egos. Another key point to remember is that a lot of what is happening in cyber-crime has to do with physical world activities like registering a fake company, recruiting money mules, dropping a fake ATM machine on a street corner in New York, and so on.

But much more work is needed to turn the tide against the proliferation of cyber-crime. This takes the form of more focused capacity building for police, prosecutors and judges. And every country has to have a proper legal framework to address challenges in cyber-crime.

In terms of legal framework, I'd like to give you a global view of the different legal instruments that are in place regionally. One could argue that the world today is pretty fragmented in that we have blocks of different countries adopting different regional legal instruments. For example, some countries have adopted the Council of Europe's Convention on Cybercrime, while others abide by the rules of the Shanghai Cooperation Organisation (SCO), which is led by Russia and China. One could also argue that in addition to this being a fragmented approach, this represents a differentiated approach to the same problem. Differentiated by what, you may ask? Well differentiated by ideologies these blocks basically represent as well as competing ideologies on how cyber-space should be run.

This is one reason why I believe that it is highly unlikely that we will come to a common legal framework in addressing cyber-crime. One cannot help but wonder what the UN's role in all this would be. Perhaps the UN should be the body that would help to "interoperate and facilitate" between different blocks. With regard to international instruments that are in place to govern interstate relations, it is often useful to look at how different elements are positioned along a spectrum of conflict intensity. At one end of this spectrum, the Tallinn Manual seeks to provide clarification on the use of force and armed attacks in the cyber context. Up until recently, there was not much clarity on this.

I remember a couple years ago I was sitting in the office of the General Manager of a certain agency in the NATO HQ in Brussels, and I asked him whether we could apply NATO Article V in response to a cyber-attack. The key term in Article V is armed attack, so essentially what I was asking is “Could a cyber-operation amount to an armed attack?” Back then the answer was “no”, but we know now the consensus is a cyber-operation is tantamount to an armed attack. There are two main bodies of law that are relevant here: Jus ad bellum sets out criteria states must consult before engaging in war, and once states are in an armed conflict, just in bello governs the conduct of war. Article 51 of the UN charter guarantees the right of the state to “use force” when acting in self-defence against an armed attack.

As far as I know, we have not witnessed a cyber-incident that is tantamount to an armed attack; at least not yet. Most of the cyber incidents fall below the threshold of an armed attack. This is where the Law of Countermeasures could be useful. Countermeasures are acts that would otherwise be wrongful acts that the “injured state” takes against the “responsible state” solely for the purpose of compelling the “responsible state” to stop its own wrongful acts.[4] It is important to note that countermeasures cannot be construed as a “use of force”, a point we will come back to slightly later. What I’d like to do now is to talk about the implications for states given what we have now.

First, for a state to respond with countermeasure or self-defence, attribution is essential. You have to know who did what to you. If this goes to an international court or tribunal, the burden of proof is on the “injured state” though not to the level of “beyond a reasonable doubt” but it has to be “clear and convincing”. Hence, the role of intelligence is really critical here, and given the challenge of technical attribution I think it is important a state combines other sources of intelligence like SIGINT, HUMINT, etc. This applies to anticipatory self-defence as well where a state can only engage in anticipatory self-defence when it is clear on the intention and capability of its adversary. Needless to say, intelligence is all about discovering the adversary's intention and capability. Now some may argue we could use the "Plea of necessity" to circumvent the issue of attribution because what is important here is not so much of who and what caused this bad situation, but rather what you need to do to mitigate the harm. This has relevance to the active cyber-defence discussion, but to cut straight to the point, my opinion is if you read Article 25 of the Inter-national Law Commission Articles on State Responsibility, you will get a sense that the practical application of the "Plea of necessity" is extremely challenging. You could only use it in truly exceptional circumstances, and one has to demonstrate that the measure taken is the only one available.

Given that attribution can be challenging and time consuming, it makes sense that states possess the ability to take a few hits and continue to function under these degraded conditions. This is why resilience is such an important component of national cyber-power. Let's go back to the point I made earlier that countermeasures, when taken, cannot be construed as a "use of force". What that means is if another state knocks out a major portion of your country's power grid with a cyber-attack, which to me is a clear use of force, and you respond in kind, that is, take out their power grid, it would render the countermeasure unlawful. Hence, the ability of states to combine instruments of national power like diplomatic, economic, politics in their response would be critical to this.

At the end we have to recognise that none of these legal instruments discussed is a panacea for all the problems we will be facing, in fact, there is always a risk that this would end up being a constant "tit for tat" where every state is making the case that it is the victim state and therefore is justified to take action. This increases the possibility of conflict escalation.[5] What is really needed is behavioural norm development and confidence building measures where the focus is on practical measures to mitigate the risk of conflict escalation. Historically, norm development and confidence building measures, especially confidence building measures, have been the work of states. I would argue private sector has an important role to play with this, and here is why.

I have attended a number of cyber policy maker and regulator conferences in the EU, and on a number of occasions there have been suggestions by conference attendees that Cisco could help with influencing countries to adopt the Council of Europe Cybercrime convention. This underscores the perception that multi nationals like Cisco, which have a global footprint, should have global influence to steer the deliberations toward a certain outcome.

To conclude, one of the things we have to remember is while governments usually own the goal of cyber-stability, they do not necessarily own all the means to shape norms of conduct in the cyberspace. Most of the technical know-how is in the hands of private sector, and it is going to be interesting to see how governments and private sector can come together on this issue.

Networks on Fire: Defending Critical

Government Networks Many government and commercial networks are now in a state of widespread and persistent compromise. An analysis of 193 compromise assessments in government organisations over a six month period showed 97% were compromised by malware, 75 per cent had command and control traffic leaving their networks, and 31 per cent were compromised by an advanced, persistent threat.

Today's threat actors are nation states, organised criminals and hack ativists. They leverage the Internet to conduct reconnaissance, conduct their attacks and hide their true origins. They target users with dynamic, polymorphic malware via multiple attack vectors. Cyber security has never been more critical. Use of the Internet and other technologies are enabling new operational models that open up governments in vastly different ways, providing citizens with greater speed and access to information but also providing attackers with a perfect platform for conducting cyber-espionage and intelligence gathering.

At the same time the threats are getting more complex, the attackers are becoming more persistent. Attacks have become extremely targeted – in the malware signatures that are seen in our customer's environments, 70 per cent of them are seen only in that organisation, created for that specific attack on that specific target alone. A new model of cyber security is needed to protect against this changing threat landscape.

What is the problem government networks face today? Every government network is a potential target and possible avenue into critical networks. The challenges for governments include budgets, cyber security skills capacity, [6] detection of attacks against critical networks, attribution of threat actors, and ensuring all critical layers are protected adequately.

Despite a focus on cyber security, the solution is not free spending on more security controls but finding the right controls. Planning cycles are often long, and funding can come at the expense of more visible initiatives.

Threat actors are using zero day attacks and previously unknown malware. According to a 2013 Pokémon Institute report on The State of Advanced Persistent Threats, commercial organisations on average have experienced approximately 9 separate APT-related incidents in the past 12 months. In addition, the report states that 68 per cent of respondents indicate that zero-day attacks are their organisation's greatest threat. These same respondents also overwhelmingly report that advanced cyber-threats have successfully evaded their traditional IDS and AV solutions. These same threat tactics and threat actors also target government agencies.

Protection of critical networks against cyber-warfare requires detection of unknown threats. NATO is considering and developing rules of engagement for defining cyber-war policies, but all government networks need strong defences against the types of zero day and highly advanced threats that are likely to be utilised by state actors against other governments.

Attribution of threat actors is a challenge, as the weaknesses of Internet connected systems make it easy to maintain plausible deniability. Identifying who is attacking may be of high importance in developing an effective response. Finally, it is a real challenge to protect and secure all critical layers. One layer is not enough in the new threat world. The cost and complexity is high, and defences need to adapt continuously to new attacks. Risks and repercussions Today, there are no real risks or repercussions to aggressors from attacks on other nations or theft of intellectual property. The attackers are safe within their own borders, protected by weak law enforcement and judicial capabilities, and widespread weaknesses in Internet connected systems. International agencies have no significant power in many jurisdictions where attacks are routed, making investigation, attribution, and containment of these enemies problematic.

In the past, espionage was expensive, difficult, and extremely risky for the individuals and potentially the countries involved. The advent of the Internet changed all that by dramatically lowering the bar for entry into the world of espionage. Geographic distance, cultural adaption and threat of capture, have all disappeared in cyberspace. This change also creates a low barrier to entry for organised crime and terrorists to also use online capabilities to steal or destroy. How should governments change their IT acquisition regulations? According to the Verizon DBIR, there were 1367 confirmed data breaches in 2013. The average number of self-detected intrusions fell from 37 per cent in 2012 to 33 per cent in 2013.

Organisations are now less likely than before to detect these intrusions themselves, as the attackers become more sophisticated and stealthy.

The 2013 Mendicant M-Trends report on breach investigations found that the average time from initial breach to detection is 229 days. One breach went undetected for 6 years. Good enough is no longer good enough. The adversaries have enormous amounts of time to find ways to break in; to defend, requires well-trained teams to identify attacks immediately, prevent them when possible, and mitigate them as quickly as possible when breached to stop data leakage and minimise impact.

You still need good security practices for the basic attacks. But fundamentally, the static defences of the past do not move quickly enough.[7] And that includes the very static IT Acquisition processes with long lead times – a defence against inappropriate acquisitions becomes a means to prolong the static defences.

The reality is that the attacker will map out your static defences, find a pathway to bypass them, and launch their attack. They will bypass your static defences before you deploy them, and moreover, when static defences are active, they will only work against known threats.Most government processes for acquisition are slow, with multiple approvals, approval bodies, review committees, risk reviews, tender processes and so on. Attackers are faster – they don't have to worry about compliance requirements – they just care how they are going to get past whatever defences are in place while maintaining plausible deniability. When defenders change something to catch their latest tactic, they will evolve quickly to evade that.

Acquisition processes need to support the defenders evolving their defences regularly because what works today would not necessarily work tomorrow, and learning from successful attacks needs to happen immediately to prevent the next attack from succeeding.

Governments should work to incorporate security standards into acquisition planning and contract administration. This is a critical step that will enhance the cyber security posture of the government. Security standards should be designed to combat advanced cyber-threats targeting both known and unknown vulnerabilities. These standards should emphasise automated, proactive and dynamic defence by incorporating signature-less, proactive defence.

Recommended attributes of such tools include the ability to:

- Identify and block in-bound zero day attacks across multiple threat vectors;
- Expose the entire attack life cycle by correlating intelligence across various threat vectors;
- Block outreach from a compromised host to its command and control centre;
- Prevent the exfiltration of data and the download of additional malware;
- Eliminate false positives; and
- Produce complete forensic details.

Tools that provide automated sharing of indicators of compromise in near real time should also be included in standard requirements. These enable new threats to be detected more rapidly, and the extent of attack campaigns to be identified.

In addition, governments need on-going mandatory training and education for contracting officers and other procurement and acquisition officials about evolving cyber-threats with an emphasis on the techniques, tactics and procedures used by sophisticated cyber-adversaries. This will allow them to make informed decisions. Governments should also support initiatives that enable rapid and flexible acquisition of new cyber security capabilities outside of traditional system integration processes. What baseline standards should be enforced for government networks?

Government baseline standards serve as a role model to incant commercial networks with best practices for cyber security. These will improve the posture of the country if critical infrastructure and other key industries are adequately protected.

It is critical to adopt measures that defend against advanced cyber-threats. Incorporating emerging best practices that use behavioural or virtualisation techniques into a security framework and adopting the framework will place governments in a better position to identify and block sophisticated threats.

One example of a best practice that incorporates these approaches into an organisation's defensive posture is the recently released United States NIST Special Publication 800.53 Rev4, Security and Privacy Controls for Federal Information Systems and Organisations, Security Control 44 (SC-44, which defines Detonation Chambers, found in Appendix F-SC, page F-214). In addition to governments, the use of Detonation Chambers as a security control has received widespread adoption across Fortune 500 in the commercial world.

The Australian Signals Directorate (ASD) Strategies to Mitigation Targeted Cyber Intrusions should also be noted in relation to the use of detonation chambers as a best practice for modern defences.[8] The weakest link is usually human, and this can take the form of ignorance of the threat, and an unwillingness to accept how creative attackers can be. In today's threat environment, every government organisation is a likely target for organised crime, activism and nation-state sponsored spying. Sophisticated attackers are well organised and will leverage the human and technical weakness, and they will harness any weak government department in order to attack other departments where there is some form of trust or other dependency.

Increasingly, the connectedness of government makes the breach of one department useful for attacking another.

Take an example of military defence, the use of air power. Air supremacy depends on planes being able to take off, and knowing accurate weather conditions is essential to battle planning. The network feeds for meteorological information, and the source of that information itself are therefore a significant dependency and communications risk for an air force.

Every department creates some risk for others and the higher the bar across all departments, the stronger the whole will be. Governments need a comprehensive approach to bring agility, situational awareness, and expertise to the protection of all layers of their critical infrastructure, with no department left behind. India's International Cyber security Strategy India's international cyber security strategy flows out of its domestic imperatives and priorities. India has the third largest Internet user base in the world, estimated at around 200 million and poised to grow rapidly with the continued increase in smart phone usage as well as new technologies such as 4G.[9]

As Prime Minister Modi pointed out in his speech at the BRICS Summit in Brazil, [10] India considers cyberspace to be a source of great opportunity but cyber security to be an equally great concern. This is not without reason. The government is looking to cyberspace as the main medium to improve and empower the citizen through various e-governance schemes as well as creating feedback mechanisms. Banking, communications and e-tailing are just some of the sectors that have been encouraged to leverage the benefits of cyberspace in providing efficient services.

The threats to the security of cyberspace emanate from various quarters; from hackers to criminals to state sponsored actors. Given the borderless nature of cyberspace, the threats have to be countered through international co-operation. At the same time, capabilities and capacities have to be built up within the country in the areas of law enforcement, forensics and jurisprudence.

The very nature of a borderless cyber-world created by technological and economic innovations is now seen as a construct that questions the very nature of the nation state system. As cyberspace becomes as much a vehicle for transporting ideas and information as it is for transmitting data, much of the heartburn is over the state's lack of control over such a potent medium. This has led to a certain duality of approach in many states, calling for complete control within national territories while endorsing the idea of cyberspace being subject to minimal control internationally. While not as engaged with the intricacies of cyber security and Internet governance as it should be, India has viewed cyberspace as a global commons "which no one state may own or control, and which is central to life as we know it today". This hands off approach is no longer tenable, in part because of the reality that cyberspace requires some governance and regulation. Many states that previously championed this perspective now sing a different tune. The United States, for instance, now contends that while cyberspace might superficially resemble other global commons like air, sea and space, the physical infrastructure was the property of different entities making such comparisons moot. In the speech referred to above, the Prime Minister described cyberspace as a global public good, which would logically necessitate some discussion and negotiation on mutually agreeable norms and practices.

India has held the position that such discussions should follow the principles laid down in the Tunis Agenda, which gives primacy of position to governments when it comes to resolving issues that are primarily in their domain. The Agenda was prescient in noting that "Policy authority for Internet-related public policy issues is the sovereign right of States", and that "they have rights and responsibilities for international Internet-related public policy issues". With most Internet-related public policy issues increasingly impinging on the sovereign right of states, a suitable mechanism and framework needs to be drawn up to ensure the continuance of cyberspace as a domain that is open, global and secure. It is to this end that India proposed a Committee for Internet-Related Policies (CIRP) to the United Nations in 2011. This would be a more permanent form of the UN Group of Governmental Experts (UN GGE) that has had three iterations so far and presented two reports. While the UN GGE has done sterling work in laying out a roadmap from Cyber Confidence Building Measures (CBMs) to norm making, its cyclical nature and the turnover in members constrain its abilities to perform a more durable role. It has also outsourced the work of implementation to sub-regional organisations that have varying degrees of expertise and capacity. In Asia, the two main multi-lateral organisations dealing with cyber security are the OIC-CERT and APCERT with a certain amount of overlap in membership. Organisations like APCERT need to be more pro-active, going beyond the two table-top exercises held a year to more intensive capacity-building programs. The ASEAN Regional Forum (ARF) has also initiated a cyber-security program designed to bring together experts from governments, international organisations, academia, and the private sector. On the whole, there is a need for a more dedicated mechanism for co-operation that covers the whole of Asia, and is Asian-led. The lack of co-operation and dialogue within the region is exemplified by the fact that India has bi-lateral cyber security dialogues with more countries outside the region than within.

At the bi-lateral level, India has cyber security dialogues with other major cyber-powers, including Japan, South Korea, the United Kingdom, France and the United States as well as the European Union. Outcomes have been in the form of training programmes, intelligence cooperation and research and development funding for joint projects. The nodal agency for securing cyberspace, [11] CERT-In has signed agreements with overseas CERTs such as USCERT and Korean Internet Security Agency (KISA).

In the short term, India's cyber security goals include building up capacities at home to provide a safe and secure cyberspace, and forging co-operative relationships internationally – bilateral as well as multi-lateral as part of that goal. Issues that have to be tackled over the long term include the re-structuring of Internet governance to better reflect the requirements of the times and the establishment of norms and conventions to moderate the excesses by way of cyber-intrusions, which, if left unchecked, could have unforeseen consequences. Enhancing ASEAN-wide Cyber security: Time for a Hub of Excellence?

The ASEAN ICT Master plan 2015 (AIM2015) envisions creating a global Information and Communications Technology (ICT) hub. The grouping's ambition is to distinguish itself as a region of high quality ICT infrastructure, skilled manpower and technological innovation. In support of these plans, member states should spur the creation of a cyber-security hub of excellence in the region as part of a wider comprehensive cyber security strategy. Lack of region-wide cohesiveness National and regional moves to adopt comprehensive cyber security strategies have been somewhat slow and fragmented across the globe. To date, ASEAN's efforts to adopt a comprehensive regional framework for cyber security are equally piecemeal.

This lack of region-wide cohesiveness does not help the region's security and impairs the ASEAN Economic Community Blueprint to become a single market and production base, a highly competitive economic region, and one that is fully integrated into the global economy. Indeed, an ASEAN-wide comprehensive cyber security framework has yet to be developed, official public documents are vague, the 2014 schedule for ASEAN official meetings does not include cyber security, and the precise extent of discussions and proposed initiatives is difficult to ascertain. Creating a Regional hub of Cyber security Professionals Congruent with ASEAN's aims to develop a workforce with high-level ICT proficiency, member states should develop a pool of cyber security professionals to effectively respond to regional and international cyber security challenges. This could be achieved through a range of approaches and programmes including

ASEAN cyber security scholarships (like those proposed under the Mactan Cebu Declaration and AIM2015 for an ASEAN ICT Scholarship programme to attract ICT talent); education on cyber security issues at the earliest possible age as well as incorporation in school curricula; the further development of "ASEAN Cyber kids Camp"; and initiatives to encourage and attract talent to choose ICT as a career.

Innovative initiatives like Coder Dojo could also be considered by ASEAN member states as a novel way to attract young talent for the purposes of regional cyber security. Coder Dojo is a cost effective and largely community-driven global movement sweeping across Europe and the United States with more than 15,000 children learning to write software in more than 35 countries. Currently, there is one in the ASEAN region (Bandung, Indonesia), five in India and eight in Japan. It runs free not-for-profit coding clubs in local communities and regular sessions for young people to learn how to code and develop websites, apps, and programs in a fun environment.[12]

In China for instance, one out of three school children already want to be a "hacker" when they grow up – hackers are the new cool, the new rock star. To attract such young talent, "Dojos" also organise tours of technology companies and introduce guest speakers to talk about their careers. Its focus on young girls and women in technology at DojoCon2013 in April this year is particularly noteworthy for the ASEAN region.ICT experts and innovators.

AIM2015 calls for the establishment of a database of ICT experts and innovators within ASEAN, which could be harnessed for cyber security professionals. Furthermore, accrediting IT and cyber security professionals with a regionally-recognised certification should also be considered to allow for regional cohesiveness. As it stands, ASEAN has completed eight Mutual Recognition Arrangements (MRAs) to facilitate the free movement of skilled labour in the region, albeit to varying degrees of cooperation in recognition of qualifications. However, of the eight professional groups listed, computer scientists and IT professionals are not listed (although engineering services are included).It is also worth considering the European Commission's recent proposal under the February 2013 Cyber security Strategy of the European Union of a roadmap for a "Network and Information Security Driving Licence". If implemented, this would be a voluntary certification programme to promote enhanced skills and competence of IT professionals. Furthermore, the Commission plans to organise with the support of the European Network and Information Security Agency (ENISA) in 2014, a "cyber security championship" where university students across the region will compete in proposing network and information security solutions.

Finally, to stimulate a culture of security and data privacy by design, the Commission recommends the introduction of training on network and information security, secure software development, and personal data protection for computer science students.

Fostering a "win-win solution" Such measures will further increase the attractiveness of ASEAN for foreign direct investment and enhance the region's competitiveness. ICT is regarded as a growth sector for the region, employing nearly 12 million people and contributing more than USD32 billion to ASEAN's GDP, with figures expected to increase by 2015.

These initiatives will also address the development divide, help alleviate poverty, and create employment opportunities in line with the social development goals of the ASEAN Community and the Millennium Development Goals of the United Nations. While there is no one-size-fits-all approach for this developing area, it is in the common interests of ASEAN states – and the wider international community - to adopt such regional initiatives for cyber security to tackle cross-border cyber threats. The current lack of region-wide cohesiveness and a comprehensive framework is detrimental not just to the realisation of the ASEAN Economic Community but also to the overall security of the ASEAN region. Significantly, it will also impede current and future international cooperation efforts on cyber security that are required to deal effectively with the cross-border nature of cyber incidents. *Originally published as RSIS Commentaries, No. 133/2013 dated 18 July 2013.

Securing Cyberspace: Whose Responsibility?

The defacements of websites of governments and businesses are a great nuisance to the victims. However, Anonymous, the network of hackers behind these defacements, declared its intention to create more than just nuisance. In a video published in 2013, the network threatened to attack the financial sector of Singapore[13] to "cause financial loss". It remains to be seen whether Anonymous is able to carry out cyber-attacks that would result in significant financial damage. The fact, however, is that critical infrastructure – whether in the finance, transport, energy, or utilities sector – is highly vulnerable. In 2012 for example, the so-called Shimon virus caused severe disruptions by wiping out data from thousands of computers at Saudi Aramco, the largest oil producer in the world. Allegedly carried out by Iran, a state-actor, it took the company two weeks to recover from the attack. Critical infrastructure vulnerabilities. It has been demonstrated that when critical infrastructure is attacked severe disruptions can follow. Further aggravating this situation is that more and more machines connect to cyberspace and become remotely controlled. These include control systems of gas and oil pipelines. In the not too distant future, even more devices will be interconnected ranging from those critical for national security as well as household goods and cars. When targeted jointly in a mass attack, even private consumer goods could turn into a national security threat. Given the likely increase in vulnerabilities governments worldwide agonise over the right approach to making

* Originally published as RSIS Commentaries, No. 210/2013 dated 12 November 2013 Effective Public-Private Cooperation for successful Cyber-crime Investigations – Capacity Building against Cyber-crime.

cyberspace more secure. From governments' point of view, protecting critical infrastructure poses two difficulties. First, in many countries, the operation of critical infrastructure as well as the physical and intangible components of cyberspace is held in private hands. Due to private ownership, governments often do not exercise immediate operational control. Even standard-setting for the Internet is not always carried out by national governments, or inter-governmental bodies, but in open standards organisations such as the Internet Engineering Task Force, where governments have limited say. Second, governments and the private sector have divergent interests: Governments on the one hand are concerned with ensuring national security while maintaining or creating an environment conducive for economic activity.

The private sector on the other hand has as its main objective making profits and serving shareholder interests. In terms of security, it does what it deems "enough" which may not necessarily be sufficient. In general, every extra dollar spent on security decreases corporate efficiency and shareholder value in the short-term. Incentives to invest in additional security measures are often only recognised once perpetrators have successfully compromised systems. This can be too late in the case of a serious cyber-attack that may cause substantial damage.

Government lead or private sector starring?

In the context of assigning roles, two diametrically opposing views have emerged. The first argues that corporations have made huge efficiency gains through the computerisation of operations. For example, banks can operate their business more efficiently by allowing their customers to make e-transactions from their homes without interacting with a clerk. Similarly, utilities providers no longer send staff to manually activate valves or switches located far from central operation sites. Rather, the same operation is commanded remotely from a machine, with minimal human action. For these reasons it is argued that the private sector should not only reap the efficiency gains of such automation and computerisation but also share the burden of hardening the infrastructure on which they depend.[14]

The opposing view puts forward that securing the nation is one of the most fundamental tasks of governments. Nobody would expect the operator of a hydroelectric power station to protect its dams against ballistic missiles from adversaries. It is argued that no other standard should apply to figurative cyber-missiles that could result in similar damage. Framework for PPP: collaborate, facilitate, regulate Arguably, it would be reasonable to share the burden of protecting cyberspace in public-private partnership (PPP). However, there is no magic formula for assigning the roles that governments and the private sector should assume. The culture of governance differs substantially between countries ranging from very little public sector involvement to heavy regulation. None-the less, a three-pronged framework could help in this endeavour: there is need for collaboration, facilitation and regulation.

First of all, close collaboration at all levels is crucial. Exchange of information and best practices, or collaboration in screening and analysing malicious Internet traffic between Internet Service Providers and governments' Computer Emergency Response Teams (CERTs) can reduce cyber-threats. Secondly, governments can facilitate the implementation of cyber security measures by providing reliable guidelines and by creating the right incentives. Investments in additional measures could be awarded tax breaks and low interest loans could be provided to companies that invest in the resilience of their systems. Furthermore, governments could consider cyber security measures that are in place when granting contracts to businesses.

Last but certainly not least, cyber security will likely not be achieved without any regulation at all. Obviously, corporations tend to loath being regulated since regulation can be burdensome and inhibit profit-making. However, governments can develop regulation in close cooperation with the private sector. Richard Clarke, former Special Adviser to the US President for Cyber security, suggests "smart regulation" is also possible: regulatory end-goals are defined but the best avenues to reach such goals are co-developed with the private sector. Equally important, legislative processes need to be accelerated to provide timely guidance to narrow the gap between ill-boding technological advances and regulation. The faster governments react, the less the chance of damage.

Admittedly it is a difficult task to balance the interests of governments and the private sector. However, close public-private partnership can prevent mere cyber-nuisance from transforming into a national security threat and finally lead to a win-win situation: an environment conducive for economic activity in a secure nation.

My focus is different from many of the other experts, and is on the narrow subject of cyber-crime. This area of interest describes the practical challenges of real crime using the Internet or exclusively on the Internet which affects real citizens across the world. It deals with groups of identifiable criminals, often operating in organised groups, who exploit computer and network vulnerabilities to commit crime against our friends, family and neighbours who have minimum knowledge and expertise to mount a coherent defence.

Many of the other experts clearly demonstrate expertise and knowledge in the area of cyber-warfare and cyber security. There has been a significant body of research[15] which has been undertaken by all these experts over the last few years with specific focus on what constitutes an act of cyber-warfare, when would a state be reasonably and legally authorised to respond to acts of cyber-provocations and what rules of engagement would cover any response.

I have an industry background and I have spent the last decades of my career working in the area of cyber-crime. Initially, this was in the area of combating child pornography in the International Network of Internet Hotlines (INHOPE). More recently this was as Industry Coordination in 2 CENTRE, the Cybercrime Centres of Excellence Network for Training, Research and Education, encouraging close collaboration between academia, law enforcement and industry in cyber-crime investigations. I have worked as acyber-crime expert for the European Commission, the Council of Europe, the Organisation for Security & Cooperation in Europe and the United Nations Office for Drugs & Crime in Vienna. I understand and appreciate the need for states to focus on the development of agreed international protocols as they relate to acts of cyber-warfare and attacks against states. We need methods and agreed protocols to reduce tensions and to de-escalate cyber-conflicts. Nonetheless, cyber-crime is happening around us daily and cyber-crime investigations are a huge challenge for law enforcement, prosecutors and judges today.

The Internet is global, has no borders and is changing, adapting and evolving. Governments and national law enforcement are challenged by the transnational dimension of the Internet. At the same time, harmful and illegal content and activities on the Internet cross national borders and directly affect citizens.

In Europe, the European Cybercrime Centre (EC3) based in Europol in The Hague is the focal point in the EU's fight against cybercrime, contributing to faster reactions in the event of online crimes. EC3 commenced its activities on 1 January 2013 with a mandate to tackle cybercrime with specific focus on crime committed by organised groups to generate large criminal profits such as online fraud, crime which causes serious harm to the victim such as online child sexual exploitation and crime which affects critical infrastructure and information systems in the European Union.

A typical online crime can span a wide range of countries with a long list of participants in the criminal chain, each with limited knowledge of upstream and downstream participants and most often the perpetrator(s) are not located in the same countries of the victims. Indeed a complex network of international connections can be created and maintained through a range of third countries by the criminal enterprise with minimum cost and technical knowledge. In some cases computers owned by innocent victims are used in the criminal plot to attack other victims or host illegal content.

The range of illegal activities on the Internet continues to evolve. Unsolicited email (SPAM) causes significant impact on network efficiencies with large 46 volumes of bandwidth, email servers and staff time being taken up in managing and restricting such communications. Many of the skills learned in this area are then applied to other areas of concern such as child abuse and intellectual property violations. Child Sexual Abuse Material (CSAM) continues to grow as Internet usage continues to grow.[16] Malware also causes significant impact on end users with new major concerns in mobile space and increased impact on desktop based systems. Many countries are concerned by the impact of online gambling and the loss of exchequer revenues if taxes related to online gambling are lost. A separate area of huge growth is that of online drugs including illegal drugs, prescription drugs (available on the Internet without prescription) or fake drugs[17] which can be damaging. Online crime continues to evolve and recently we have witnessed an increase in attacks in mobile devices and on online extortion through ransom ware. Trans-national cyber-crime investigations are challenging, and there is a need for national law enforcement agencies to work closely with each other internationally in order to successfully prosecute online crime. Few law enforcement agencies are actively funded or are encouraged to cooperate with foreign agencies, and a range of barriers need to be surmounted.

Appropriate legislation is a major concern. There are few international instruments on the legal definitions of cyber-crime and procedural instruments are equally effective and it is important to ensure that national legislation is comparable internationally. One of the earliest international instruments is the Council of Europe Cybercrime Convention, which was created in 2001 and many regional and national instruments have been created since. However, responding to the challenge of cyber-crime is not exclusively a role for law enforcement. Since 1999 an international NGO called INHOPE, the international network of Internet hotlines has worked to protect children and remove online child abuse material from the Internet and simultaneously empower faster investigations by law enforcement. In 2013, the INHOPE network consisted of 49 Internet hotlines in 43 countries where 170 analysts processed 1, 210, 893 reports of illegal content and 54, 969 reports were assessed to contain unique URLs of child sexual abuse material. One example of swift international collaboration enabled by the network occurred in June 2013 when the Irish Hotline.ie had a major success in cooperation with INHOPE colleagues at Taiwan's Web547 hotline. Hotline.ie received an anonymous report about a forum posting involving 520 child sexual abuse material (CSAM) videos. Hotline.ie traced the videos to Taiwan and forwarded the details to the Web547 hotline. Their analysts uncovered a further 408 locations on this service containing more CSAM. In all, 908 video and picture archives were reported to law enforcement agencies and the relevant Internet service provider, resulting in the rapid removal of the illegal material from the Internet.

Cyber-crime investigations today are further challenged by the increase in the workload of cyber-crime investigation units, the increased complexity of the cases which are being handled, the reduced resources available in the current global economically-challenged climate[18] and the high expectations from citizens and the judiciary in the quality, efficiency and effectiveness of the criminal investigation.

Investigators have insufficient training options in IT forensics and cyber-crime investigations, and in Europe, generally rely on courses provided by Europol and/or Interpol. A number of countries have developed their own law enforcement cyber-crime training programmes either alone or in conjunction with academic institutes. Law enforcement has also availed of a large number of training courses, seminars, conferences and hands-on training provided by different industry players in locations throughout the world. These methods are not scalable or sustainable and do not follow a training path or provide a standard assessment of knowledge or competence. Therefore, it is difficult to measure the usefulness and effectiveness of these efforts. Current international cross-coordination of training activities is limited and relies on a few individuals to drive the activities. The 2Centre network was created in order to provide academically accredited training in a modular format 48 developed in cooperation with law enforcement and industry targeted at the cyber-crime forensics investigator. These centres of excellence collaborate in a network to ensure minimum duplication of effort, high quality training and research, shared with others in the network to ensure consistency and scalability compatible with cultural and linguistic sensitivity. One of the greatest challenges on the Internet today is increasing user confidence and security, which is hampered by large scale highly visible malware attacks. As far back as 2009, the Australian Cyber Security Report highlighted concerns in these areas when they said that "Australia's national security, economic prosperity and social wellbeing are critically dependent upon the availability, integrity and confidentiality of a range of information and communications technologies ICT". This view would be common among many countries of the world. The report went on to state that "the production, sale and distribution of malicious code has become a prolific criminal industry, making malware stealthier, more targeted, multi-faceted and harder to analyse and defeat". This is further compounded by the fact that the report also confirmed that "there is a growing array of state and non-state actors who are compromising, stealing, changing or destroying information and therefore potentially causing critical disruptions to Australian systems.

The distinction between traditional threat actors – hackers, terrorists, organised criminal networks, industrial spies and foreign intelligence services – is increasingly blurred".

It is not clear the level of determination or resources that will be available to an adversary. Some of these adversaries might be state actors. The disclosures by Edward Snowden, former NSA consultant, have dramatically increased concerns by users and even states around the world about Internet security, confidentiality and privacy. The software programming vulnerabilities uncovered in the Secure Sockets Layer have further increased uncertainty.

As a result of these disclosures, the issues surrounding national security is broadly discussed in society today, and it is clear that the widespread collection of data on the Internet – both private and open-source intelligence – provide higher levels of profiling and tracking than ever before. Large volumes of traffic, subscriber and billing data is often stored by Internet industry stakeholders and disclosed to authorised state agencies based on democratic laws adopted by national parliaments. These same parliaments provide oversight that such systems function properly.

It is important to differentiate between data retention and data profiling conducted by national security in different countries and the activities required for the investigation and prosecution of criminal acts. In areas indicated before, such as online child abuse or attacks against computer systems, there is an on-going need for access to data records in order to investigate online crimes, identify offenders by gathering evidence and for the exoneration of innocent third parties.

Many reasonable and proportionate strategies have been painstakingly developed over the last decade for effective cooperation between the Internet industry and law enforcement to support criminal investigations. It would be a great pity if they were disbanded or disrupted as a result of widespread fears and concerns about overreaching national security agencies across the world.

Internet Governance: Views from the Internet Society

Noelle de Guzman

The year 2014 marks a critical point in Internet governance. On the one hand, the United States' recent announcement that it will relinquish stewardship of the Internet's technical back-end, the Internet Corporation for Assigned Names and Numbers (ICANN), could bring forth a more globalised and inclusive model of Internet oversight. On the other, the upcoming ITU Plenipotentiary Conference, where the foundational ITU treaties will be renegotiated and possibly revised, might also bring the global resource one step closer to fragmentation and state control.[19]

There are several factors which motivate organisations like the Internet Society to continue to advocate for decentralised Internet governance. One of these is sustainability. Underlying the Internet's immense growth and mass adoption is its open and interoperable architecture, a feature that has enabled low-barrier connectivity and innovation at the edges of the network. Integral to this end-to-end model is the collaborative approach by which Internet resources are managed – unlike other global communication platforms, there is no centralised authority for the Internet. This is reflected in the distributed and bottom-up manner by which global bodies such as the Internet Engineering Task Force develop Internet standards and protocols, as well as in the loose structural makeup of multi-actor meetings like the Internet Governance Forum.

The future of Internet governance as underlined by the first United Nations' World Summit on Information Society (WSIS) in 2003, the Internet's growing utility to society and economy has increased the range of stakeholders who each have an interest in its 73 oversight. Consequently, Internet governance has become more multi-faceted, with activities that range from technical standards coordination to regulation and advocacy – an ecosystem that similarly requires the participation and cooperation of various groups and entities.

The outcome document of WSIS 2005, the Tunis Agenda, had delineated distinct and separate responsibilities for each major Internet stakeholder group. It has, for instance, recognised the authority of states in Internet policymaking. These provisions however remain hotly contested in many circles. And as the 2012 World Conference on International Telecommunications (WCIT) in Dubai demonstrated, states themselves have yet to reach a consensus on their role in Internet governance. Yet there are also indications of progress. Recent events such as the Net Mundial in Brazil (April 2014) allude to the continuing efforts by governments, private sector players, technical communities, civil society groups and other entities to work together to advance the multi-stakeholder model of Internet governance.

The Net Mundial Multi Stake holder Statement, a product of a two-day debate and discussion among 1, 480 delegates from across the world, outlines a number of guidelines for future Internet governance. It can in some ways be considered as enhancement to existing principles in that it calls for a governance model that is not only transparent and accountable, but must enable the meaningful participation of all stakeholders, both on the discussion and the decision-making table. This means inclusiveness that is backed by policy and operating at the global, national as well as local levels. It also means addressing the interests of existing Internet users as well as those who are not yet online. The Net Mundial Statement takes a different tack to the Tunis Agenda in that it recognises the varying functions that different stakeholders have in different contexts – it allows for flexibility in collaboration, with roles being identified and agreed on according to the issues at hand. Its provisions are relevant to cyber security practices on two fronts: Firstly, it calls for better coordination between technical and non-technical communities to enable both groups to better grasp the policy implications of technical decisions, and the technical implications of policy decision-making. This is relevant in areas like jurisdiction and law enforcement assistance, which still needs more involvement from network operators and software developers. Secondly, it aims to ground efforts to ensure Internet security and stability in universal human rights principles – a demand backed by a parallel resolution released by the UN Human Rights Council in June 2014. It stressed that the rights that people have offline must also be protected online[20] – this includes freedom of expression, such as the freedom to hold opinions without interference, and to receive and impart information and ideas; freedom of association, including through social networks and platforms; and privacy. Balancing freedom and security.

A number of challenges in Internet governance, particularly in cyber security, stems from the fact that cyberspace is made up of infrastructure which are physically located – and thus can be easily controlled – in sovereign jurisdictions. At the same time, it is also made up of virtual properties that defy geographic boundaries. This means that every attempt to control the Internet's physical layers inevitably has extraterritorial effects.

Online security, a concern that for institutions is closely tied with issues of sovereignty and corporate control, can at face value, be easily viewed as oppositional to the notion of an open and borderless network of networks. But it is, as many Internet stakeholder groups have pointed out, a false dichotomy. The Internet's interconnected and unfragmented space lies at the heart of its resilience and at the root of its social and economic value. Efforts to limit risks by creating 'walled gardens'[21] would greatly restrict its current and future utility – to start, balkanising the Internet can and will cause information inefficiencies across networks. The high degree of interdependencies on the Internet means that security needs to be approached from the perspective of managing risk – taking into account threats as well as their likelihood and impact. A good starting point is to assume that there is no absolute security – there will always be vulnerabilities, and our concept of 'secure' has to take into account residual risks that are considered acceptable in a specific context. Balancing openness and security requires a common understanding of the problems at hand, and of where the vulnerabilities lie – is it end-user devices or user-behaviour or the infrastructure or the underlying telecoms networks – so as to determine where suitable solutions, whether these are technical, policy, economic or social, can be found.[22]

At the same time, security paradigms should be grounded on protecting the Internet as a global asset, rather than simply on preventing perceived harm. The same properties that open up opportunities for malicious activity online – accessibility through open platforms, permission-free innovation, and its global reach – are also the ones that underpin the Internet's success and its value to users. This means that security solutions should be designed and implemented in ways which seriously considers the potential effect they might have on the 'good side' of the Internet.

The Internet has allowed us to become more efficient, it has enabled new forms of production and distribution, and has given rise to economic models such as open source software. It also has the potential to be a significant instrument in addressing social ills and other global challenges. Thus, the end goal of cyber security solutions should be to make the Internet more resilient. These should not undo the progress that we have made in making the Internet a beneficial tool for everyone, and should not stunt the Internet's growth and potential.

Ultimately, it is people that hold the Internet together: the usefulness and effectiveness of security measures is heavily dependent on the actions of many actors and entities. The social component of cybercrime cannot be fixed without user engagement. Neither can tools like encryption technologies be beneficial if they are not widely adopted. It is important to consider the costs and benefits of our actions for other stakeholders – and this always entails a balancing of interests, of national security with human rights, and of economic, developmental, and other relevant concerns.

References

1. Churcibaan C. (1971). On the facility, and morality of measuring social change. Accounting Review XLVI, 1: 30-35.
2. Clarke A- and Rosen R- (2001). Length of stay: how short should hospital care be?European Journal of Public Health 11: 166-170.
3. Coh. C., Patuwo B. E., & Hu M. Y. (1998). The human factor in advanced manufacturing technology adoption: an empirical analysis. International Journal of Operations & Production Management 18, 1: 87-106.
4. Conner K. R. (1991). A historical comparison of resource-based theory and five schools of thought within industrial organisation economies: do we have a new theory of the firm? Journal of Management 17: 121-154.
5. Cooper C. A. & Rhodes W. W. (1978). Measuring the efficiency of decision making units. European Journal of Operational Research 2, 6: 429-444.
6. Cornelius N. and Gooch L. (2001). Performance management: strater, systems and rewards. In Human resource management: a managerial perspective, 2nd ed., edited by Nelarine Cornelius, pp: 141-177. Thomson Learning. London.
7. Cooper C. A. & Rhodes W. W. (1978). Measuring the efficiency of decision making units. European Journal of Operational Research 2, 6: 429-444.
8. Conner K. R. (1991). A historical comparison of resource-based theory and five schools of thought within industrial organisation economies: do we have a new theory of the firm? Journal of Management 17: 121-154.
9. Cooper C. A. & Rhodes W. W. (1978). Measuring the efficiency of decision making units. European Journal of Operational Research 2, 6: 429-444.
10. Cornelius N. and Gooch L. (2001). Performance management: strater, systems and rewards. In Human resource management: a managerial perspective, 2nd ed., edited by Nelarine Cornelius, pp: 141-177. Thomson Learning. London.
11. Corston R. & Colman A- M. (1996). Gender and social facilitation effects on computer competence and attitudes toward computers. Journal of Educational Computing Research 14: 171-183
12. Cox T. and Blake S. (1991). Managing cultural diversity: implications for organisation a competitiveness. The Executive 5: 4 5-56.

13. Cronbach L. J. (1951). Coefficient alpha and the internal structure of tests. Psychometrica 16: 2, 97-334.
14. Corston R. & Colman A- M. (1996). Gender and social facilitation effects on computer competence and attitudes toward computers. Journal of Educational Computing Research 14: 171-183.
15. Cox T. and Blake S. (1991). Managing cultural diversity: implications for organisation a competitiveness. The Executive 5: 4 5-58.
16. Cronbach L. J. (195 1). Coefficient alpha and the internal structure of tests. Psychometrica 16: 2, 97-334.
17. Caldas, S. J. & Bankston III, C. (1998). The inequality of separation: Racial composition of schools and academic achievement. Educational Administration Quarterly, 34 (4), 533-557.
18. Carpenter, H. H. (1971). Formal organisational structural factors and perceived job satisfaction of classroom teachers. Administrative Science Quarterly, 16 (4), 460-465.
19. Chapman, J. & Boyd, W. L. (1986). Decentralisation, devolution and the school principal: Australian lessons on statewide education reforms. Educational administration Quarterly, 22 (4), 28-58.
20. Connolly, T., Conlon, E. J. & Deutsch, S. J. (1980). Organisational effectiveness: A multiple constituency approach. Academy of Management Review, 5 (2), 211-217.
21. Crow, G. M. & Pounder, D. G. (2000). Interdisciplinary teacher teams: Context, design and process. Educational Administration Quarterly, 36 (2), 216-254.
22. Cunningham, J. B. (1977). Approaches to the evaluation of organisational effectiveness. Academy of Management Review, 2 (3), 463-474.

India and ASEAN: A Framework for Comprehensive Engagement

There are more factors working towards a synergy of interests between India and the states comprising the Association of South-East Asian Nations (ASEAN) than most other regional entities in the Asia-Pacific region.[1] This is not always evident largely because relations were, for almost three decades, dormant and clouded by the political climate of the Cold War, the different priorities of India and the ASEAN states, and the deep divisions and conflicts within the South-East Asian region. That situation has changed in the past few years, opening up the possibilities for structural linkages and comprehensive engagement between the two sides.

This is not to argue that India or the ASEAN states do not currently have greater stakes in cooperation with the United States and Japan—which along with the European Union shape global economic and security structures, provide the markets, capital and technology—or that China with its rapid growth, large trade prospects, and the strategic challenges and security problems it poses is not crucial. However, India-ASEAN relations if nurtured can have a special tenor because of the gravitation of a number of strategic, economic and political factors. It is essential that all-round ties be steadily deepened so that both emerge stronger not only to face the post-Cold War challenges in the areas of security, politics and economy, and the problems accruing from deep asymmetry of power in the international system, but also to shape the future of Asia and the world.

India and the states of ASEAN are well-placed to expand their cooperation. They do not have any bilateral territorial disputes, security fears or conflicts. The new environment provides great opportunities to expand a cooperative agenda that will in turn enhance their common good as well as individual autonomy, leverage and status in the global order. They share many common social, political and economic problems, besides a long land and maritime boundary. They need to maintain peace and expand prosperity through an uncertain and complex post-Cold War security and strategic climate. Together they could enhance Asia's ability to cope with rapid social and economic change, democratisation, and maintain stability in multi-ethnic states. Growing high level political exchanges and dialogues indicate that this is being realised in both India and ASEAN.

Strategic Imperatives for Cooperation:

(i) Strategic Uncertainty

The world has vast stakes—economic, security, political—in the Asia-Pacific region beginning with India and moving eastward through South-East Asia. It has some of the largest and key states of the world within its ambit—Japan, China, India, Indonesia, Korea,

Russia, and the United States. The economies of the region are dynamic. Huge trade and investments ties, financial and information networks span across the area, making it politically and economically one the most vital regions of the world. There is thus a heavy concentration of vital interests of almost all the major powers, including those of Britain, France and Germany.[2] Given the fact that the region has the world's largest concentration of population, much of the fate of the world will be decided by what happens here and how existing and emerging challenges are tackled.

Peace and stability in this region is crucial if economic dynamism is to persist through the coming decades. This is, however, not guaranteed. A series of sovereignty disputes and military issues have led to an uncertain and complex security environment. New powers are emerging and the strategic order is mobile and shifting. The region has to create a new balance of power amidst conditions that are rapidly changing. The breaking down of the Cold War induced ideological, military, economic and diplomatic barriers; the dynamic growth of the region's economies; and resurgence in power of the regional states is creating a new environment that requires new structures of peace and stability.[3]

Rapid economic growth in the region implies that the major economic powers will be keenly involved in Asia. Two, it will mean the rise in the power of a series of large Asian states, the consequent power shift, and the need for restructuring the global structures that seek to maintain the status quo of the old post-World War II balance of forces. Three, such a shift will entail a possible clash of interests between the established North—North America and West Europe—and the Asian South. Japan, which already belongs to the Northern tier, will be increasingly torn between these two worlds and is ultimately likely to be a factor in restructuring the existing global institutions.

The resurgence of Asia is likely to give rise to other tensions and challenges as well. Strong economic and politico-military competition among the major players in the region is possible since economic power will be translated into military power by many of the states with serious security implications. And finally, rapid modernisation could have a destabilising internal impact on some of the major states, with regional security implications. The post-socialist states such as China and in Indo-China are particularly prone to such tensions, but it could as well hit post-Suharto Indonesia, and the Korean peninsula as it moves towards unification. India with its complex social and democratic policy has been prone to such strains as well.

Clearly, significant efforts have to build inter-state institutions and establish universally acceptable norms for state conduct and intra-state government if the region is to remain stable and peaceful through the coming decades.

(a) Uncertainties About Major Powers: The high speed capitalist growth in the region was, during the Cold War, buttressed by US presence and power. China's growing power is now seen by many in Asia as creating uncertainties about the long-term stability of the old order. The rapid growth in China's overall national power has both positive and negative features for Asia. It is positive because it involves the development of the largest population concentration in a single state and contributes to overall global development. Its significantly open door economic reform has opened up one of the largest markets for

Asian and the world's industry. An economically advancing, reforming and prosperous China is good for Asian stability and security. It is also important in creating a global and an Asian equilibrium of forces that is essential if peace and security is to prevail, and a balance of power created.

However, the growth of China's power, both economic and military, has led to an assertive foreign policy, to use of force or threat of use of force in settling outstanding territorial[4] disputes—as in the Paracels and Spratlys, and in the Taiwan Straits. China's desire for unification with Taiwan and Taiwan's desire to maintain its independence can be a major destabilising factor in the region unless properly handled by all. The rapid economic growth in China has been accompanied by strong growth in its defence budget since 1989, and the modernisation of its nuclear forces, and growth of force projection capabilities, including its Navy. The recently published China's White Paper on Arms Control and Disarmament indicates a general Chinese desire to concentrate on development, expand cooperation and security, and settle disputes peacefully. But clearly, China's actions—including its transfer of missiles to Pakistan and Saudi Arabia—and the rise of its power are factors that are of serious security concern for many Asian states. The South-East Asian states have been directly affected by China's territorial claims in the Spratlys and the growth of its military power. India too is directly affected given the fact that China continues to occupy large portions of Indian territory and maintains claims on an entire Indian province—Arunachal Pradesh.

This concern about China is compounded by the problems of systemic and leadership transitions. There are genuine fears of instability, and given the increasing weaknesses and tensions within the ruling Communist Party, the People's Liberation Army (PLA) has emerged as the principal guarantor of stability and national unity. The crucial role of the PLA within China means in foreign policy terms an assertive China on sovereignty and territorial issues. How to translate the growing political and economic ties that most regional states have with China into constructive peace ties remains a key challenge. How to harness China's power for Asia's overall prosperity, security and autnomous development will be a major challenge in the coming years. It will almost certainly require a policy of engagement accompanied by more balanced equilibrium of forces in Asia, with both India and ASEAN as strong elements of such a balance.

The United States retains enormous influence on the region's economy, politics and security. It has the dominant military presence in Asia and maintains its old Cold War alliance system. America's continuing engagement in regional affairs is seen by most countries as beneficial for the continent's stability and prosperity through the difficult post-Cold War transitional phase. However, tensions between the US and China or Russia; a breakdown in US-Japan ties; persisting tensions in US-Iran and US-Iraq relations can complicate the role of the United States in the region. Stable relations among the major powers is an essential requirement for Asian peace through the coming decades. Moreover, barring its allies in the region, the rest of the states of Asia clearly have to safeguard their security interests on their own. US presence in East Asia may, therefore, be necessary but is not sufficient for many of the ASEAN states—Vietnam being the most prominent example. This is largely true for India as well.

There are internal pressures on the US to reduce its Asian presence. If this comes about suddenly, it would clearly be destabilising for Asia. What Asia needs is neither US hegemony nor isolation but a continued engagement to bolster universal norms, cooperative structures, non-use of force, stable ties among all major states, and an end to great power hegemonism. For the present, the Bush and Clinton Administrations have ensured that American power would not retreat from Asia-Pacific and that both its alliance system, forward deployment of forces, and politico-and economic commitments to maintain its leadership and position in the region would be maintained, though important changes in existing defence sharing arrangements and reductions in forces are underway. America's friends and allies in Asia are not certain how long this would be sustained. New rationales have to be found in the US to sustain the Cold War alliances now that the Soviet Union has disintegrated and Communism is no more a force. Credible reasons have to be given to neutralise the opposition within America for subsidising the security of Japan and other allies in the Asia-Pacific many of whom are currently running large trade surpluses with the US.

But the very fact that the US plays such an important ideological and strategic role in the region makes China nervous and insecure. Efforts to develop a Theatre Missile Defence System by the United States and Japan are highly disturbing to China whose deterrence capability is undermined. This could lead to a series of destabilising developments. A structure of cooperation and peace in which the US, Russia, China, Japan, India are all engaged and find equally beneficial is necessary for Asian stability and peace.

But that alone is not enough. Serious cooperative security building efforts that benefit all states are necessary as well. The ASEAN Regional Forum (ARF) process which the ASEAN has initiated is, therefore, of great importance. The ARF is currently concentrating on confidence building through greater military transparency and dialogue, and on preventive diplomacy. India has supported the process and now that it has formally joined the group, it hopes to actively promote such efforts within the ARF and the Council for Security Cooperation in Asia Pacific (CSCAP) to create a better security climate in Asia. The process has a better chance of succeeding being an ASEAN rather than a great power promoted endeavour. The fact that the United States, Japan, China and Russia have backed the process is important for its success. The ARF's work is not easy. If the major powers violate international norms or use force, the organisation—like the United Nations—would find itself in a bind. Nonetheless, its consultative role is an important initial step towards constructing a framework of cooperative security in Asia-Pacific.

(b) Weapons of Mass Destruction: The important role nuclear weapons play in the defence and foreign policies of the five major powers—four of whom are active in the Asia-Pacific region: the US, China, Russia and France—are a principal source of insecurity. The indefinite extension of the nuclear Non-Proliferation Treaty (NPT) and the Comprehensive Test Ban Treaty (CTBT) have indicated the continued determination of the nuclear weapon states to perpetuate the weapons in order to buttress their security, diplomacy and dominant role in regional affairs. It is a situation that breeds political distrust and dominance, military insecurity, and techno-economic controls on developing states. It also breeds insecurity among the major powers.[5] The efforts to develop a Theatre Missile Defence System by the United States and Japan is an example and this in turn would make China nervous by undermining its deterrence capability.

India is surrounded by nuclear and missile powers. It is, therefore, keenly interested that issues of arms control and disarmament do not adversely affect its interests. Persistence of the present asymmetric nuclear order is not acceptable to India on political, security, and moral grounds. Its position on both the NPT and on the CTBT reflect its long established policy on the issue, and its insistence on nuclear disarmament. However, since nuclear disarmament is not on the agenda of the N-5 states, India would clearly have to take appropriate measures—including building a minimum deterrence capability—to ensure its security and political autonomy. In such a situation India would expect the ASEAN states to treat India's nuclear programme in the same light as they do those of the N-5.

(c) Territorial Problems Among the Regional States: A series of territorial problems continue to sour the relations and act as potential flash-points in the region. Problems exist between China and Japan, China and ASEAN, within ASEAN, Russia and Japan, India and China. In addition, the problems in regard to the unification of China and Korea are explosive in nature. The Spratlys dispute has already become a point of friction. In the coming years the nations have to evolve a system of confidence building, peacefully negotiated settlement on the basis of adjustments, and even neutral arbitration to resolve some of the issues if the region is to evolve into a zone of peace.

The effect of these three factors has been a rapid rise in defence expenditure, arms acquisition and modernisation of forces, especially naval, air power, and missiles throughout the region. This is already underway in China, Taiwan, the Korean peninsula and South-East Asia. India has always supported peaceful settlement of disputes, observance of international norms and legal procedures, diplomacy and non-aggressive defence policies. Its support would considerably streng-then the peace and security building efforts of the ASEAN in the Asia-Pacific region.

(ii) Economic Imperatives for Cooperation

While India has made substantial gains in some areas and maintained an over 5 per cent growth rate through the 1980s and 1990s, there are several important lessons that it can learn from the East Asian experience as a whole, including the ASEAN experience.[6]

Rapid economic growth and increasing interdependence is shaping a new resurgence in Asia. Many of the states in the region share certain fundamental elements that have produced great success. These include a partnership between state and industry, high rates of savings and investments, high priority for education, health care, human resources development and infrastructure; the rigours of the market counter-balanced by rising incomes and care for the most disadvantaged; strong and efficient regulatory mechanisms to guide a market-friendly economy; the values of discipline and frugality—not different from the Protestant ethic that shaped the development of capitalism in Europe—and authoritarian rigour in the corporate, labour and political sectors to ensure stability.[7] Japan, Korea, Taiwan, Singapore and now Malaysia have shaped the contours and contents of an "East Asian economic model"—an engine of growth and a source of ideas for the development and modernisation of South-East Asia and China. Many of the ideas and experiences have relevance for a modernising India, though politically the democratic model the country has adopted demands that they be suitably adapted.

It is this all pervasive modernisation and growth, the shrinking of poverty and rising living standards, the rapid urbanisation and the development of the economic is news of the state that has raised the promise of the Asian Century. Japan, South Korea, Taiwan, Singapore are already among the advanced global economies. China, the ASEAN states and India are moving towards such a goal. This has enormous implications for the world. It will drastically cut down global poverty, raise incomes and open up huge markets for economic expansion globally. India as the second largest country in the world and ASEAN with its 400 million people are enormously important for shaping Asia's and the world's future. Their increasing cooperation is of immense strategic value.

Accompanying this growth has been a rapid process of regional integration—a key measure to pool resources, avoid internecine competition, enhance global competitive edge and reduce security problems. Throughout Asia—and the world—regional economic cooperation, even as states open out to the whole world, is the trend. This is born of a real need to consolidate the competitive capabilities of states by creating larger markets, pooling economic, technological, natural and human resources. The European Community and North American Free Trade Area (NAFTA) are the products of this need even among the most developed techno-economic powers.

Intra-Asian trade has been rapidly growing in the past decade. The Association of South-East Asian States (ASEAN)/ the ASEAN Free Trade Area (AFTA) and the South Asian Preferential Trade Area (SAPTA)/South Asian Association for Regional Cooperation (SAARC) are the two most advanced politico-economic efforts in the direction. The Asia-Pacific Economic Cooperation (APEC) which is seeking to promote free trade, the newly promoted Indian Ocean Rim, are major efforts at various stages of evolution. These are necessary organisations that promote trade, development and security building. By bringing together a group of neighbouring states that may have different kinds of frictions, regional organisations help expand the peace process and promote development. This dual feature of regionalism has been best underlined by the enormous success of the European Union process. Major nations such as France, Germany, Britain and Italy that were not at peace with each other for centuries have today developed a structure of interdependence in economics, defence and foreign policies, and research and development that rules out conflict.[8] The same positive effects can be seen in the expanding ASEAN process which has bridged the previous divide between Indo-China and the rest of South-East Asia and dampened political and territorial problems among the member-states.

Comprehensive ties between India and the ASEAN states would, therefore, have a positive impact on Asia. Paul Krugman has rightly argued that the thrust for growth in South-East Asia in the next phase of development has to come from rising productivity and technological innovation.[9]

Close economic ties and technology cooperation have been identified as among the six key areas of Indo-ASEAN cooperation. Serious Indo-ASEAN technological collaboration is one way this can be achieved. However, current linkages are weak. Much work would have to done to improve telecommunication ties, shipping, air and railway links, banking, financial and tariff issues, and setting up institutionalised procedures before the two sides develop substantial economic interdependence.

Political Imperatives for Cooperation

(a) To Build Stable Multi-Ethnic States: Most Asian states—in this case India and the ASEAN countries—face a common problem: how to build stable, tolerant and secular state structures in conditions of multi-ethnicity and externally induced complications. Indeed through much of Asia and the world, multi-ethnicity is the dominant feature of states, and not the West European tradition of single-ethnic/nation state which itself is undergoing changes as a result of labour migration. India, Malaysia, Singapore, Indonesia, Myanmar, the Philippines, Thailand and Cambodia are, therefore, the world's laboratories for ways to build stable, integrated states based on the shared identities of the people which at the same time preserve ethnic and cultural diversities.

Given the nature of migration and the presence of large communities of Chinese, Indians, Vietnamese, Thais, etc., in different parts of Asia, the issues of stable inter-state ties and intra-state ethnic stability are closely intertwined. Asia has to work towards the stability and security of strong, secular, federal multi-ethnic states if it is to remain secure and stable in the coming years. Cries of self-determination are a negative feature for Asia. What is needed instead is a protection of rights of all communities in decentralised, federal but integrated state systems.

(b) The Challenge of Democratisation: The other key political challenge that confronts both India and the ASEAN states—though in different ways—is how to build stable, democratic state structures in conditions of a rising tide of expectations for better life and greater liberty. Indeed, through much of Asia, the struggle between pressures for democratisation against existing authoritarian state structures or oppressive socio-political conditions is a reality. In East Asia, this has assumed a new twist with the division along democracy-authoritarian political lines. Human rights abuses are common in many of the states. In Myanmar, Indonesia, and Indo-China, there is a rising pressure for political change and expansion of political rights.[10] Jail and labour conditions must improve throughout India and ASEAN, freedom of expression and dissent must be protected, and laws have to be reasonable and transparent.

Without such changes there is every prospect that socio-economic-political fissures will be aggravated. Demands for self-determination and human rights would also secure external backing, jeopardising national unity and sovereignty. Militancy, insurgency and terrorism have wracked many parts of India and the ASEAN region in the past and continue to do so even now. Only through steady democratisation, decentralisation and provision of caring and efficient governance can the integrity of state structures and stability be preserved.

The sharing of experiences among India and the ASEAN states and common endeavour in building secular, federal, decentralised and democratic political systems would enhance political stability and security throughout the region.

Indo-ASEAN Ties

The year 1996 was a landmark year for Indo-ASEAN cooperation. In July, at the fifth ASEAN Summit, India became simultaneously a Dialogue Partner as well as a member of the ARF at the summit in Jakarta, Indonesia.

India and ASEAN have enormous prospects to advance cooperative political, economic, technological and military ties. The absence of conflict on vital issues and the presence of common challenges make it possible to rapidly expand ties between the two peoples. It is necessary that this window of opportunity to build strong relations be grasped, and institutional mechanisms created to advance them on a long-term basis, and impediments removed. The two sides had identified four broad sectors of cooperation during their Sectoral Dialogue Partnership phase—trade, investment, science and technology, and tourism. To these, two others have been added following India becoming a Dialogue Partner in July 1996—infrastructure and human resources. Overall, the following areas would clearly need focus through the coming years:

— Regular high-level political dialogue and exchanges.
— Rapid expansion of trade, investment and tourism ties.
— Improving communication links: road, railroad, shipping and air links, and telecommunication links between India and the ASEAN states. A joint India-ASEAN effort to promote the Southern Eurasian Railway grid that would link South-East Asia through India and Central Asia to Europe would have enormous impact on raising trade and tourist links through Eurasia. Transportation of goods would become faster and there would be huge economic and peace dividends. Investments would not be large since much of the existing network would be utilised, upgraded where necessary and gaps filled out. High speed rail and modern communications would be used.

— Expansion of military-to-military ties through high level visits and joint exercises; co-production of select categories of weapon systems.

— Joint research and development of select dual-use technologies.

— Setting up of a joint group to discuss proliferation of weapons of mass destruction and to control the flow of drugs and illegal arms.

— Since 1991, India has paid special attention to its relations with the Asia-Pacific region: South-East Asia, Japan, China and Korea. Economic ties with Taiwan are growing following the establishment of trade and cultural offices. India became a Sectoral Dialogue Partner of ASEAN in 1992 and this improved relations. Prime Minister Rao's visit to South-East Asia in 1993 and 1994 and Foreign Minister I.K. Gujral's visits in 1996 have underlined the importance India attaches to its ties with ASEAN. The ASEAN states have reciprocated through a large number of visits—the most recent being that of Prime Minister Mahathir Mohammed.

In his statement in Jakarta in July 1996, Gujral laid out India's policy direction while calling for all-round cooperation. The expanding ties with ASEAN have also helped greater involvement in the Pacific region. India is keen to enter the APEC and is keen to participate in the Asia-Europe Meeting (ASEM). These are new post-Cold War institutions. For India, participation in these bodies would contribute to the modernisation, prosperity and security building process in the region.

Indo-ASEAN trade and investment ties have grown rapidly in the 1990s (See Table 1). Indo-ASEAN trade in 1995 was valued at over $5 billion and approved investments at over $2 billion. There is immense scope for enhancing this further. Current Indian exports to ASEAN and investments would have to be raised systematically to secure greater balance. New Indian investments in the Philippines are positive recent developments. Some problems in enhancing cooperation flow from the slowness of decision-making and implementing structures in India. Some of these flow from infrastructural bottlenecks, others are systemic. However, it is also necessary that the ASEAN states provide political and organisational backing and thrusts to deepen the two-way process.[11] Clearly close attention would have to be paid to existing bottlenecks and ways to overcome them if the opportunities for cooperation are to be translated into structural bonds.

However, ever since India became serious about building strong ties with East Asia and the Pacific states as part of its new post-Cold War economic and political strategy, it has faced certain hurdles, at times on the ground that it is not a Pacific power, that its participation in the Asia-Pacific cooperative ventures was intrinsically—however inexplicable—linked to that of Pakistan and since this would bring Indo-Pakistan tensions into the region, India would have to wait. Mental blocks driven by Cold War mindsets, religious motivations, and competitive feelings, have been obstacles to faster development of Indo-ASEAN ties.

Much of this is changing. Singapore and Thailand's growing interest in trade and investment ties; Malaysia's interest in expanding economic and defence relations; strong political ties with Vietnam; and friendly ties with Indonesia, the Philippines, Cambodia and Laos are positive factors. Indo-Myanmar relations have improved in recent years for pragmatic reasons despite continuing sympathy and support in India for Aung San Suu Kyi and the National League for Democracy. Existing defence relationships between India and the region are playing an important role in changing existing perceptions of each other. Moreover, India, Malaysia, and Indonesia cooperate within the G-15, and India, Malaysia, Indonesia, Vietnam, Singapore, and other South-East Asian states are members of the Non-Aligned Movement. Finally, India's entry into the ARF and its becoming a Dialogue

Partner of ASEAN ahead of, and unlinked to, Pakistan has dealt a major blow to flawed linkage theories and removed an important irritant in Indo-ASEAN relations. Indeed, Pakistan does not have either a land or a maritime border with South-East Asia, few economic ties, low political relations, and no strategic, geo-political or economic relevance for Eastern Asia. The attempt to bring it in and link it to India's entry was detrimental to the growth of the relationship. India would similarly be sensitive to the attitude of the ASEAN states towards its entry into the APEC and ASEM.

On the security front, it is essential that the necessary steps India and ASEAN may take to enhance their external security do not cause misunderstanding. A constant dialogue on security issues, and defence cooperation would be required. Both India and the ASEAN states seek a nuclear weapon free world, but their perception of the utility of the NPT and the CTBT—which the ASEAN states have endorsed and India has not—or Nuclear Weapon Free Zones are different. India's nuclear posture will be guided by the need to ensure security and maintain its independence and autonomy in the international system. Clearly the existing non-proliferation regimes fail to address the threats posed by the nuclear weapon states, particularly China and Pakistan; they seek to perpetuate an adverse asymmetry of power between the N-5 and India with both political and security consequences; and they do not have an early disarmament as a goal.

It would be necessary to ensure that the steps India may take in the nuclear and missile sectors to preserve its security and political interests do not cause frictions and that ASEAN understands their logic and does not see them as aimed against it—since they are not. India understands ASEAN's effort to keep South-East Asia denuclearised through the South-East Asian Nuclear Free Zone (SEANFZ) but does not see Nuclear Free Zones as addressing the key issue of concern—the possession of nuclear weapons by the N-5. India, however, has supported the Zone of Peace Friendship and

Neutrality (ZOPFAN) since 1972 as a measure that would enhance the overall security of South-East Asia.

A continuing dialogue between the two sides is also necessary so that their respective defence modernisation does not become a source of controversy as it was attempted over the Indian Navy in the 1980s. Grand military modernisation and power projection strategies by some of the major powers would inevitably lead to defensive responses by others. The ARF would have to deal with such issues so as to ensure that an arms race does not grip the region. Steady defence modernisation within a defensive military strategy is the desired framework for the Asia-Pacific states.

As far as India's approach towards military developments in the Asia-Pacific region is concerned, it has displayed prudence and understanding over the Spratlys issue, the Australia-Indonesia security agreement, and the modernisation of ASEAN defence forces. It has backed ASEAN's expansion to include all ten countries of South-East Asia and sees it as an important step for enhancing peace and security. India seeks a balanced, cooperative order in Asia. A strong India is in ASEAN's strategic interest, just as a strong ASEAN is in India's—as long as both are cooperating, interdependent, have no disputes, and are working together on regional and global issues.

What positions some of the ASEAN states adopt on the Kashmir issue would also be a factor in shaping the relationship. India has always treated the ethnic problems in South-East Asia with understanding and the yardstick of its own ethnic realities. Its only concern has been that no ethnic community must be discriminated against in any state. It has sought to resolve the Kashmir problem politically and democratically under conditions of a large and dangerous insurgency that has received full support from Pakistan.[12] A failure by the ASEAN states to understand the complexities of the ethnic issues, the danger posed by armed secessionist movements and trans-border terrorism, and India's efforts to solve the grievances through political dialogue can only have a deletrious effect on relations.

Over the past years, India has improved and deepened its relations with all its neighbours in the subcontinent, the Gulf, and South-East Asia. Relations with China have improved and the two countries are engaged in resolving the outstanding disputes though the task is by no means easy. Ties with the US, Europe, Japan and Russia are growing and friendly. Over the past year, the new United Front government in New Delhi has through unilateral[13] trade and tariff and other concessions been galavanising the SAARC and SAPTA process. Thus, a settlement of the Ganges waters sharing problem with Bangladesh has been attained. India has even unilaterally relaxed visa rules for many categories of Pakistani tourists. It has taken a keen interest in the Indian Ocean Region (IOR) initiative. Relations with Pakistan alone have remained frozen though there are signs that the new Nawaz Sharif government may be interested in more meaningful talks to lower tensions and improve trade ties. India sees itself as a force for stability and peace in Asia and its role and capability is of immense strategic significance for the rest of the world.

The opportunities and need for Indo-ASEAN cooperation clearly far outweigh the scepticism and problems. Closer coordination and dialogue will help overcome differences from erupting and lay the foundations for strong Indo-ASEAN ties in the coming years.

12 February, 2016 PM Modi's Sojourn to South East Asia: Reinvigorating the Partnership in the New Millennium Dr. Rajiv Ranjan* Prime Minister Narendra Modi's visit to Kuala Lumpur to attend the 13th ASEAN-India Summit and 10th East Asia Summit from 21 to 22 November 2015 was PM Modi's second interaction with ASEAN Members, first being at Nay Pyi Taw, Myanmar in November 2014 for the 12th ASEAN-India Summit. He also undertook an official visit to Malaysia on 23 November 2015 and held bilateral dialogue

with his Malaysian counterpart Dato Sri Mohd Najib Tun Abdul Razak. PM Modi thereafter paid an official visit to Singapore on 23-24 November 2015 to commemorate the 50th anniversary of bilateral relations and elevate this relationship to strategic partnership. PM Modi's participation at both the ASEAN-India Summit and the East Asia Summit and bilateral visit and meetings with leaders signifies the importance that India attaches to ASEAN and its role in the region. India's historical and civilisational contacts and geographical proximity with nations of Southeast Asia (SEA) portray the significance of the region. The economic miracle of the Asia and inspiring economic growth of some ASEAN countries attached economic viability to the region. The rise of China as economic and military power and its growing foothold in the region attested strategic importance of the region. India's 'Look East' Asia policy, in 1990s, was premised on economic and political ICWA Issue Brief 2 | www.icwa.in considerations, to focus on her neighbours in the east. The 'Look East' policy catalysed the India's engagement with SEA nations. India became a sectorial dialogue partner of ASEAN in 1992, which was upgraded to full dialogue partnership in 1996. Since 2002, India had annual Summits with ASEAN. ASEAN and India-ASEAN commemorated the 20th anniversary of dialogue-level partnership and the 10th anniversary of Summit-level partnership under the theme 'ASEAN-India Partnership for Peace and Shared Prosperity' on December 20-21, 2012, in New Delhi. Although, the 'Look East' policy accelerated the India's relations with ASEAN, "rise of a number of new powers in Asia, notably China, the re-balancing or 'pivot to Asia' strategy of the United States"1 has entrusted India to adapt to these momentous changes and thereby a re-energised policy, 'Act East' unveiled by Prime Minister Modi to harness the opportunities and tackle the strategic challenges. India's engagement with SEA nations, while pursuing 'Act East' is the manifestation of India's interaction with the region for millennia and endeavours to rejuvenate the linkages with the region. India is also actively participating in the regional integration initiatives like,

East Asia Summit and East Asia Forum and ASEAN Community. India is also part of negotiations on the Regional Comprehensive Economic Partnership Agreement (RCEP), which includes ASEAN and its other five Free Trade Agreement (FTA) partners, Australia, China, Japan, South Korea and New Zealand. The RCEP, which accounts for 24 present of the global GDP, over 45 present of the world's population and almost 30 present of the world's output and trade, will be India's largest trading block. Evolving Regional Architecture: India and ASEAN The first ASEAN-India Summit was held in Phnom Penh in 2002 to promote regional peace and stability and foster closer economic and developmental cooperation. Since then, both India and ASEAN have travelled a long way. India-ASEAN trade increased to about $ 76.5 billion in 2014-15 and ASEAN remains the largest investment partner – both for inward and outward flows2. Since 2002, India has annual Summits with ASEAN; along with China, Japan ICWA Issue Brief 3[14] | www.icwa.in and Republic of Korea have also similar arrangement with ASEAN. India has acceded to the TAC (Treaty of Amity and Cooperation in Southeast Asia). Source: http://www.asean.or.jp The signing of the TAC by India in 2003 is recognition of India by ASEAN as a major player in the region and the strong commitment and valuable contribution India has made and is making to regional peace, stability and prosperity3. There are 30 Dialogue Mechanisms cutting across all the sectors including 7 ministerial level meetings4. In 2012, India and ASEAN commemorated 20 years of dialogue partnership and 10 years of Summit level partnership with ASEAN with a Commemorative Summit in New Delhi under the theme 'ASEAN-India Partnership for Peace and Shared Prosperity' on December 20-21, 2012. India upgraded its partnership with ASEAN to "Strategic Partnership". Trade and Economic Partnership Trade and economic consideration has been one of the driving forces of India's engagement with SEA nations. ASEAN has become India's fourth largest trading partner. Trade and investment flows between ASEAN and India gradually increasing but remained relatively low compared with other dialogue partners of ASEAN. The annual trade registered an average growth of 22 per cent per annum in the decade till 2011-12, but has stagnated ICWA Issue Brief 4 | www.icwa.in thereafter.5. The total trade between ASEAN and India has decreased by 5.4 per cent, from US$71.8 billion in 2012 US$67.9 billion in 20136. At the 10th ASEAN - India Summit in November 2012, the Leaders set the target of US$100 billion by 2015 for ASEAN-India trade. According to Ministry of External Affairs, India-ASEAN trade was at approximately US$ 76.52 billion in 2014-157. India exports product worth US$ 31.8 billion which accounts for 10.55 present of India's export in 2014-15, while it was US$ 33.1 billion in 2013-148. Thus India's export to ASEAN region has declined by 3.99 present. India imports from ASEAN are gradually increasing thereby the trade balance is negative. In 2014-15, India imported goods worth US$ 43.3 billion which was US $ 41.2 billion during 2013-14. ASEAN accounts for approximately 12.5% of investment flows into India since 2000. FDI inflows into India from ASEAN between April 2007-March 2015 were about US$ 32.44 billion. Whereas FDI outflows from India to ASEAN countries, from April 2007 to March 2015 was about US$ 38.672 billion10. India nevertheless, is the 10th trading partner to ASEAN, accounting for only 2.7 percent of total ASEAN trade11. The statistics indicates that there are unexplored opportunities for India to increase trade with ASEAN countries. This includes trade in services. Source: Based on Data provided on http://www.asean.org/ ICWA Issue Brief 5 | www.icwa.in India and ASEAN are constantly engaged in improving their economic relations. At the 2nd ASEAN-India Summit in 2003, the Leaders signed the ASEAN-India Framework Agreement on Comprehensive Economic Cooperation. The Framework Agreement laid a sound basis for the establishment of an ASEAN-India Free Trade Area (FTA), which includes FTA in goods, services and investment. ASEAN and India, in 2009 signed the ASEAN-India Trade in Goods (TIG) Agreement in Bangkok. The signing of the ASEAN-India Trade in Goods Agreement leads the way for the establishment of one of the world's largest free trade areas (FTA). India ASEAN FTA, having market of almost 1.8 billion people with a combined GDP of US$ 2.8 trillion, sought to liberalise the trade norms and ease trade barriers. Plait asserts that "India-ASEAN goods FTA have a specific problem in this regard. Its Rules of Origin (ROO) insist on simultaneous satisfaction of Regional Value Content (RVC) and Change in Tariff Heading (CTH) criteria. None of the other ASEAN FTAs insist on both, but merely ask for satisfaction of either criterion. Simple and easy rules are essential for increasing utilisation of FTAs"12. Chand Rima Sikdar and Bishwjit Nag in their study stipulates that even India-ASEAN FTA[15] is fully implemented India would experience a 1.07 per cent fall in GDP and a 58.6 per cent fall in employment13. Parthapratim Pal and Mitali Dasgupta also note that India is unlikely to benefit in the short term from the India ASEAN FTA. However, they are in the view that "some advantages for India in the long term, especially if India becomes a hub for service exports to the ASEAN region"14. Palit suggests that it's important to make domestic industry and businesses active stakeholders in the various trade agreements that India is signing with the ASEAN and its individual members to gains from FTAs. The ASEAN-India Agreements for Trade in Services & Investments signed in 2014 is expected to further enhance trade and benefit India. ASEAN and India have agreed, at 12th AEM-India Consultations, 23 August 2015, Kuala Lumpur, to review the ASEAN- India Trade in Goods (AITIG) Agreement to ensure that it is trade facilitative and relevant to the current global trading practices. The Ministers endorsed the Scope of the Review of the AITIG Agreement, which includes: (i) implementation issues; (ii) facilitation measures; (iii) to take into account other negotiations on further liberalisation of ICWA Issue Brief 6 | www.icwa.in trade in goods; iv) sharing and exchanging of trade data and; (v) promoting AITIG Agreement to the stakeholders. India also has bilateral trade agreements with Singapore, Malaysia and Thailand. With Singapore and Malaysia, India has signed comprehensive economic cooperation agreement on 27th May 2003 and 1st July 2011, respectively. India has framework agreement of trade with Thailand. It is interesting to note that India had trade deficit each year with its trade partners Singapore, Malaysia, Indonesia, Thailand and Myanmar. Therefore, FTA with these countries further deteriorates the trade balance. India must hasten the process of trade negotiations with CLMV countries to exploit ASEAN-India FTA in goods signed in 2009, as only by 2018 the provisions of FTA in goods with Cambodia, Lao PDR, Myanmar and Viet Nam will become operational16 and India has only trade surplus with these countries, to neutralise the trade deficit. A third Plan of Action (POA), adopted at 13th India-ASEAN Summit, 2015 intends to foster 'collaboration to strengthen regional financial stability and contribute to reforming the global economic and financial architecture to safeguard the regional and global economies from future crises'17. Strategic Partnership ASEAN-India partnership has exceeded the sphere of functional cooperation to cover political and security dimensions, validating David Mitrany's 'functionalism theory' for regional integration. India participates in a number of consultative meetings with ASEAN under the ASEAN-India Dialogue Relations, which include Summit, ministerial meetings, senior officials meetings, and meetings at expert's level. India also participates in dialogue and cooperation frameworks initiated by ASEAN, in the ASEAN Regional Forum (ARF), the Post Ministerial Conference (PMC) 10+1, the East Asia Summit (EAS), Mekong-Ganga Cooperation and Bengal Initiative for Multi sectorial Technical and Economic Cooperation (BIMSTEC), thereby enhancing regional dialogues and providing impetus to regional integration. ICWA Issue Brief 7 | www.icwa.in India and ASEAN, to strengthen their engagement signed 'the ASEAN-India Partnership for Peace, Progress and Shared Prosperity19', which sets out the roadmap for long-term ASEAN-India engagement, at the 3rd ASEAN-India Summit in 2004 in Vientiane. Three Plan of Actions (POA) have been developed to implement the Partnership. The POA (2004-2010) and POA

(2010-15) successfully implemented provision of the Partnership. A third POA was adopted at 13th India-ASEAN Summit, 2015 and "lays out priorities and measures to be undertaken by both sides to further deepen and enhance their political security, economic and socio-cultural ties as well as to realise the full potential of the ASEAN India strategic partnership in all areas of common interests". POA (2016-2020) further tend to intensify the India-ASEAN strategic engagement. The POA calls both India and ASEAN to strengthen the EAS, with ASEAN as the driving force, broaden the cooperation on strategic, political and economic issues of common interest, to promote peace, stability and economic prosperity in the region.[16] ASEAN also encourages India to actively participate and co-chair joint exercises and activities organised by the East Asia Summit, ASEAN Regional Forum (ARF), and ASEAN Defence Ministers' Meeting-Plus (ADMM Plus). India and ASEAN support the implementation of the Southeast Asia Nuclear Weapons Free Zone (SEANFWZ) Treaty as an effective instrument towards the promotion of international peace and security.

Amitendu Palit observes that India's engagement with SEA nations is driven largely by "strategic economic priorities including spotting and exploiting untapped energy and mineral resources, business and trade interests for integrating into the regional supply chains, ensuring the safety of economic traffic along sea lanes of communication and other vital economic matters" While Sanjaya Baru is of view that SEA nations' engagement with India has "strategic factors as well". Baru asserts that the "end of the Cold War and the emergence of China as a major power have alerted a range of countries in Asia, including Japan, Korea, Singapore, Indonesia, Malaysia and Thailand to consider closer relations with India". It is clear, thus the engagement between India and SEA nations is not guided by interests of one but strategically, economically and politically imperative for both, India and SEA nations. ICWA Issue Brief 8 | www.icwa.in India's engagement with SEA nations is not uniformity across the spectrum. Countries, like Singapore, Indonesia, Vietnam and Malaysia have strategic partnership with India while other strategically crucial country Philippines and culturally close nation Cambodia are yet to become strategic partners. Connectivity The Connectivity is one of the major features of India-ASEAN relations. Cultural connectivity and physical connectivity immensely influence the policies of both partners while engaging with each other. There are numbers of physical connectivity projects with ASEAN countries. Kaladan Multimodal Transit Transport Project, piloted and funded by Ministry of External Affairs, India, aims to develop Port/IWT between Sittwe and Kaletwa along Kaladan River and Road form Paletwa to Indo-Myanmar border (Mizoram).

References

1. Day, C., Harris, A., & Hadfield, M. (2001). Grounding knowledge of schools in stakeholder realities: A multi-perspective study of effective school leaders. School Leadership & Management, 21 (1), 19-42.
2. Department of School Education and Literacy, Ministry of Human Resource Development, Government of India. 'Working Group Report on Secondary and Vocational Education: 12th Five Year Plan (2012–2017) '.
3. Daniels S. (1997). Back to basic with productivity techniques. Work Study 46, 2: 52-57.
4. Day G. S. (1994). The capabilities of market-driven organisations. Journal of Marketing 58: 37-52.
5. Delaney J. T. & Huselid M. A. (1996). The impact of human resource management practices on perceptions of organisational performance. Academy of Management Journal 39, 4: 949-969.
6. Delery J. E. and Doty D. H. (1996). Modes of theorizing in strategic human resource management: tests of universalistic, contingency, and configurational performance predictions. Academy of Management Journal 39: 802-835.
7. Journal of Operations & Production Management, Vol. 14 No. 5, pp. 35-51
8. Fahy J. (2000). The resource-based view of the firm: some stumbling blocks on the road to understanding sustainable competitive advantage. Journal of European Industrial Training 24/2/3/49: 4-104.

9. Farer & Grosskopf S. (1994). Measuring productivity: a comment. International Journal of Operations and Production Management 14, 9: 8 3-88.

10. Fazio R. H., Jackson J. R., Dunton B. C., & Williams C. J. (1996). Variability in automatic activation as an unobtrusive measure of racial attitudes: A bonafide pipeline. Journal of Personality and Social Psychology 69: 1013-1027.

11. Fey C. F., Bjorkman. and Pavlovskaya A. (2000). The effect of human resource management practices on firm performance in Russia. International Journal of Human Resource Management 11, 1: 1-1 8.

12. Gerhart B. and Milkovich G. T. (1990). Organisational differences in managerial compensation and firm performance. Academy of Management Journal 33: 663-691.

13. Ghobadian A- and Aservorth J. (1994). Performance measurement in local government- concept and practice. International Journal of Operations & Production Management 14, 5: 35-51.

14. Gamoran, A., & Dreeben, R. (1986). Coupling and control in educational organisations. Administrative Science Quarterly, 31 (4), 612-632.

15. Goddard, R. D., Sweetland, S. R. & Hoy W. K. (2000). Academic emphasis of urban elementary schools and student achievement in reading and mathematics: A multilevel analysis. Educational Administration Quarterly, 36 (5), 683-702.

16. Gray, J., & Wilcox, B. (1995). Good school, bad school: Evaluating performance and encouraging improvement. Buckingham, UK: Open University Press. Greenfield, W. D. Jr. (1995). Towards a theory of school administration: The centrality of leadership. Educational Administration Quarterly, 3 (1), 61-85.

The ASEAN Regional Forum: From Dialogue to Practical Security Cooperation

Abstract This article examines to what extent the Association of Southeast Asian Nations (ASEAN). Regional Forum (ARF) has moved beyond dialogue to practical security co-operation. Focusing on terrorism, maritime security and disaster relief as key areas of ARF activities in the past few years, the paper offers four arguments: first, while the ARF primarily remains a forum for regional security dialogues and confidence building,[1] its participants have slowly become prepared to proceed with practical security co-operation, albeit only in limited ways. To the extent that desktop and field exercises take place under ARF auspices, most have been organised in the area of disaster relief. This implies, second, that for the most part ARF participants are still pursuing capacity building and operational security responses outside the Forum. Third, the ARF's cautious embrace of practical co-operation is not the outcome of ASEAN's exercise of diplomatic centrality but the result of initiatives pursued by a small group of ASEAN and some non-ASEAN states. Fourth, at least in the short term, any expectations that participants might organize significantly more demanding practical activities under ARF auspices are premature.

Introduction

The Association of Southeast Asian Nations (ASEAN) Regional Forum (ARF) was one of the most conspicuous additions to the evolving security architecture in the Asia-Pacific in the 1990s. However, from the very outset, assessments of the ARF have been shaped by questions over its usefulness and future direction (e.g. Lifer 1996; Lim 1998; Tan et al 2002). A key issue has been when and how the ARF would move beyond confidence building to preventive diplomacy, the second of the three stages of security co-operation envisaged in the 1995 ARF Concept Paper (for example, Tay and Talib 1997; Desker 2006). In the event, given the very diverse political outlooks of participant states and their different vulnerabilities, even defining preventive diplomacy proved a major challenge (Ball and Acharya 1999). Participants thus only arrived at a consensus position in 2001, which could be considered quite conservative and cautious, in line with the principle that the ARF advances at a pace comfortable to all. Participants' failure to move unequivocally beyond dialogue and confidence building, while nevertheless recognizing the overlap between confidence building and preventive diplomacy, reinforced widespread criticisms of the ARF as a 'talk shop'. Interestingly, more recent literature has nevertheless been positive about the ARF's contribution to regional security. For instance, Johnston (2008) has highlighted the ARF's apparent early success in socializing China. Other scholars have similarly emphasised its alleged importance as a 'norm-brewery' (Katsumata 2006) and the significance of its normative framework for maintaining regional stability and security (Heller 2005). Significantly, it has also been argued that the ARF in fact meets the expectations of participants as regards mutual reassurance (Kawasaki 2006). Those explaining the limited achievements of the ARF and its low-level institutionalisation under ASEAN leadership have squarely pointed to the pursuit of regime security by some ARF participants (Khong and Nesadurai 2007), or focused on the effects of domestic coalitions (Solingen

2008). Significantly, irrespective of whether assessments of the ARF are more positive or critical, the research to date generally maintains that the ARF has not been moving forward its cooperative security agenda to extend to concrete and practical security cooperation.

Such cooperation can be understood in at least two ways: either as cooperative activity that is designed to provide a framework for further individual or collective action, or in terms of multilateral activity in preparation for and possibly extending to operational exercises and responses under ARF auspices.[2] While focusing on both, this article is particularly interested in establishing to what extent the ARF has embraced practical cooperation in the second sense outlined above. There are three main reasons for doing so. First, since 9/11 the ARF has increasingly dealt with non-traditional security issues that in the view of most governments have required practical responses. Secondly, the ARF involves many more officials and experts than it did in the past. Particularly noteworthy in this regard is the growing role of defence officials, who meet relatively frequently and in many cases are advocates of practical cooperation. Third, participants remain rhetorically committed to the ARF as the 'main multilateral political and security forum in the region'. For ASEAN countries especially, this raises the question of what the ARF should best do to remain relevant.

The article is divided into five sections. The first provides a brief overview of how the ARF's activities have expanded in recent years. The following three sections then examine to what extent the ARF has addressed in practical terms the three non-traditional or transnational issues that have dominated its agenda since 2001: terrorism, maritime security and disaster relief. The fifth section examines factors influencing practical security cooperation in the ARF.

The article offers four conclusions. First, while ARF activities continue to mainly focus on security dialogue and confidence building, ARF participants as a whole have slowly become more content not only to engage in discussions and exchanges designed to impact on practices, but also to proceed with practical exercises organised multilaterally under the ARF banner. To the extent that such exercises have recently been organised under ARF auspices, these have occurred in the fields of maritime security and, in particular, disaster relief. Second, this implies that operational security responses undertaken by participants are still conducted outside the ARF. Third, this cautious embrace of practical cooperation has coincided with changes in ASEAN's declaratory position on the issue, but for now it seems more the outcome of political initiatives pursued by a minority of ARF states in response to changing circumstances and challenges than the consequence of ASEAN's actual enthusiasm to turn a new leaf. Finally, hopes or expectations that participants will soon organize more demanding practical activities under ARF auspices—involving most or all participants—are likely to be disappointed.

The ARF agenda since 9/11

ARF participants have for years debated about how to advance the Forum's activities with respect to the road-map sketched for the regional arrangement by ASEAN in the 1995 Concept Paper (ASEAN 1995) in terms of a progression from confidence building to preventive diplomacy (PD), to the elaboration of approaches to conflict.[3] Yet the security dialogue of ARF participants has for long also focused on specific regional security issues and those international security concerns that affect the Asia-Pacific, including the situation on the Korean Peninsula, the progress attained in moving beyond the Declaration on the Conduct of Parties in the South China Sea, events in the Middle East and the proliferation of weapons (including small arms and weapons of mass destruction).

Since the end of the last millennium, the ARF's agenda and activities have expanded significantly.[4] To illustrate, during the eighth ARF (July 2000 – July 2001), for example, activities were limited to the organisation of the annual ministerial meeting; discussions at the ARF Senior Officials Meeting (ARF SOM); two Intercessional Support Group meetings on Confidence Building Measures (ISG CBMs); the fourth Meeting of Heads of Defence Colleges and Institutions; three seminars (on civil-military cooperation, CBMs on conventional weapons and approaches to confidence building); two expert group meetings relating to CBMs); one workshop on piracy; and one on humanitarian assistance.

Seven years on, ARF activities had multiplied to include the following: the annual ministerial meeting; the ARF SOM, two meetings of the Intercessional Support Group on Confidence Building Measures and Preventive Diplomacy (ISG on CBMs and PD; which replaced the ISG on CBMs); the eleventh ARF Meeting of Heads of Defence Universities/ Colleges/Institutions; regular ARF Defence Officials' dialogues; inter-sessional meetings on both counter-terrorism and transnational crime (ISM CT-TC) and disaster relief (ISM-DR); a yearly ARF Security Policy Conference; various seminars (focusing on energy security, cyber terrorism, narcotics control and anti-personal landmines); workshops (on CBMs and PD, and the management of small arms and light weapons, or SALW); a training programme and a round table discussion relating to maritime security, an experts meeting on peace keeping; and a desktop exercise on disaster relief. The planned activities for the period until December 2009 reveal a further possible deepening of the ARF focus on maritime security and non-proliferation and disarmament, as participants have also agreed on intercessional meetings in these areas. This development in turn testifies again to the confluence of traditional and new security challenges after the 9/11 attacks.

ASEAN Regional Forum (undated) for an overview of ARF Track I activities.

While the ARF agenda reflects diverse security interests pursued by participants, its widening is of course also the consequence of global and regional circumstances and developments, and calls to respond to these. Partly as a result, ARF activities—workshops, seminars or similar—have concomitantly also dramatically risen in number. In particular, participants have devoted much more attention to non-traditional security issues that tend to be transnational in nature, even as conventional security concerns have remained on the agenda. The counter-terrorism focus of the ARF in the wake of the 9/11 attacks, reinforced by the Jemaah Islamiyah (JI) bombings perpetrated in Bali, Indonesia, in October 2002, is an example in case. Similarly, the acts of armed robbery and piracy committed in Southeast Asian waters earlier this decade had a catalytic effect as regards re-energizing discussions about maritime security.[5] A series of natural disasters, especially the 2004 Indian Ocean tsunami, which brought significant destruction and loss of human life to the region, subsequently raised important issues about the region's disaster relief cooperation. Acknowledging that the ARF dialogue and activities have clearly revolved around many other issues (e.g. counter-proliferation), it is posited here that after 2001, ARF participants have focused above all on terrorism, maritime security and disaster relief. With regard to all three issues, the question has been how ARF participants might be able to make a contribution to addressing perceived threats and challenges and whether this would involve them going beyond dialogue.

Terrorism

ARF participants responded to the 9/11 attacks by demonstrating political solidarity with the United States, as expressed in the undertaking 'to use all necessary and available means to pursue, capture and punish those responsible' for the attacks and 'to prevent additional attacks' (ARF 2001a). While not defining terrorism, 3 there was, as officials noted in December 2001, 'general agreement that ARF participants view all acts of terrorism as an attack on humanity and completely unjustifiable regardless of any motivations, committed wherever, whenever and by whomever, and a profound threat to international peace and stability' (ARF 2001b). Officials also clearly stated their collective commitment to 'cooperate at the regional level towards joint practical counter-terrorism measures' (ARF 2001b). In April 2002, participants of the ISG on confidence-building measures (CBMs) agreed that 'terrorism had become an immediate, direct and long term threat to the peace and stability of each and every country in the region and the world at large' (ARF 2002a). Participants at the ninth ARF in July 2002 released a Statement on Measures Against Terrorist Financing, in which they politically committed themselves to freezing terrorist assets in line with UN Security Council Resolution 1373 in particular, and to enhancing their international cooperation with respect to information exchanges. They also agreed (ARF 2002b) that 'further collaboration was needed to support capacity building, in particular to enhance participants' capability to counter terrorism, especially in areas such as legal assistance, financial measures and practical law enforcement cooperation'. To discuss counter-terrorism.

On new and old terrorism in Southeast Asia, see Tan (2007).

Cooperation, participants established an Intercessional Meeting on Counter-Terrorism and Transnational Crime (ISM CT-TC), which was initially chaired by the United States and Malaysia. These moves suggested the ARF's collective securitisation of terrorism. However, the ARF consensus could not hide the divergent state responses to terrorism, and some countries—especially Indonesia—initially seemed to lack the kind of political resolve in the war against terror that the United States demonstrated and sought from others (Abuzz 2003, Ch. 5).

The Bali bombings of October 2002 reinforced the ARF's commitment to counter-terrorism. In this regard, Australia and Singapore hosted in June 2003 an ARF workshop on managing the consequences of a major terrorist attack. It included an interactive desktop exercise that dealt with a hypothetical attack involving the use of chemical and radiological disbursement devices in densely populated areas. Without explicitly referring to Jemaah Islamiyah, the tenth ARF ministerial meeting termed terrorism a menace to the security of nations and peoples around the world, and again emphasised the importance of regional capacity building (ARF 2003a). Ministers also adopted a key document on cooperative counter-terrorist action that had emerged from ISM CT-TC deliberations. Here (ARF 2003c) possible measures to strengthen border security were organised along four headings (movement of people, goods, document security and general measures). Most of the proposed measures were to be taken nationally (such as strengthening law enforcement and intelligence capabilities) and bilaterally (for example, intelligence sharing and extraditing terrorists). No time table for or guide to implementation was agreed, however. Interestingly, while they also called for enhanced efforts and commitment to combat terrorism, such efforts were to be taken 'in a more comprehensive manner on a voluntary basis, taking into account resources and capacity of ARF participants' (ARF 2003c, my emphasis). While the ARF statement on border security served to provide a framework for cooperative activities in relation to counter-terrorism within the ARF, movement towards significantly closer practical cooperation was not straight forward, not least given different sensitivities to the political effects of both the war against terror and the war against Iraq, domestically and within the region. Based on further discussions in the ARF ISM CT-TC, ministers next issued a statement on strengthening transport security against international terrorism at the eleventh ARF in July 2004. However, while setting out a range of measures and incorporating numerous pledges regarding concerted and collective action to enhance transport security (ARF 2004b), the language employed was somewhat weaker than that in relation to border security, raising questions both about the level of political commitment to implement the measures identified and existing capacity to do so. A further year on, ministers vowed to enhance practical cooperation through better information sharing, intelligence exchange and the promotion of document integrity and security. However, this followed the admission that significant constraints had been affecting information and intelligence sharing in the context of the ARF, including political will, national sovereignty, the rule of law and respect for human rights. Reflecting existing sensitivities,[6] it was decided that the type of intelligence to be shared among ARF participating countries would focus at the preliminary stage on 'strategic intelligence' and only subsequently on 'tactical intelligence' (ARF 2005b). That said, it would appear that no comprehensive updated list was always immediately available on national contact points for information exchange and intelligence cooperation (ARF 2006a).

ARF participants have since 2006 focused on terrorism as a long-term challenge. To this purpose, the fourth ISM CT-TC, organised in Beijing in April 2006, discussed terrorist trends and developed recommendations focusing on promoting inter-faith and inter-cultural dialogues; strengthening links with the Shanghai Cooperation Organisation; and focusing more on the overlapping areas between terrorism and transnational crime (such as money laundering and drug trafficking). At the thirteenth ARF in July 2006, foreign ministers followed up and adopted the ARF Statement on Cooperation in Fighting Cyber Attack and Terrorist Misuse of Cyber Space, and the ARF Statement on Promoting a People-Centred Approach to Counter-Terrorism. The fifth ISM CT-TC reinforced the emphasis on 'soft approaches' by discussing ideas on how to promote inter-civilisation dialogue as an approach to counter-terrorism. As in previous years, these deliberations were subsequently fed into a statement on the topic issued by the Philippines as ARF Chair in August 2007. Possibly fearing that participants might be drifting away from even very limited concrete practical cooperation, the United States submitted to the sixth ISM CT-TC a proposal for an ARF Work Plan for Counterterrorism and Transnational Crime, with a view to building regional capacity in counterterrorism and to focusing the ARF on concrete cooperation. Notably, though the meeting resolved that the future work of the ISM CT-TC should be practical, action oriented and concrete, those participating expressed only 'support in principle' (ARF 2008a) for the US proposal. Following further discussion, ministers ultimately agreed to support the idea for the ARF work plan on CT-TC, but instructed their senior officials to work out the details, including a list of lead countries or co-sponsors, as well as specific projects. For their part, ARF foreign ministers also reaffirmed their commitment to countering terrorism with the involvement of civil society, the private sector as well as mass media (ARF 2008b).

By organizing numerous multilateral exchanges to discuss and promote higher standards in guarding against terrorism, the ARF has contributed political impetus to region-wide counter-terrorism efforts. That said, desktop exercises relating specifically to transnational terrorism were not regularised under the ARF banner. Indeed, to put the ARF's counter-terrorism endeavours into perspective, it is also useful to note, without aiming to be comprehensive in scope however, that there have quite a few bilateral, sub regional and broader regional frameworks outside the ARF in which its participants have either agreed or pursued decisions, capacity building and even operational responses in relation to counter-terrorism.

Relevant national efforts continue, including the passing of legislation and operations by security forces. The former include Cambodia's 2007 Counter terrorism Law and the Philippines' 2007 Human Security Act. The latter include Manila's military and law enforcement efforts to eliminate safe havens in the Sulu Archipelago and Jakarta's raid of suspected JI strongholds on Poso.

At the broader regional and sub-regional level, counter-terrorism cooperation has of course taken place in fore such as APEC. Following many years of deliberations and cooperation in this area, ASEAN signed a Convention on

Counter Terrorism Convention in January 2007.[7] This requires six instruments of ratification to enter into force. The convention specifies cooperation in conformity with the domestic laws of the parties involved with respect to a considerable number of areas, including early warning, prevention of terrorism and the development of regional databases. Its Article XIII deals with extraditable offences. Smaller relevant frameworks building on momentum of the ARF include the Bali Regional Ministerial Meeting on Counter-Terrorism (BRMM-CT), which was led by Australia and Indonesia and convened in February 2004 specifically to translate existing political commitments into practical collaborative actions, albeit outside the ARF framework. Its follow-up was the Sub-Regional Ministerial Conference on Counter-Terrorism (involving Australia, Indonesia, Malaysia, the Philippines, Singapore and Thailand) in March 2007. As regards capacity building, Indonesia in particular has benefited from the establishment of the Jakarta Centre for Law Enforcement Cooperation (JCLEC). Other regional centres involved in building up capacity have comprised the Southeast Asia Regional Centre for Counter-Terrorism (SEARCCT) in Kuala Lumpur and the International Law Enforcement Cooperation (JCLEC) in Bangkok, with explicit blessings from ARF participants.

Bilateralism seems to have proved most suitable for the pursuit of practical cooperation. Australia, for example, has concluded Memorandums of Under-standing (MoUs) on counter-terrorism cooperation with Indonesia, Philippines, Malaysia, Thailand, Brunei and Cambodia. These bilateral counter-terrorism programmes have focused on information exchange and capacity building, not least to further improve border security. Canberra even signed a Status of Forces Agreement with the Philippines in 2007, allowing Australian troops to come for 'combined training, exercises or other activities mutually approved', but this agreement had not yet entered into force at the time of writing. The United States clearly also continues to offer very substantial and wide-ranging bilateral assistance in the field of counter-terrorism. For instance, Washington has assisted Indonesia in developing a credible regime against money laundering and terrorism finance. As regards US bilateral terrorism training with the Philippines, activities are now being organised under the auspices of the Security Engagement Board, a security consultative mechanism established in 2006 for bilateral cooperation on non-traditional security concerns. As the Balikatan exercises implemented under the 1951 Mutual Defence Treaty are no longer considered to offer a legitimate framework to combat terrorism insofar as they are supposed to address conventional and external armed threats only, there has been some momentum behind a proposal for a new counter-terrorism framework entitled Kapit Bisig ('Linked Arms') consisting of three components: (1) humanitarian and civil affairs; (2) security assistance and training; and (3) operations. As with the Balikatan framework, the US remains barred from undertaking independent combat operations in the Philippines, but bilateral training in the field

- For an analysis of APEC's developing security role, see Ravenhill 2007.
- Joint training is in accordance with the 1999 RP-US Visiting Forces Agreement.

is unproblematic. Also, Washington has used the State Department's Rewards for Justice Programme to pay for information that led to the killings of Abu Sayyaf Group (ASG) leaders Khadaffy Janjalani and Abu Solaiman.

In short, then, while the ARF has conducted a number of activities in relation to counter-terrorism, its record on practical concrete counter-terrorism has to date remained quite limited. Most of the ARF Statements relative to terrorism do not in effect establish very consequential frameworks. To the extent that concrete counter-terrorism measures have been identified in recent years, participants have not been shy at least to implicitly point to unresolved disagreements or a lack of resources and capacity to which there are no clear solutions. Though one desktop exercise relevant to counter-terrorism was undertaken under ARF auspices, actual capacity building fostered within the context of the ARF has thus been much more limited than that offered within other settings or arrangements. Unlike members of the Shanghai Cooperation Organisation, ARF participants have certainly not engaged in collective practical counter-terrorism activities such as live military exercises (de Haas 2007). To be fair, the latter should also not have been the expectation given the ARF's status as a regionally specific vehicle of cooperative security.

Maritime security

The ARF's early focus on maritime security was much boosted as a consequence of increasing apprehension among some participants about possible maritime terrorism after 9/11, particularly given recurrent piracy incidents in the Malacca Strait (Johnson and Valencia 2005). Finding consensual positions on matters of maritime security has not always been straightforward for ARF participants given different positions regarding maritime-based threats that in part reflect differences in perspective between coastal and maritime states (Mak 2006a; 2006b).[8] However, they nevertheless managed to adopt an ARF Statement on Cooperation Against Piracy and Other Threats to Maritime Security, which was released at the tenth ARF ministerial meeting in June 2003. Significantly, the statement identifies maritime security as 'an indispensable and fundamental condition for the welfare and economic security of the ARF region' (ARF 2003b). ARF participants have also viewed maritime security as multidimensional, encompassing maritime terrorism, piracy, maritime transnational crime involving arms smuggling, drug trafficking, illegal immigration via maritime routes and maritime pollution.[9]

The 2003 statement contained several further political commitments. For instance, participants agreed that it was necessary to 'step up broad-based regional cooperative efforts' among all institutions concerned (including naval units, coastal patrol and law enforcement agencies). Also, participant countries would 'endeavour' to achieve effective implementation of relevant international instruments such as United Nations Convention on the Law of the Sea (UNCLOS), and the Convention for the Suppression of Unlawful Acts Against the Safety of Maritime Navigation (SUA 1988). The latter convention obliges contracting governments either to extradite or prosecute persons alleged to have committed acts such as seizing ships by force or perpetrating acts of violence against persons on board ships. As it stands, several ASEAN countries—including Indonesia, Malaysia and Thailand—have yet to accede to SUA 1988. Tellingly, ARF participants only encouraged bilateral and multilateral maritime cooperation on the basis of respecting territorial integrity, sovereignty, sovereign rights and jurisdiction and in accordance with principles of voluntary participation and agreement—in areas such as personnel contact, information exchanges and exercises; and providing technical assistance and capacity building (ARF 2003b). Participants also agreed that neither the statement nor any act carried out in pursuit to it 'should prejudice the position of ARF countries with regard to any unsettled dispute concerning sovereignty or other rights over territory' (ARF 2003b), thus highlighting in effect the unresolved competing maritime claims such as exist for the northern part of the Malacca Strait.

In 2004, ARF participants highlighted the critical importance of sea transport infrastructure and services. In March, officials again emphasized (ARF 2004a) the 'need to give serious attention to combat piracy and armed robbery at sea, and to develop a multilateral framework for achieving cooperation in the region'. However, no mention of maritime security was made in the ARF Chairman's statement released at the subsequent ministerial meeting in Jakarta in July 2004, reflecting profound disagreements on the issue which had come to a head over the testimony given by the Commander of US Pacific Command (PACOM), Admiral Thomas Fargo, to the US House of Representatives in relation to an American-led Regional Maritime Security Initiative (RMSI) that was said to serve the operationalisation of the Proliferation Security Initiative and the US State Department's Malacca Strait Initiative. Admiral Fargo had justified the initiative with respect to the need to gain an awareness of the maritime domain and to fight threats using the maritime space. According to Fargo, PACOM was 'looking at things like high-speed vessels, putting Special Operations[10] Forces on high-speed vessels, putting, potentially, marines on high-speed vessels so that we can use boats that might be incorporated with these vessels to conduct effective interdiction...' (Fargo 2004). While Singapore had voiced support for RMSI, Malaysia and Indonesia were critical of the initiative.

Nonetheless, at an ARF workshop in September 2004, co-chaired by Malaysia, Indonesia and the United States, participants reached 'general agreement and understanding' that 'piracy and armed robbery against ships, criminal activity such as smuggling and the potential for terrorist attacks pose a threat to maritime security' (ARF 2004c). They also stressed the urgent need to develop an accurate and timely information system and to apply a cooperative approach in the form of bilateral, trilateral or multilateral arrangements. One such arrangement already existed by then: Malaysia, Indonesia and Singapore had started implementing coordinated naval patrols (Operation MALSINDO) in July 2004.

In the event, ARF countries agreed to enhance their maritime security cooperation by focusing on four areas: cooperative frameworks; common understandings of threats; information exchange, mechanisms, policies and procedures; and national capacities (ARF 2004c). However, this intent to cooperate was formulated against the backdrop of their recognition of obstacles to maritime security cooperation, such as 'lack of political will, a lack of trust between countries, the difficulties in exchanging classified information, and a lack
Following clarifications made by Admiral Fargo in May 2004, the RMSI was further developed as a cooperative undertaking

(USPACOM 2004). These obstacles remained but some headway in relation to developing a framework for maritime security was nevertheless made in another ARF workshop, co-hosted by Singapore and the US in March 2005.

Denoted a CBM in its own right, the workshop sought to develop concrete 'solution sets'. It combined an operational demonstration by Singapore in relation to container screening and inter-agency counter measures against 'small boat threats' as well as 'larger rogue vessels' (ARF 2005a) with efforts to flesh out a practical agenda within and outside the ARF. In terms of multilateral cooperation, the meeting brought about agreement that the role of the International Maritime Organisation (IMO) might be one possible catalyst for maritime cooperation, in areas of situational awareness, information sharing, personnel training, capacity building and technical cooperation. As regards operational solutions, there was no consensus that existing cooperation among some participants should extend to joint (rather than coordinated) patrols and include pursuit arrangements. At the same time, several participants supported the expansion of maritime-related activities by the Five Powers Defence Arrangements and the Western Pacific Naval Symposium.

Singapore used the workshop to brief on the role of the Regional Cooperation Agreement on Anti-Piracy and Armed Robbery against ships in Asia (ReCAPP), which was regarded as controversial in Malaysia and Indonesia. Proposed originally in 2001 by then Japanese Prime Minister Junichiro Koizumi, the ReCAPP initiative aims, among other things, to prevent and suppress piracy and armed robbery against ships on the basis of information sharing, capacity building and operational cooperation.9 ReCAPP also allows for contracting parties to extradite persons who have committed armed robbery against ships as well as for capacity building in the form of joint exercises. Against this backdrop of at times controversial maritime cooperation, participants also formulated proposals for maritime cooperation within the ARF.

One such proposal focused on achieving consensus on three key principles to guide future maritime security dialogue and cooperation. First, the primary responsibility for the safety and security of key waterways such as the Malacca and Singapore Straits would lie with littoral states. Second, there would also be a role for other stakeholders, though this was not specified. Third, participants would proceed to develop maritime security[11] cooperation on the basis of consultation and in accordance with international law (ARF 2005a). These principles were in essence affirmed as guiding principles at the Fourth Asian Security Summit or Shangri-La Dialogue, and also absorbed into the August 2005 Batam Statement by Indonesia, Malaysia and Singapore (Singapore Ministry of Foreign Affairs 2005). Reflecting the continued commitment to this consensus, recent statements by the ARF Chairs have also reaffirmed that maritime security.

The ReCAAP Agreement was finalised in November 2004 and entered into force in September 2006. Indonesia and Malaysia have preferred not to sign and ratify the agreement, indicating instead their apparent preparedness to cooperate with the Singapore-based ReCAAP Information Sharing Centre, which is an independent international organisation. The ReCAPP Contracting Parties in early 2009 are Bangladesh, Brunei Darussalam, Cambodia, PRC, India, Japan, South Korea, Laos, Myanmar, Philippines, Singapore, Sri Lanka, Thailand and Vietnam.

A second idea, put forward by Singapore, focused on organizing an ARF maritime security exercise as an operational CBM in 2006 (ARF 2005a). Though the initiation of ARF maritime security exercises had first been suggested in the 2003 ARF Statement on Cooperation Against Piracy and Other Threats to Maritime Security and despite 'general agreement and understanding' regarding the usefulness of bilateral and/or multilateral initiatives in relation to training (ARF 2005a), participants organised two ARF maritime capacity building workshops in 2005 but remained reluctant to pursue the proposal for an operational exercise at sea. As was noted the following year (ARF 2006a): 'It was agreed that future collaborative maritime activities especially those concerning joint maritime exercises will be carefully studied and consulted between and among concerned countries, with the view of achieving consensus'. Significantly, Singapore's determined push for an ARF Maritime Security Capacity Building Exercise still met reservations even when the original proposal was trimmed to a shore exercise. The exercise ultimately obtained the go-ahead, however, 'using a fictitious scenario and a fictitious map with an exercise area that falls within international waters which will not infringe on the territorial sovereignty of any country' (ARF 2006b). Representatives of twenty-one ARF participants then gathered in Singapore in January 2007 to conduct professional exchanges as well as table top and simulation exercises (Singapore Ministry of Defence (MINDEF) 2007). By the time of writing, this kind of shore exercise has not been repeated.

ARF participants have undertaken further capacity-building measures and even operational responses, but such cooperation has not been organised under ARF auspices. Singapore and Indonesia, for instance, established a cooperative system to generate real-time surveillance of the Singapore Strait, and all three littoral countries also launched the so-called 'Eyes in the Sky' (EiS) initiative in September 2005 to attain better maritime domain awareness over the Strait of Malacca. As part of the Malacca Straits Security Initiative, the EiS involved the establishment of a Combined Maritime Patrol Team and an EiS Operations Centre in each of the three states.[12] The security situation in the Sulu-Celebes tri-border region, where Indonesia, Malaysia and the Philippines meet and which has widely been considered to constitute one of the world's major ungoverned territories fuelling transnational challenges, 10 has also prompted bilateral maritime cooperation. Indonesia and the Philippines have conducted coordinated patrols ('Corpat Philindo'), while Malaysia and the Philippines launched a similar arrangement known as Ops Phimal in June 2007. That said, while the former takes place only four times a year, the latter is organised even only twice (Storey 2007).

The lack of funds and capabilities faced by most Southeast Asian states has also prompted some of the major regional players to offer bilateral training and to enhance existing capabilities.[13] An important role in this regard has been played by Japan, which has been concerned about piracy since the mid-1990s (Bradford 2004). With a primary focus on the Strait of Malacca, Tokyo has relied on its sophisticated Coast Guard to foster cooperation with civilian maritime counterparts.

For a detailed discussion, see Greenwood (2006) and in particular Rabasa (2007).

The Japan International Cooperation Agency (JICA) has funded training seminars organised by the Japanese Coast Guard. Japan has also made available patrol boats to both Indonesia and the Philippines, making this the first time that the Japanese government 'ever used official development assistance to transfer weapons' (Samuels 2007, 80).

The United States Pacific Command too has worked very closely with Indonesia and the Philippines with regard to maritime security. It has provided both training and equipment, including radar and patrol craft, as well as assistance designed to increase cooperation among the littoral states. Training has included maritime interdiction operations involving, for instance, US naval vessels, Tentara National Indonesia (TNI) patrol ships and members of Indonesia's Naval Special Warfare Unit (KOPASKA) (US Embassy Jakarta 2006a). Addressing the use of the Sulawesi Sea by regional networks, the two countries have also conducted bilateral exercises that included maritime interdiction operations, involving Special Operations Command Pacific (SOC-PAC) and, on the Indonesian side, members of Indonesia's Marine Corps Special Warfare Unit, DEN JAKA (US Embassy Jakarta 2006b). To allow Indonesia to promote maritime security and thwart transnational crime, Washington has furthermore provided Jakarta with financial assistance to build a new training centre at the Indonesian Marine Police Training Facility. The US government has also made available thirty patrol boats for Marine Police as part of its strategy to build the capacity of partners (Gates 2008).

Moreover, to address insecurity in the Sulu Sea tri-border region, Washington has helped establish 'Coast Watch South'—a high-tech surveillance system involving radar and patrols. According to Mark Valencia (2008), this involves P-3 Orion surveillance planes, unmanned aerial vehicles, spy satellites, fast patrol boats and helicopters. The US has also set up a maritime interdiction co-ordination centre in Zamboanga. Bilateral maritime exercises with Manila often focus on interdiction. Japanese and US efforts at strengthening the maritime capacity of littoral states have been reinforced by Australian assistance. Canberra has, for instance, offered the Philippines twenty-eight high-speed boats for Coast Watch South (Storey 2007).

In addition, Australia organizes maritime exercises (such as Kakadu IX in 2008) to improve maritime interoperability with the regional states of Singapore, Malaysia and Thailand. Observers from the Philippines and Indonesia also attend. In addition, not only are a number of ASEAN countries participating in CARAT— which stands for Cooperation Afloat Readiness and Training—but some (Brunei, Cambodia, Indonesia, Malaysia, Philippines, Singapore, Thailand and Vietnam) also participate in the Western Pacific Naval Symposium, which also now focuses on operational exercises against the new security challenges.11 Members of the Five Power Defence Arrangements (Singapore, Malaysia, Australia, United Kingdom and New Zealand) have also undertaken such operational exercises since 2004.

While most maritime security cooperation takes place outside the Forum, a stock taking of ARF activities and issues relating to maritime security was11 WPNS had 19 members in 2007. Singapore hosted both the inaugural and the second WPNS multilateral sea exercise. The first involved ships from eight WPNS navies (Australia, Canada, France, India, Japan, Malaysia, Singapore and Thailand).[14]

Driven in part by legal-political debates about permissible uses of a country's Exclusive Economic Zone (see Djalal, Yankov and Bergin 2005) as well as concerns about illegal fishing, Indonesia used the opportunity to call for the creation of an ISM on Maritime Security. The establishment of this ISM was fairly controversial among ARF participants, but it was ultimately agreed in 2008.

Disaster relief

Having provided one of the early settings for possible ARF cooperation, the ISM on Disaster Relief was suspended at the turn of the century amid apparent differences surrounding the involvement of regional militaries in relief operations. There were then also difficult questions about whether regional or international disaster relief should even require the consent of the affected country, but ARF participants dismissed these with reference to the principle of sovereignty. As the co-chairs of the third ISM-DR (ARF 1999) formulated it, 'National and multilateral military capabilities should be engaged in disaster relief operations according to the concrete circumstances and the regulations in each country, in a transparent manner, but only upon the request of the country suffering damage'.[15] This reaffirmed the respect for sovereignty made explicit in the 1994 Oslo Guidelines on the use of military and civil defence assets in disaster relief, which also emphasized the core principles of humanity, neutrality and impartiality.

The ISM DR was reconvened in 2005 in response to the devastation and immense human losses resulting from the Indian Ocean tsunami in December 2004 as well as the international relief effort that this natural catastrophe prompted. Among other issues, the relief operations had for instance highlighted the reliance on bilateral efforts and raised questions about the use of foreign military assets.12 Indeed, a total of thirty-five countries had provided military or civil defence aid to countries affected by the tsunami, making for significant coordination challenges. In Indonesia's case, the tsunami had brought TNI Commander General Endriartono Sutarto to initially approach his counterparts in Australia, Malaysia, New Zealand, Singapore and the United States to request external assistance. However, Jakarta later insisted that foreign military assets would have to be withdrawn within ninety days. The objective in reconstituting the ARF ISM DR was thus to work towards effective mechanisms to achieve substantial reduction of disaster losses in lives and in social, economic and environmental assets as well as to respond jointly to disaster emergencies through concerted national efforts and intensified regional and international co-operation. The focus on disaster relief has remained very relevant. Since the 2004 tsunami, Southeast Asia has seen more minor natural catastrophes, especially in the Philippines and Indonesia, 13 where foreign militaries have again been deployed, and significant devastation of the Ayeyawaddy Delta by Cyclone Nargis in May 2008.

At the twelfth ARF in July 2005, foreign ministers welcomed the idea of stand-by arrangements for disaster relief, albeit under the auspices of the United

For an extended discussion, see Stockholm Inter-national Peace Research Institute [SIPRI] (2008).

In February 2006, a landslide devastated part of Leyte, Philippines, killing more than 1, 100. In Indonesia close to 6, 000 were killed in an earthquake in May 2006 that left many more affected.

Nations, including rehabilitation and reconstruction efforts in the medium and long term (ARF 2005c). They also looked forward to the expeditious establishment of regional mechanisms on disaster reduction, such as the ASEAN Agreement on Disaster Management and Emergency Response. Notably, in this agreement, ASEAN countries had emphasized the need to respect scrupulously the principle of sovereignty and had accorded the affected state primary responsibility when responding to disasters (ASEAN 2005b). They had also made a rhetorical commitment to developing and implementing operational measures, including the establishment of monitoring, assessment and early warning systems as well as standby arrangements for disaster relief and emergency response. Significantly, as regards possible standby arrangements, the ASEAN countries were clear that they would make assets available on a voluntary basis only. The development of standard operating procedures for regional cooperation and national action was also mooted. In addition, an ASEAN Co-ordinating Centre for Humanitarian Assistance was to be established to facilitate cooperation among parties.

To advance the ARF's role—which ASEAN governments wanted to be consistent with their own multilateral framework—in disaster relief, the Head of the ARF Unit in November 2005 emphasized the basic need to exchange information on disaster management and to set up an ARF database of assets and capabilities. He also stressed the importance of continuing with regional capacity building, and to advance civil-military cooperation. To promote ARF cooperation in disaster relief, and to coordinate the implementation of relevant recommendations of various ARF meetings, a number of so-called 'shepherds' then stepped forward, initially comprising Australia, Indonesia, Malaysia and the United States (ARF 2005d). China and the European Union (EU) subsequently also assumed such a role.

The Yogyakarta and Central Java tectonic earthquake in May 2006 occurred too early for the ARF's position on disaster relief to have significantly moved forward. Accordingly, the practical response again essentially relied on bilateral assistance. The US Pacific Command, for instance, deployed a military medical unit.[16] However, against the backdrop of the rescue and assistance activities in response to the earthquake, ARF participants released the ARF Statement on Disaster Management and Emergency Response. This suggested that ARF participants would endeavour to enhance cooperation that supports and complements existing regional and international disaster management and emergency response mechanisms in four areas: risk identification; disaster prevention and prepared-ness; emergency response and disaster relief; and capacity building (ARF 2006c). The document also stated that participants would work towards the development of an ARF regional standby arrangement for immediate humanitarian assistance, including standard operating procedures (SOPs).

The continued promotion of disaster relief cooperation by ARF participants has had three thrusts. First, China called for an ARF disaster relief modality that would introduce a framework consisting of appropriate norms, rules and procedures as well as a regional database of relief resources. This initiative led Disaster relief has of course also been addressed outside the ARF. In 2006, for instance, the Oslo Guidelines were updated. It has also featured, for instance, at the Tokyo Defence Forum (Japan Ministry of Defence 2006).

Secondly, Indonesia has promoted the creation of an ARF Standby Arrangement (SA) for immediate humanitarian assistance. Responding to some concerns regarding the nature of the commitments associated with the SA, Indonesia has underscored that in its view commitments to the SA would be non-binding and that contributions would be voluntary. The third initiative has seen Australia in particular propose SOPs for humanitarian assistance and disaster relief (HADR) in order to provide a speedy and efficient response to natural disasters, including the use of military assets. Canberra has insisted that while civilian agencies might enjoy overarching responsibility in disaster relief efforts, the military often has the best capacity to respond swiftly to immediate disaster relief needs. The idea that the ARF could fill a niche role in promoting civil-military cooperation has attracted some support among the ARF constituency. That said, Indonesia has noted the importance of the respect for sovereignty in the promotion of civil-military and inter-agency coordination among disaster relief stakeholders. One of Indonesia's specific concerns has apparently focused on the weapons systems carried by foreign military assets during relief operations. Against this backdrop, Indonesia and Australia organised the first ARF Disaster Relief desktop exercise at the Naval Command and Staff College in Jakarta on 1 – 2 May 2008 in order to validate draft HADR SOPs. This represented an important step towards enhancing concrete cooperation in this area. The scenario for the exercise was a natural disaster in a fictitious country that suffers volcanic eruption, an earthquake and a tsunami and needs external assistance. The primary objectives of the exercise were to improve civil and military coordination in disaster relief and to promote understanding and cooperation among ARF participants in situations in which a coordinated multinational response would be required. The event was judged a success although Mongolia and Myanmar did not participate (ARF 2008b).[17]

Cyclone Nargis occurred merely hours after the Indonesian-Australian exercise finished. Within days, Myanmar's obstruction of easy access for international relief workers to cyclone-devastated areas in the Ayeyawaddy Delta raised the question whether the international community should intervene by invoking the responsibility to protect (Hacked 2009; also see Selth 2008). Senior officials of ARF participants thereupon stressed the 'importance of speeding up the arrangements to receive and deploy aid, material and relief personnel to the stricken areas' (cited in Kyodo 2008). In the event, Myanmar's authorities resisted external pressure to admit foreign military assets to facilitate humanitarian assistance to the delta, but they agreed to ASEAN's push to facilitate disaster relief involving the wider international community.

Myanmar's problematic response to Cyclone Nargis raised in pronounced fashion for ARF participants how to deepen their cooperation regarding disaster relief. At the fifteenth ARF in Singapore, ministers called for greater civil-military coordination for major, multinational disaster responses through training, information sharing and multinational exercises. They also 'recognised that military assets and personnel, in full support and not in place of civilian responses, have played an increasingly important role in regional disaster responses' (ARF 2008b). The foreign ministers moreover requested their senior officials to develop operational procedures in the form of ARF Strategic Guidance for Humanitarian Assistance and Disaster Relief.

SOPs, complement the existing General Guidelines on Disaster Relief Cooperation, and may include a focus on a possible ARF Standby Arrangement. Ministers also asked the Co-chairs of the ISM on DR to draw up a disaster relief work-plan aimed at coordinating ARF-wide or sub-regional training for disaster preparedness, and to explore the feasibility of an ARF humanitarian assistance military and civil defence assets template that would be bilateral and voluntary, though it would function only as one possible tool (ARF 2008b).

Significantly, ARF ministers also agreed that several basic principles should continue to apply:

(1) the affected country has the primary responsibility to respond to the humanitarian needs following natural disasters;
(2) where needed, the affected country should facilitate humanitarian assistance from other countries and international organisations to achieve the overall objective of coordinated, timely and effective disaster management and relief;
(3) external assistance should be based on a request from the affected country; and
(4) disaster relief efforts should be undertaken under the latter's overall coordination (ARF 2008b).

These principles indicate that among ARF participants there remain considerable reservations about possible disaster relief roles assumed by other regional states. Plans originally put forward by the Philippines and the United States to conduct an operational exercise under ARF auspices were realised in May 2009. The first ARF live disaster relief exercise, termed Voluntary Demonstration of Response (VDR), was civilian-led but also involved foreign militaries. It featured a hypothetical powerful typhoon and involved a table top exercise, a maritime search and rescue demonstration by the Philippine Navy, Philippine Coastguard and the Japanese Coast Guard, as well as the provision of medical assistance and engineering and construction work. Activities on the ground, which would appear to have involved personnel from the Philippines, Indonesia, Papua New Guinea and the United States, seem to have dove tailed the focus of Balikatan 2009, a bilateral exercise organised by Manila and Washington. Most ARF participants are said to have sent to VDR only observers, however, including the vast majority of the ASEAN countries.

Moving towards more practical cooperation: advocates and constraints

As regards dealing with the transnational challenges addressed in this article, ARF participants have clearly engaged in limited forms of practical cooperation under the Forum's auspices. Apart from establishing some parameters and reference points for such cooperation, participants have also organised a small ASEAN since 2005, organised ASEAN Regional Disaster Emergency Response Simulation Exercises (ARDEX): in Selangor, Malaysia (ARDEX-05); along Tonle Baasac River in Cambodia in September 2006 (ARDEX-06); in Singapore in October 2007 (ARDEX-07); and in Thailand in August 2008 (ARDEX-08). Scenarios for these simulations have included a flood disaster, a multi-story apartment collapse, and a typhoon disaster. These simulation exercises form part of ASEAN's endeavours to prepare for the implementation of the ASEAN Agreement on Disaster Management and Emergency Response (AADMER).The recent field exercise in the Philippines means that ARF participants have now taken practical cooperation furthest in the area of disaster relief. This development represents considerable progression for the ARF. After all, practical cooperation was not really envisaged when the ARF was founded as a vehicle for advancing cooperative security modelled on the experience of ASEAN; it is an experience that is generally associated with regional political-security dialogue, confidence building and norm shaping. This raises the question as to whether practical cooperation within the ARF will not only continue, but also expand and deepen.

There are perhaps two reasons to be optimistic in this regard.[18] First, the ARF's collective rhetorical commitment to concrete and practical cooperation is now explicit, albeit more recent than some of the desktop exercises that have been organised. In the 2008 Singapore Declaration participants vow 'to undertake concrete and practical cooperation to address issues of common interests, with the view to build capacity, develop expertise and enhance coordination in areas that can contribute to the region's collective security objectives' (ARF 2008c). Also, some ARF participants are discussing whether practical cooperation in relation to non-traditional security issues could be a step to moving unambiguously from confidence building to preventive diplomacy. At face value, this seems to bode well as regards the ARF's future orientation. However, it may still take time truly to bridge the longstanding divide on the issue of practical cooperation that has existed between a group of activist states and the silent majority of ASEAN countries. The ARF's more ambitious—albeit still limited—practical cooperation is effectively the result of initiatives that have been pursued by only a few participants, which are keen to increase the Forum's overall relevance. As the submissions to the ARF Annual Security Outlook (ASO) demonstrate, a number of non-ASEAN countries have consistently been calling for the ARF to embrace concrete and practical activities. In 2005, for instance, while acknowledging that the ARF dialogues had yielded recommendations for practical measures, Australia posited the need for an 'agreed ARF work plan' in order to take the ARF beyond recommendations (ARF ASO 2005: 15). Canada favoured practical measures in relation to non-proliferation and suggested that the ARF should consider practical ways to collaborate in terms of training for and participation in peace support operations (ARF ASO 2005: 21). In 2007, Canberra indicated that Australia would 'continue to work for the evolution of the ARF from the region's principal forum for security dialogue and cooperation into a body with the institutional and operational capacity to respond effectively and meaningfully to regional security developments' (ARF ASO 2007: 1). Similarly, the United States in 2007 called on the ARF to 'continue to strengthen its institutional capacity to form and implement appropriate solutions' to non-traditional security threats (ARF ASO 2007: 116). Japan has also been keen for the ARF to commit to concrete cooperative actions (Yuzawa 2007).

In contrast, as a grouping, ASEAN has been considerably more reluctant to even represent the ARF as a site for dialogue and cooperation. In 2002, ASEAN foreign ministers still regarded the ARF only 'as the key forum for political and security dialogue in the Asia-Pacific region' (ASEAN 2002). The joint communique of the thirty-sixth ASEAN foreign ministers' meeting then re-cast the ARF as 'a unique and indispensable forum for political and security dialogue and cooperation' (ASEAN 2003), but it took a further two years until all ASEAN ministers explicitly 'recognised the need to forge concrete cooperation among ARF countries in building capacity and capabilities in order to better cope with challenges' (ASEAN 2005a, my emphasis). Also, ASEAN ministers only in 2007 'encouraged the forging of more concrete and practical cooperation among ARF countries in building capacity and capabilities in order to better cope with numerous challenges, including in counter-terrorism, disaster relief, maritime security, non-proliferation and disarmament of weapons of mass destruction and energy security, among others' (ASEAN 2007, my emphasis).

This language obfuscated serious divisions among ASEAN countries[19] in relation to practical cooperation under the ARF banner. After all, as this article makes clear, among ASEAN states, it is only Singapore, the Philippines and Indonesia that have played a role in organizing ARF desktop and field exercises. Indeed, other ASEAN countries have mostly remained cautious about and at times opposed to practical cooperation that has been proposed. This is not necessarily a surprise, as ASEAN states have diverse security interests and they have not least for that reason held different views about how best to foster regional security and what shape regional order should take. Notably, Singapore and the Philippines, given their particularly close security relations with the United States and Australia, have understandably been keen to respond constructively to longstanding demands that the ARF move beyond dialogue and allow the non-ASEAN countries a greater role in the management of regional security. For various reasons, this enthusiasm has not been fully shared within ASEAN though, even if many members recognize the need to alleviate pressure in this regard.

Notably, the establishment of the ASEAN Political and Security Community (APSC, formerly ASEAN Security Community or ASC), strongly promoted by Indonesia, was designed to allow the Association to become more relevant as a limited security organisation and to help address the numerous diplomatic challenges to its position as the ARF's primary driving force. In the event, however, the initial ideas even as regards dealing with new security challenges proved too ambitious to carry full consensus. The compromise that is the Declaration of ASEAN Concord II (Bali Concord II) has thus been the source of some disappointment (Sukma 2010), not least because it continues to inhibit ASEAN from assuming a more pro-active security role. The ratification of the ASEAN Charter in 2008 has not fundamentally changed this state of affairs. There are thus real questions about whether all ASEAN states will want to follow up the ARF's declared commitment to practical cooperation even in its circumscribed form. Within this broader context, there are at least two specific reasons why some participants may be cautious about and may even resist proposals for more and deeper practical security cooperation under ARF auspices.

First, several ARF participants at most have limited capacity and resources. Clearly, a lack of capacity and restricted capabilities may prevent the participation in or organisation of multilateral activity. It is no coincidence that:

(1) the only counter-terrorism desktop exercise under ARF auspices was organised in Australia;

(2) the only maritime security shore exercise organised to date took place in Singapore; and the only field exercise in relation to disaster relief was hosted by the Philippines, involving above all US forces already present because of Balikatan 2009. Indeed, while the attendance at the maritime security shore exercise was quite respectable, ARF countries actually participating in VDR were few in number.

This suggests that for some participants repeat exercises and a stronger record of cooperation under ARF auspices probably depend on prior capacity building, including training, and material assistance. For others this state of affairs implies considerable limitations on security cooperation among participants. Not surprisingly, rather than to pursue practical security cooperation within the ARF, many participants therefore feel more disposed to take advantage of capacity building in bilateral as well as various mini-and multilateral contexts outside the Forum.[20] Even if the region will benefit from that, there will remain ARF participants that continue to lack the capacity to take part meaningfully in practical multilateral cooperation for some time.

Second, multilateral cooperative activity in the ARF has suffered from a lack of trust among participants, many of which are concerned about the possible disregard or erosion of the basic principles of inter-state conduct such as sovereignty and non-interference. As this article showed as regards counter-terrorism cooperation, for example, ARF participants have hesitated to share information and intelligence in a multilateral setting. The ARF's response to maritime challenges also pointed to the need to take into account the particular sovereignty concerns of two of the major coastal states: Malaysia and Indonesia. Indeed, the basic normative framework that ARF participants have agreed as underpinning maritime security cooperation revolves around paying due regard to sovereignty. The debate about what role the ARF might play in relation to disaster relief has been similarly shaped in so far as some participants maintain that sovereignty is seen by some as imposing unambiguous limitations on what those willing to assist are able to do—even at the invitation of affected countries.[21] The use of foreign militaries and their assets on their territory has been especially problematic for some ARF participants, not least because different militaries still operate on the basis of very different SOPs (for example as regards weapons systems carried during relief operations). Consequently, countries such as Indonesia have noted the importance of the respect for sovereignty in the promotion of civil-military and inter-agency coordination among disaster relief stakeholders. There is no reason to believe that further efforts devoted to concrete and practical security cooperation will not remain circumscribed by a wider wariness within the ARF concerning the legal, political and potential security ramifications of relevant collective decisions.

Conclusions

This article has examined the extent to which the ARF has moved towards becoming a forum for practical security cooperation. To this end, it focused on how the ARF has approached cooperation in three key areas: terrorism, maritime security and disaster relief. It argued that in relation to combating terrorism the ARF has formulated a number of reference points and core ideas for concerted action. However, ARF participants have found difficult even limited practical counter-terrorism cooperation within the Forum's multilateral setting, leaving participants to focus primarily on other settings in order to organize cooperation in relation to practical counter-terrorism measures. As regards maritime security,

ARF discussions have yielded basic agreement on a normative framework to guide cooperation within the Forum and other institutional contexts. Singapore's tenacity in organizing a maritime security shore exercise in 2007 in some ways signified a major step forward in promoting practical cooperation among ARF participants, but given the initial opposition to an ARF maritime security exercise doubts must remain about the possibility to run further iterations. And again, capacity building and surveillance activities to improve maritime security have really been pursued outside the ARF. The Indian Ocean tsunami led to sustained efforts within the ARF to promote practical cooperation in disaster relief. While this might also attest to the greater import increasingly given to human security by ARF participants, efforts to push the ARF's role in disaster relief have exposed sensitivities on a range of issues, especially as regards respect for sovereignty and security concerns about having foreign troops providing assistance in affected states. Given that the organisation of desktop and field exercises has hitherto depended on the initiatives and political will of the ARF's more activist participants, it seems reasonable to assume that these still limited forms of practical cooperation will continue as long as the activist states are happy to continue to promote them. However, in view of the constraints identified in this article, one may also be forgiven for remaining sceptical in the short to medium term about whether the ARF will be able to maintain, let alone build on, its current record of limited practical cooperation.

References

1. Griffith, J. (2002). Is quality/effectiveness an empirically demonstrable school attri, bute? Statistical aids for determining appropriate levels of analysis. School Effectiveness and School Improvement, 13 (1), 91–122.
2. Guest D. &Hoque K. (1994). The good, the bad, and the ugly: human resource management in new non-union establishments. The International Journal of Human Resource Management 5, 1: 1-14.

3. Guest D. (1987). Human resource management and industrial relations. Journal of Management Science 24, 5: 503-521.
4. Guest D. (1989b). Personnel and HRM: can you tell the difference? Personnel Management, January: 48-51.
5. GUEST D. E. (1997). Human resource management and performance: a review and Research agenda. International Journal of Human Resource Management, 83: 263-276.
6. Guest D. E. (2001). Human resource management: when research confronts theory. International Journal of Human resource Management, November: 920-1106.
7. Hall, J. W. (1972). A comparison of Halpin and Croft's organisational climates and Likert and Likert's organisational systems. Administrative Science Quarterly, 17 (4), 586-590.
8. Hendry C. & Petrigrew A. (1990). Human resource management: an agenda for the 1990s. International Journal of Human Resource Management, 1: 17-44.
9. Huselid M. (1995). The impact of human resource management practices on turnover, productivity, and corporate financial performance. Academy of Management Journal 38, 3: 63 5-672.
10. Hunt S. D., Chonko L. B., & Wood V. R. (1985). Organisational commitment and marketing. Journal of Marketing 49: 112-126.
11. Hendry C., Woodward S., and BRADLEY P. (2000). Performance and rewards: out the stables. Human Resource Management Journal 10, 3: 46-62.
12. Huselid M. A. and Becker B. E. (1996). Methodological issues in cross-sectional and panel estimates of the human resource-firm performance link. Industrial Relations 35, 3: 410-424.
13. Ichniowski C., Shaw K., & Prennushi G. (1997). The effects of human resource management practices on productivity: a case study of steel finishing lines. American Economic Review 87, 3: 291-313.
14. Inn K. Rowland and G. Ferris (Eds.), Research in personnel and human resource management, vol. 10: 271-299. JAI Press. Greenwich, CT.
15. Ichniowski C., Shaw K., & Prennushi G. (1997). The effects of human resource management practices on productivity: a case study of steel finishing lines. American Economic Review 87, 3: 251-369.
16. Kane B. and Palmer L . (1995). Strategic HRM or managing the employment relationship? International Journal of Manpower 5, 6: 6-21.

17. Kangis P. and Williams D. G. S. (2000). Organisational climate and corporate Performance: an empirical investigation. Management decision38, 8: 531-540.
18. Kaplan R. S. (1983). Measuring manufacturing performance: a new challenge for managerial accounting research. The Accounting Review, October 686-705.
19. Kaplan R. S. and Norton D .P. (1992). The balanced scorecard-measures that drive performance. Harvard Business Review, January-February 71-7 9.
20. Kaplan R. S .and Norton D. P. (1993). Putting the balanced scorecard to work. Harvard Business Review, September-October. 134-142.
21. Kaplan R. S. and Norton D. P . (1996). Using the balanced scorecard as a strategic management system. Harvard Business Review, January-February 75-85.

States with Military Doctrine, Policies, or Organizations

ALBANIA

Albania views cyber-attack as an emerging threat and is drafting a national cyber strategy. A Cyber Coordinator will be located in the prime minister's office. In 2010, the Albanian Ministry of Defence created the Inter-Institutional Maritime Operational Centre, with responsibility for civil emergencies, airspace control, and developing a cyber-defence capability. In 2011, the United States and Albania launched a joint initiative under United States Agency for International Development to improve Albania's ability to prevent and respond to cyber security incidents. As part of the programme, Albanian officials attended workshops held by the Carnegie Mellon Software Engineering Institute to assist the Albanian government in creating a national computer emergency response team (CERT).

ARGENTINA

Argentina has both civilian and military agencies with a cyber-security mission. Argentine military officials have stated that information warfare capabilities should include both defensive measures to protect domestic networks and offensive measures to disrupt those of the enemy. The task of developing joint military doctrine for communications and electronic warfare falls on Jefatura VI (responsible for command, control, communications, information technology, and interoperability) of the armed forces. The Argentine Army's Communications and Computing Systems Command includes "Computer Science Troops" who implement a comprehensive doctrine that includes "cybernetic operations" for the cyberspace battlefield.[1]

AUSTRALIA

The Department of the Prime Minister and Cabinet, which assumed the responsibility from the Attorney General's Office in December 2011, coordinates Australia's cyber security policy. An Assistant Secretary is part of the Cyber Policy and Homeland Security Division under this department and is responsible for cyber policy and crisis management serving as the Cyber Policy Coordinator for whole-of-government cyber security initiatives. Australia planned to release a white paper by the end of 2012 that will lay out the state's relationship with and approach to cyberspace, likely future opportunities and challenges, and its strategic interests in cyberspace. The Cyber Security Strategy was released in 2009. It identified seven strategic priorities: developing threat awareness and response, changing civilian security culture, promoting public–private partnerships, securing government systems, pursuing international engagement, creating an effective legal framework, and building a skilled cyber workforce.

The Defence Signals Directorate supports national cyber security initiatives such as CERT Australia and the Trusted Information Sharing Network for critical infrastructure. Australia's Cyber Security Operations Centre was established in 2010.21 It is part of the Department of Defence under the Defence Signals Directorate. Its staff of 130 is comprised of specialists from the Signals Directorate, the Attorney General's Department, the Federal Police and the Australian Security Intelligence Organisation. The mission of the centre is to advise the government on how best to protect the country from cyber threats by disseminating information and coordinating incident response operations. It is complemented by a national CERT established in 2010 that serves as a single point of contact for cyber security-related information.

The Australian Security Intelligence Organisation established a cyber-investigations unit in March 2011. It focuses on response and intelligence regarding "state-sponsored cyber-attack". Australian police worked with Indonesian police to set up the Cyber Crime Investigation Centre in Jakarta in July 2011 to improve detection of cybercrime and promote bilateral coordination on cybercrime law enforcement. Australia has also developed, with domestic internet service providers, a voluntary industry code on cyberspace designed to reduce botnets and malware in consumer computers.

AUSTRIA

The Austrian Ministry of Defence cited cyber security as a major component of the defence strategy and has plans to restructure cabinet offices to include a cyber-component. Austria's recent national security strategy, Shaping Security in a New Decade, released March2011, addresses contemporary threats, including cyber security.[2] The Abwehramt, Austria's military intelligence organisation, cites electronic defence, including malware protection, as one of its core responsibilities. It has been reported that Austria does not anticipate conventional military attacks to be a significant threat in the future and is refocusing its defence on cyber security as a result, and is building a cyber-defence structure consisting of 1, 600 soldiers.

BELARUS

Belarusian military doctrine refers to cyber conflict or cyber warfare as "information confrontation", which is seen as having the potential to be one of the main external threats facing the state. New elements of the armed forces, including new special operations forces, will be created to respond to new challenges and threats such as cyber-attack. The new forces will focus on mitigating the risks from cyberspace to military security while also using it effectively as a new battlefield. These units will be considered special operations units and will focus on "information security, confrontation, and counteraction". The military is developingcyber capabilities for defence and early warning of cyber-attack. The armed forces are responsible for ensuring informational security and, in wartime, for informational confrontation and counteraction against enemy forces. Belarus's agreement on cooperation with the Commonwealth of Independent States contains a provision on mutual assistance in the event of a cyber-incident.

BRAZIL

Brazil's National Defence Strategy, issued December 2008, identified cyber technology as a strategic sector for national defence. The strategy calls for the establishment of an organi-sation dedicated to enhancing cyber capabilities in industry and the military. The strategy stresses the importance of indigenous cyber capabilities and technological self-suffi-ciency. The technologies considered particularly important are those used in submarines and weapons systems. Brazil plans to develop indigenous cyber capabilities by building capacity in educational institutions and in the military to enhance communication among components of the armed forces.

Brazil's International Security Office is responsible for the security of public administration networks. In 2010, the International Security Office announced that the Brazilian Army had created an inter agency cyber security centre, the Centre of Cyber Defence, to protect critical military, governmental, and information infrastructure. The Centre will be staffed by 140 members of the army, air force, and navy when it becomes fully operational, but the current number of staff is unclear. In 2012 the Centre received $45 million from the government for its operations. The Cyber-Warfare Communications Centre is part of the Centre of Cyber

Defence and has been purchasing virus and cyber-attack simulators for military training purposes. Brazil has established the Cyber warfare Communication Centre, led by a brigadier general, in response to numerous attacks on Brazilian military networks.

Brazil's regional engagement on cyber security recently included a conference for the Organisation of American States (OAS) Inter-American Committee Against Terrorism (CICTE) on the creation and management of computer security incident response teams (CSIRTs). The Brazilian Intelligence Agency and the Department of Information Security and Cooperation contributed to educating CICTE members. In 2010, Brazil and the United States signed a defence cooperation agreement. Areas of cooperation will include cyber security, as Brazilian personnel have participated in US Department of Defence-sponsored workshops and virtual exercises on cyber defence.

CANADA

Canada issued its Cyber Security Strategy in October 2010. The strategy has three pillars: securing government systems, collaborating to secure vital cyber systems outside the federal government to strengthen resiliency, including for critical infrastructure, and helping Canadians to be secure online. Public Safety Canada, the agency responsible for public safety and national security preparedness, oversees implementation of the strategy. The Canadian Security Intelligence Service lists information security threats as one of its five priority areas. "Brazilian army to get cyber warfare training and security support from Panda Security", Security Week, 28 September 2010.

OAS CICTE, "CICTE's first cyber security program CSIRT training course held in Brazil", www.cicte.oas.org/Rev/En/events/Cyber_Events/CSIRT%20training%20course.asp.[3]

US Department of State, "U.S.–Brazil defence cooperation agreement (DCA)", 12 April 2010; US National Defence

University, "NDU college cyber professors: Duvall, Saunders and Hurley, are honoured by the Office of the Secretary of Defence Network and Information Integration Department of Defence Chief Information Office", 22 December 2011. Canada, Canada's Cyber Security Strategy, 2010.

Public Safety Canada, "Government of Canada launches Canada's cyber security strategy", 3 October 2010.

Canadian Security Intelligence Service, "Our priority areas", www.csis.gc.ca/ prrts/index-eng.asp.

The strategy also addresses international engagement between the Department of National Defence and allied militaries on cyber defence best practices. The Canadian Armed Forces Information Management Group is responsible for the protection of the armed forces' computer and communications networks. Subsidiary organisations include the Canadian Forces Network Operation Centre as well as a centre for electronic warfare and signals intelligence. In June 2011, Canada created the Directorate of Cybernetics to build cyber warfare capabilities for the armed forces.

CHINA

In 2012, China's State Council issued a set of new cyber security policy guidelines calling for intensified efforts to better detect and handle "information emergencies", reduce internet crime and better protect personal information. Several ministries in China have responsibility for cyber security, including the Ministry of Public Security and the Ministry of Industry and Information Technology, both of which are overseen by the State Council. The Ministry of Public Security is responsible for investigating cybercrime and responding to emergencies. The Ministry of Industry and Information Technology is responsible for regulation and development, and has domestic responsibilities similar to those of the Department of Homeland Security in the United States; it sets standards, holds exercises, carries out inspections on network security, and operates the national CERT.[4]

China's State Council's Information Office issued a white paper in 2011 on national defence that built upon on previous documents. It tasked the military to "maintain its security interests in space, electromagnetic space and cyber space". The strategy calls for "a new type of combat capabilityto win local wars in conditions of informationisation". It states that the "fighting capabilities of the armed forces in conditions of informationisation have been significantly raised".[5] In May 2011, the Ministry of National Defence announced that the army had established an "Online Blue Army" to improve the network security of the military forces.

COLOMBIA

The Colombian Ministry of Foreign Relations established an inter-agency working group on cyberspace in 2005. After the Ministry of Information and Communications Technology identified gaps in cyber security, the working group, with input from the Ministry of Foreign Relations and the Ministry of the Interior and Justice, assigned cyber security responsibilities to the Ministry of Defence. Colombia created a national CERT in 2009. The Ministry of Defence is the lead agency in operating the CERT, although legislative, judicial, and international matters are the responsibility of the respective agencies. The Directorate for Criminal Investigations within the National Police Force, for example, now has a cybercrime investigations unit known as the Technology Investigations Group.

The CERT is part of a larger national cyber security policy to coordinate public and private sector cyber defence. In 2009, the Ministry of Defence called for a national cyber strategy with new tools for prevention, response, and defence. It recommended creating a joint doctrine to govern both military and police operations in cyberspace. Defence capabilities would include not only early alerts of attack on both public and private infrastructure and information, but also the ability to repel such attacks and to conduct cyber-attacks against aggressors. In November 2011, the Ministry of

Defence ran attack simulations supported by the OAS, to test capabilities and strengthen the reaction of the state in the face of a large-scale attack.

CROATIA

According to the Strategic Defence Review, Croatia will be creating a Signals Unit that will be responsible for a stationary, network-information, and encryption signal systems. The Security and Intelligence Agency, a part of the Ministry of Defence, ensures the government's internet security. Croatia has had a national CERT since 2009.[6]

CUBA

The Cuban government holds a monopoly on telecommunications and controls internet traffic. The Ministry of Informatics and Communications has prioritized the development of indigenous information technology to enhance cyber self-sufficiency and cyber security against potential external threats. Cuba hopes to prevent cyber-attack by developing national software and migrating state institutions to domestic, rather than imported, software and computers.

DEMOCRATIC PEOPLE'S REPUBLIC OF KOREA

Sources suggest that the Democratic People's Republic of Korea invests significant resources in its offensive cyber capabilities, though progress in this area is difficult to determine due to the lack of information on the subject.

DENMARK

Danish cyber strategy is defensive and focused on protecting military computer systems from exploitation or disruption. Military doctrine references cyberspace as a military battle space. The Danish Defence Agreement 2010–2014 calls for the establishment of a computer network operations unit, to promote Denmark's cyber capabilities and to protect the information technology of the armed forces from cyber-attack by 2014. The Defence Intelligence Service is responsible for finding and countering cyber threats and is planning to establish a cyber-warfare unit. The role of the army's 3rd Electronic Warfare Company is to disrupt or exploit enemy communications.

ESTONIA

The Cyber Security Strategy Committee was formed after Estonia was the target of the "first-ever co-ordinated cyber-attack against an entire country" in May 2007, and released the Cyber Security Strategy in 2008. The Committee is chaired by the Ministry of Defence in cooperation with the Ministry of Foreign Affairs, the Ministry of Internal Affairs, the Ministry of Education and Research, the Ministry of Justice, and the Ministry of Economics. The strategy seeks to decrease vulnerability in cyberspace, prevent cyber-attack, and restore critical infrastructure as quickly as possible in the event of an attack. To this end, the strategy identifies the following goals: to establish a multilevel system of security measures, expand expertise in information security, institute regulatory reforms, and foster international cooperation. A unit within the Ministry of Economic Affairs. The Ministry of Defence coordinates Estonia's cyber defence.

The Defence League, a voluntary national defence organisation, is organised and trained by the Ministry of Defence. The Defence League's Cyber Unit has three main tasks: protection of the Estonian civilian internet, training IT specialists, and sharing information on cyber security with the public. Estonia has also created the Department of Critical Infrastructure Protection, tasked to defend public and private networks at the strategic level. It conducts risk assessments, collects information on critical infrastructure, and proposes defensive measures to counter cyber threats. Projects include mapping critical infrastructure and designing contingency plans for large-scale cyber-attack. Estonia's focus is now shifting towards the protection of intellectual property in order to preserve economic assets and advantages over the long term.[7] To protect both critical and economic infrastructure,

Estonia is building partnerships between the public and private sectors.

Estonia places significant emphasis on its North Atlantic Treaty Organisation (NATO) membership and international cooperation as means to augment and streamline its defence capabilities. Estonia proposed the NATO Cooperative Cyber Defence Centre of Excellence in Tallinn, which was launched in 2008 to promote cooperation, information-sharing, and research in the field of cyber security.

FIJI

Fiji has established a cybercrime unit in the police force. In 2010, Fiji established the Cyber security Working Group led by the Cybercrimes Unit of the national police force and the Ministry of Defence. The group, based on a public–private partnership, includes government information technology departments, the Financial Intelligence Unit (which monitors illegal activities such as money laundering), licensed operators, network services providers, and banks. Fiji has addressed online financial protection as well as online customs and tax evasion issues with the establishment of the Fiji Inland Revenue and Customs Excise Authority.

FINLAND

In March 2012, Finland's President and the Cabinet Committee on Foreign and Security Policy announced that the Security and Defence Committee will be responsible for preparing a national cyber security strategy to improve national preparedness. Finland was planning to issue the new cyber security strategy by the end of 2012—however as of December 2012 it had not been released. Finland also plans to improve cyber intelligence capabilities to track organised crime and terrorist threats. The Ministry of Defence has drafted a national cyber defence strategy proposal that would provide substantial investment to protect crucial military, government, and private sector networks. The plan increases funding for the military's Cyber Defence Unit to allow it to mount cyber-attacks on "hostile forces" as part of a "Credible Response Platform", which is likely to deploy malware, worms, and viruses against "attackers". The initial stages of the plan could be operational by 2013. Finland established a CERT, which serves as the reporting centre for information or computer security threats. It runs the national information security situation awareness system, which collects and circulates security situation reports.

In September 2012, the president of Sitra, the Finnish Innovation Fund, recommended setting up a national cyber security centre in order to improve coordination, speed up decision-making, and develop confidence in the field. He noted that Finland does not "have the ability to respond to a large-scale cyber-attack against several vitally important targets at the same time".

FRANCE

The main authority for cyber defence is the French Network and Information Security Agency, established in 2009. Its missions include detecting and reacting to cyber-attack, mitigating cyber threats by supporting research and development, and providing information to government and critical infrastructure entities. It operates under the Prime Minister and is part of the General Secretariat for National Defence. In February 2011, the Agency released the official French cyber doctrine. France's four objectives in cyberspace are to become a global power in cyber defence, guarantee information sovereignty and freedom of decision, secure critical infrastructure, and maintain privacy in cyberspace.

France's white paper on defence and national security, issued in 2008, highlighted the threat of large-scale cyber-attack against critical infrastructure as a prominent national security concern and defined new strategies for cyber defence. In the document, France describes the cyber domain as an area in which its sovereignty must be expressed fully, and states that it is pursuing a two-pronged strategy in building its defensive and its offensive capabilities.

France is also developing an offensive cyber war capability under the purview of the Joint Staff and specialised services. Both the army and the air force have electronic warfare units. Offensive capabilities are also being pursued by the intelligence services. The Analysis and Combat Centre for Cyber Defence coordinates with the Network and Information Security Agency and other agencies to monitor military networks and respond to intrusions. In addition, the Directorate for Defence Protection and Security is an intelligence agency within the Ministry of Defence that ensures the military's operational capacity by providing information about potential threats and vulnerabilities. It protects against the threats of espionage, sabotage, subversion, organised crime, and terrorism. The Directorate increasingly focuses on communicating cyber threats and vulnerabilities to network operators in the military and the defence industry in order to improve cyber security.

GEORGIA

The Georgian Ministry of Defence Minister's Vision 2012–2013 prioritizes the development of cyber security capabilities, as well as streamlining. The army has one brigade for intelligence, surveillance, and reconnaissance that includes two electronic warfare regiments. The air force has one fleet for electronic warfare communication and information systems. Georgia's National Security Concept, approved by Parliament in December 2011, identifies cyber security as a key priority, emphasizing[8] the need for rapid response and mitigation capabilities, information security, and international cooperation. Georgia has been developing a National Cyber Strategy, but as of December 2012 it was not yet finalised. Early reports indicated that the strategy will centre around five key objectives: research and analysis, a normative framework for new legislation, inter-agency coordination, public awareness and education, and international cooperation.[9]

As of June 2012, Georgia's parliament has been debating a draft bill on information security, which would define critical information systems as those systems whose function is essential to self-defence, economic security, preservation of state authorities, and/or public life, and which proposes an expanded system of classification to safeguard sensitive information. Georgia's information security efforts are coordinated by the Data Exchange Agency, which also manages e-governance and infrastructure development efforts. Georgia recently signed the Convention on Cybercrime, which entered into force in Georgia in October 2012.

GERMANY

In March 2011, the German Federal Government released a new cyber security strategy. It builds on the 2009 Act to Strengthen the Security of Federal Information Technology, the 2009 Critical Infrastructure Protection Implementation Plan, and the 2005 National Plan for Information Infrastructure Protection. The latter was Germany's first effort at a comprehensive approach to cyber security. Under the 2011 strategy, a National Cyber Security Council was established, headed by a state secretary from the Ministry of Interior, and a National Cyber Response Centre. The Ministry of the Interior has been the lead on cyber security and the Federal Office for Information Security, overseen by the ministry, is in charge of promoting the security of information technology.

The National Cyber Security Council will focus on coordinating preventive and cooperative cyber security measures. It is composed of the Federal Chancellery and state secretaries from the Foreign Office, the Ministry of the Interior, the Ministry of Defence, the Ministry for Economics and Technology, the Ministry of Justice, the Ministry of Finance, and the Ministry of Education and Research, as well as state-level representatives. Representatives from private industry as well as academia are invited as associated members. The National Cyber Security Council is responsible for coordinating defence techniques and cyber policy.

Germany's National Cyber Response Centre incorporates officials from the Federal Criminal Police Office, the Federal Police, the Customs Criminological Office, the Federal Intelligence Service, the armed forces, and critical infrastructure authorities. The Centre reports to the Federal Office for Information Security and coordinates with the Federal Office for the Protection of the Constitution and the Federal Office of Civil Protection and Disaster Assistance, (both part of the Ministry of the Interior). The Centre will not develop offensive capabilities, instead focusing on operational cooperation and information-sharing in areas of vulnerability protection and incident response. In August 2012, the Minister of the Interior announced the potential need for new cyber security legislation and that he was currently in discussions with industry.[10]

The Department of Information and Computer Network Operations of the armed forces' Strategic Reconnaissance Unit is tasked with developing cyber capabilities. In 2009, this consisted of 76 military personnel with computer science training provided by the armed forces. The unit was reportedly designed as a specialised cyber group to be trained in offensive cyber capabilities.

GREECE

In 2008, Greece established the National Authority Against Electronic Attack-CERT, as part of its National Intelligence Service. The Authority is tasked with the protection of the public sector and national critical infrastructures by means both passive and active. Three other publicly funded CERTs serve Greece: AUTH-CERT, GRNET-CERT, and FORTH CERT, all of them sharing responsibility for alerts, warnings and announcements, incident handling, and response and coordination.

The military's investment in cyber warfare capabilities began with the establishment of the Office of Computer Warfare in 1999. In 2004, the military established the Department of Cyber Defence, which in February 2011 was upgraded to the Directorate of Cyber Defence, 110 falling directly under the authority of the Chief of Defence. The Directorate is responsible for defending against acts of cyber warfare and to this end coordinates with the National Intelligence Service and the police. It is also responsible for the coordination of national and international cyber defence exercises. Greece conducted two rounds of national exercises in 2010 and 2011and participated in the NATO Cyber Defence Exercise of 2010 and 2011.

HUNGARY

Hungary's 2012 National Security Strategy identifies the need to ensure the operation of critical infrastructure networks, assess and prioritize cyber risks, raise public awareness of cyber threats, and work with international partners to protect secure information systems. The National Cyber security Centre is tasked with protecting central government systems as well as critical infrastructure from cyber-attack. It is also the home of CERT-Hungary. The Centre is part of the Prime Minister's Office and is led by the Information Security Supervisor of the Government. The Centre focuses on prevention and early detection of cyber-attack and is developing the technical capability to defend against such. It works with the public to raise awareness of cyber security, with the private sector to promote information exchange on information technology issues, and with the government to develop long-term cyber strategies. The Centre represents Hungary in international forums in cyber security exercises and information-sharing initiatives. The Ministry of Defence is responsible for information security and has developed special classes at the Zrinyi Defence Academy to build military cyber security capacity. During Hungary's Council of the European Union presidency in 2011, the Ministry of Defence hosted a European conference on cyberspace security and in October 2012 hosted the second global Cyber Security Summit, building on the first such conference held in London in November 2011.

INDIA

In November 2012, India established the National Cyber Security Coordinator as the overarching body for securing cyber systems, supported by four agencies: the National Technical Research Organisation, the National Critical Information and Infrastructure Protection Centre, the Computer Emergency Response Team, and the Ministry of Defence. The National Technical Research Organisation and the National Critical Information Infrastructure Protection Centre will be tasked with protecting critical infrastructure such as police systems, nuclear facilities, and space ground stations. The Ministry of Defence will maintain cyber security of the army, air force, and navy defence systems, and the National Cyber Security Coordinator will ensure that there are no overlapping functions or jurisdictions across the four cyber security agencies. India also has a cyber-security coordinator in the National Security Council Secretariat.

The Ministry of Communications and Information Technology released a draft National Cyber Security Policy in March 2011, much of which focuses on the protection of critical infrastructure, public–private partnerships, and research and development efforts. In line with the draft policy, a proposal under consideration by the National Security Council as of June 2012 would create the National Critical Information Infrastructure Protection Centre (under the National Technical Research Organisation), which, along with national and sector-specific CERTs, would ensure the security of the state's critical infrastructure.

India set up a Joint Working Group on cyber security, which was to establish a testing laboratory to audit and study the vulnerabilities of critical information infrastructure and establish a multidisciplinary centre for excellence. The Ministry of Defence's Defence Research and Development Organisation is developing an indigenous cyber defence system to ensure that vital sectors are safe and secure. As of May 2012, the project was reportedly about 50 per cent complete.[11] The Defence Intelligence Agency and the National Technical Intelligence Communication Centre are creating a joint team to alert the government to potential cyber vulnerabilities.

Multiple organisations within the Ministry of Defence are responsible for cyber security. The Defence Information Warfare Agency coordinates information warfare responses. In 2005, the Indian Army created the Cyber Security Establishment to secure networks at the division level and to conduct security audits. The army also established the Cyber Security Laboratory at the Military College of Telecommunications Engineering in April 2010. In July 2012, the Indian Navy announced the formation of a new cadre of information technology officers dedicated to managing, [12] administering, and protecting critical networks. The navy has said that the officers will not engage in offensive operations. The National Technical Research Organisation, along with the Defence

Intelligence Agency, is responsible for developing offensive cyber capabilities. India's National Security Advisory Board has recommended the creation of centralcyber security command modelled on the United States Cyber Command.

INDONESIA

In March 2012, Indonesia's Deputy Defence Minister announced plans for the creation of a cyber-defence unit to secure networks related to defence and military infrastructures. Indonesia has drafted cyber legislation. A 2007 decree by the Ministry of Communication and Information Technology tasked Indonesia's Security Incident Response Team on Internet Infrastructure / Coordination Centre with a wide range of cyber security functions, including advising on major cyber threats, improving national cyber defence (especially in critical infrastructure), and supporting law enforcement with regard to cybercrime.

ISLAMIC REPUBLIC OF IRAN

The Islamic Republic of Iran has put significant effort into developing cyber capabilities. In March 2012, a decree was issued establishing the Supreme Council of Cyberspace, to include heads of intelligence, militia, security, media, and the Revolutionary Guard Corps. The Council is tasked with the coordination of national cyber warfare and information security and may play a role in the effort to develop a national internet.

The acting commander of the Basiji, a paramilitary force, announced that state's cyber army is made up of some 120, 000 university teachers, students, and clerics. The Islamic Republic of Iran announced in June 2011 that it plans to establish a cyber-command for the armed forces to defend against cyber-attack and to centralize operations. Iranian officials state that the cyber command will be defensive and that it will be primarily concerned with thwarting efforts to incite dissent within the country. Iranian cyber capabilities are coordinated within the military by the Passive Defence Organisation. The Islamic Revolutionary Guard Corps also has a cyber-warfare unit. In 2010, a military commander[13] described this as the second largest cyber army in the world. The Iranian Cyber Police Unit, launched in 2011, is mainly used to police social media websites.

ISRAEL

In May 2011, Israel launched its National Cyber Defence Initiative, creating the National Cybernetic Taskforce. The Taskforce's recommendations led to the establishment of the National Cyber Directorate in the Prime Minister's Office. The Directorate's task is to ensure inter-agency coordination and expand cyber security in critical infrastructure and industry. The Directorate is developing a national cyber defence concept and appropriate regulations, and promoting international cooperation. Civilian cyber security is handled by the National Information Security Authority within the

Israel Security Agency, established in 2002 with the goal of securing critical infrastructure, formulating information security strategies, and publishing threat scenarios. It has authority over several major operators of critical infrastructure, including electricity providers, banks, and government entities, and is empowered to levy sanctions against organisations in violation of its directives. It has limited power, however, over other government entities such as the Israeli Defence Forces, issuing prescriptive guidelines but lacking formal oversight. In November 2012, Israel announced that it is creating a dual cyber security programme called MASAD, which will promote research and development for both civilian and defence purposes.

Military-oriented operations are split between the Israel Defence Forces' Unit 8200—which deals with signals intelligence and encryption—and the C4I Corps. Unit 8200 is staffed by military conscripts and officers, and it focuses on three areas of cyber security: intelligence gathering, defence, and attack. The C4I Corps is responsible for and organizing cyber defence capabilities, with teams that test firewalls and encryption. In 2009, to improve cooperation between Unit 8200 and C4I, a senior intelligence officer was assigned to the C4I's Centre for Encryption and Information Security with responsibility for assessing technological advances in cyber capabilities among Israel's adversaries. Senior military officials have said that cyber warfare fits well with Israel's military doctrine, and that it gives small states abilities once only available to superpowers.

ITALY

Italy's 2010 Annual Report on the Information System for the Security of the Republic identified cyber security as a growing challenge to national security. In June 2012, Italy held the state's first national cyber security exercise, involving the Council of Ministers, and the Ministries of Defence, Public Administration, and Public Safety, to test the security services' response to a series of simulated attacks by cyber criminals.

The Ministers of Communications, Justice, and Internal Affairs created a permanent observer group for the security and protection of networks and communications. The Data Protection Authority and the police collaborate on a regular basis to stop and prevent criminal activities involving spam and spyware. Italy does have a CERT; however it has "insufficient funds to operate on a global scale".

The Italian military has an electronic warfare unit responsible for intelligence, surveillance, target acquisition, and reconnaissance. Other elements monitoring cyber security include the Defence Innovation Centre and the Division for Information Security of the Defence Staff. Additionally, the Telematics Section of the Carabineer was established to combat cybercrime and terrorism. Italy participated in a seven-country exercise organised by the European Network and Information Security Agency in June 2012 to test national response mechanisms and to improve cross-border coordination, and it is a founding member of the NATO Cooperative Cyber Defence Centre of Excellence. Italy is a signatory of the Convention on Cybercrime and has enacted or amended legislation to provide a legal framework for combating cybercrime.

JAPAN

Japan is beginning to create new organisations and to fund research on cyber capabilities and hopes to issue a comprehensive national cyber security strategy in 2013.[14] The National Information Security Centre and the Information Security Policy Council, both established in 2005 in the Cabinet Office, are responsible for national security and emergency response systems, including guarding against cyber-attack. The Centre drafts standards, formulates recommendation, and reports to the Cabinet Secretariat. It is supported by the Government Security Operation Coordination team, which became operational in 2008. The team monitors government information systems and implements the Centre's directives. Japan's 2009 National Strategy on Information Security indicates that all government agencies must assist the team in improving cyber defences.

Japan's Ministry of Defence plans to create a 100-member cyber defence unit in 2013. Currently, the Japan Self-Defence Force has four units with 360 members responsible for protecting military computer systems. The Command, Control, Communications, and Computer Systems Command, established in 2008, will develop cyber defence capabilities at the national level. The Command's Cyberspace Defence Unit will integrate cyber defence into the military, provide coordination and technical and training assistance, and research cyber warfare options. Japan's 2010 defence white paper highlighted cyber activity as a new development in warfare and described trends in cyber warfare capabilities. In June 2011, Japan and the United States announced a bilateral strategic policy dialogue on cyber security issues. Japan's Ministry of Internal Affairs and Communications and the Ministry of Economy, Trade, and Industry established the Cyber Clean Centre to study botnets, analyse their occurrence, and develop counter measures. Internet service providers and security vendors assist with the research. In October 2011, because of attacks on Mitsubishi and other Japanese corporations, the Ministry of Economy, Trade, and Industry established the Japan Cyber Security Information Sharing Partnership to facilitate information-sharing among manufacturers of core and various public and private cyber security organisations.

KAZAKHSTAN

Kazakhstan's 2011 Military Doctrine identifies cyber terrorism and the use of information technologies and psychological warfare to interfere in Kazakhstan's internal affairs as threats facing the country. The Ministry of Communication and Information controls much of the country's IT infrastructure. In 2009, Kazakhstan established a CERT in the Ministry of Communications and Information to monitor and protect the kHz domain. Additionally, the Kazakhstan Committee of National Security has created the

Computer Crime Unit. Kazakhstan proposed creating a cyber-police agency within the Shanghai Cooperation Organisation and has participated in Collective Security Treaty Organisation discussions on efforts to combat cybercrime.[15] Kazakhstan's civil nuclear cooperation agreement with India also included a memorandum of understanding between the states' CERTs supporting coordination in the event of a cyber-attack, including mutual response to cyber incidents, the exchange of information on threats and attacks, and the exchange of human resources. It also meets with foreign CERT programmes to improve effectiveness.

LITHUANIA

In 2011, Lithuania published its cyber security strategy, the Programme for the Development of Electronic Information Security (Cyber-Security) for 2011–2019, which sets objectives for securing state-owned information resources, efficient functioning of critical information infrastructure, and cyber security for all Lithuanian internet users. Additionally, the Programme identifies the required tasks for achieving these objectives and divides responsibility for these tasks among numerous ministries. The Programme also sets a 2015 deadline for a Cyber Defence Plan to address defence institutions' critical information infrastructure, to be followed by a National Cyber Defence Plan in 2019, covering critical information infrastructure and national information resources. Lithuania has, according to its Prime Minister, established a national cyber coordinator position. Lithuania continues to develop cyber security laws. Lithuania's military doctrine classifies cyberspace as a war fighting environment and identifies "massive cyber-attack" as a potential threat to the country.

MALAYSIA

Malaysia has established national policies and organisations to promote cyber security. The National Cyber Crisis Committee, operating under the National Security Council, provides policy direction for cyber security.

Additionally, the National Cyber-Security Policy seeks to address threats to critical national information infrastructure by defining 10 critical sectors and eight policy thrusts to ensure protection. The Ministry of Defence implements information technology security policy to protect government and business from cyber-attack. Its missions include ensuring the safety of networks and preventing cyber incidents from having harmful economic effects. Cyber Security Malaysia, part of the Ministry of Science, Technology, and Innovation, coordinates national cyber security policy implementation. Cyber security Malaysia is also involved in cyber emergency response, digital forensics, and law enforcement to combat cybercrime, and provides a help centre for internet users, a training centre for professionals, and public alerts on cyber threats. To support these efforts, Cyber Security Malaysia hosts annual Cyber Crisis Exercises to assess national capabilities to withstand a cyber-attack. Malaysia continues to develop new cyber security laws in response to increased attacks against government websites. Malaysia's CERT, formed in 1997, addresses the computer security concerns of internet users and cites its goal as the reduction of successful attacks and lowering the risk of damage from cyber-attack.

MYANMAR

Myanmar established the Defence Services Computer Directorate in 1990, which was later renamed Military Affairs Security and given the mission to work on network-centric warfare, cyber capabilities and electronic warfare. Military Affairs Security[16] reportedly has received assistance from China.

NETHERLANDS

In 2012, the Netherlands Ministry of Defence released its Defence Cyber Strategy. There are six specific priorities addressed in the Strategy: acomprehensive approach, enhancing defensive capabilities, developing offensive military capabilities, improving information-gathering and security skills, improving and encouraging innovation, and continuing to foster and develop domestic and international cooperation efforts. The Strategy describes the offensive capabilities as a "force multiplier" for increasing military effectiveness and preserving an "active defence", while recognizing the reality that the use of cyber techniques as a military tool is still in its infancy.

The National Cyber Security Centre was created on 1 January 2012 with the purpose of providing expertise and advice, and monitoring threats and managing crises, and encompasses the previously existing GOVCERT. NL. The Centre has published a security checklist for supervisory control and data acquisition for industrial control systems, and the Cyber Security Assessment Netherlands report, which assesses the short-term goals and needs of the government regarding cyber security.

The Netherlands issued the National Cyber Security Strategy in 2011. The Strategy has five components: linking and reinforcing initiatives, promoting individual responsibility, creating public–private partnerships, pursing international cooperation, and striking a balance between self-regulation and legislation. It calls for annual trend reports in cybercrime and digital security, and states that a national information and communications technology "Crisis Plan" will be published in mid-2011, although as of December 2012 the report had not been publicly released. The Strategy places heavy emphasis on regulating cybercrime and launched an initiative to ensure that all information and communications technology parties report data loss, theft, or misuse. There will also be a Cyber Education and Training Centre to research cyber defence and to develop the human capital necessary to bolster a growing digital economy.

The Ministry of the Interior coordinates interdepartmental cyber security among various civilian and military units responsible for cyber issues; the Ministry of Defence will cooperate on cyber defence. The Netherlands Ministry of Defence plans to invest in the development of cyber warfare capabilities despite budget cuts in other areas. The Netherlands does not have a specific unit for cyber warfare, but Netherlands military officials say that this may change in the future. The Netherlands has a memorandum of understanding with Luxembourg and Belgium on cooperation in cyber security, including information- and expertise-sharing, cooperation on best practices, and the development of public–private partnerships.[17]

According to the 2011 annual report of the Military Intelligence and Security Service, the military established The Defence Taskforce Cyber in January 2012 in order to gather intelligence on cyber activities and threats, as well as to create closer coordination with the Signet-Cyber Unit. The National Coordinator for Counter-Terrorism[18] has expanded its mission to include a cyber-component, specifically in testing the vulnerability of internet applications against cyber-attack.

NORWAY

Norway completed the drafting stage of a National Cyber Defence Strategy in 2010. The Strategy proposes 22 measures to strengthen Norway's ability to prevent and manage cyber events. The main objectives are the following: to establish a common situational overview and understanding of the cyber threat, secure information and communications systems, raise awareness and education about the cyber threat, strengthen the ability to detect and manage incidents, combat and investigate incidents, and strengthen the coordination of cyber security.

The National Security Authority will receive a budget increase of 30 per cent in 2013. The Authority reports to both the Ministries of Defence and Justice and is responsible for preparing preventive and protective digital security measures. Norway's CERT is a department of the National Security Authority.

The Long-Term Plan for Defence, released in March 2012, states that the Ministry of Defence is to strengthen capacities in cyber defence and intelligence. In September 2012, the armed forces established the Cyber Defence Force as a "separate entity tasked with securing the Armed Forces against cyber threats".

POLAND

Responsibility for cyber security in Poland is divided between the Ministry of Administration and Digitisation and the Internal Security Service. The Ministry of National Defence also has significant cyber responsibilities for military networks. In 2010, Poland developed the Governmental Action Plan for Cyber security 2011–2016. It called for the creation of an Inter-ministerial Coordination Team for Protection of Cyberspace and a Government Representative for Protection of Cyberspace, as well as representatives from other public and private entities. The Ministry of Administration and Digitisation now has responsibility and has set up a task force for implementation. The government CERT has responsibilities for both public and private networks, including critical infrastructure. The Internal Security Service manages the CERT.

The Ministry of National Defence's Vision of the Polish Armed Forces gives greater emphasis to cyber security, and protecting information resources and the energy sector. The 2009.

Defence Strategy identifies cyber-attack as a dangerous threat. Poland will create an "Independent Information Force" in the armed forces to integrate electronic intelligence, psychological operations, and cyber offensive and defensive actions. Poland's NATO partnership is an important element of its cyber defence strategy. The Computer Incident Response System is responsible for cyber security in the Ministry of National Defence. The System is supervised by the Director of the Information Technology and Telecommunication Department, who coordinates cyber security functions and is supported by the Ministerial Centre for Network Security and ICT [information and communications technology] Services

Management. In 2011, Poland signed an agreement with the NATO Consultation, Command, and Control Agency that would facilitate the development of new technologies to counter cyber threats.[19]

REPUBLIC OF KOREA

The Korea Communications Commission announced a national cyber security strategy in August 2011, developed through the joint effort of 15 government agencies. Cyberspace will be considered an operational domain, such as land, air, and sea, which thus needs a state-level defence system. The strategy will focus on defence, i.e., prevention and detection of, and response to cyber-attack. The National Cyber Security Centre is responsible for identifying, preventing, and responding to cyber-attack. It works with the private and military sectors to prevent cyber-attack, analyse vulnerabilities, and coordinate cyber emergency response activities.

The 2008 defence white paper identified cyber security as an essential component of national defence. The 2010 white paper outlines cyber-attack as one of several non-traditional security threats. CERTs have been created at the corps level to oversee the Defence Information Systems. The white paper also details the security measures taken by the Ministry of National Defence to protect the Defence Information Network as well as the Battlefield Management System.

The Ministry of National Defence established the Cyber War Centre in January 2010. Its primary aim is to increase the security of government and financial information networks. The Ministry of National Defence has also created an independent Cyber Warfare Command responsible for defensive and offensive operations in cyberspace, and employing over 200 personnel.

According to the Korea Communications Commission, the National Intelligence Service will play the lead role in cyber issues. The Commission, along with the Ministries of National Defence and Government Administration and Home Affairs, will be tasked respectively with private sector security, national defence, and protecting the safety of the government's computer systems. Currently, more than 95 per cent of the country's households have access to the Internet. The new strategy would require encryption and data back-up in the public and private sectors, as well as other security precautions. The Korea Advanced Institute of Science and Technology established the Cyber Security Research Centre, which has assisted in detecting and defending against cyber-attack. The Republic of Korea also plans to develop offensive and defensive cyber warfare weapons, and increase manpower in the Cyber Warfare Command; the defence plan aims to boost the number of personnel to 1, 000.

RUSSIAN FEDERATION

In July 2012, the Russian Federation's Security Council released a national policy for fighting cybercrime and the creation of a national system to detect and prevent cyber-attack. Responsibility for policy, which aims to secure the country's networks by 2020, was given to the Federal Security Service.[20]

In January 2012, the Russian Federation's Defence Ministry published its "Conceptual Views Regarding the Activity of the Armed Forces of the Russian Federation in the Information Space". The strategy discusses the principles of information security and different measures to control for interference in information systems. Section 3 of the strategy assesses different rules for deterrence and conflict prevention and resolution. In March 2012, the Russian Federation announced that it was considering establishing a cyber-security command to secure information for the armed forces. In addition, the government has drafted a bill to create an advanced military research agency for cyber security.

The Military Doctrine of 2010 discusses the use of political and informational instruments to protect national interests and those of allies. The Doctrine defines the characteristic features of modern military conflict as including the integrated use of military force and non-military capabilities, and a greater role for information warfare.

SINGAPORE

The National Infocomm Security Committee formulates cyber policy and security strategy. The Singapore Infocomm Technology Security Authority oversees network security. This agency operates under the Internal Security Department of the Ministry of Home Affairs. Singapore announced in 2011 that it will create the National Cyber security Centre to combat cyber threats. Thc Singapore Infocomm Technology Security Authority will head the Centre. The Centre is planned to become fully operational in 2013–2014; phase one, the establishment of a monitoring system for critical infrastructure and emergency services sectors, was accomplished in 2011. The Authority also has a programme to recruit information technology professionals to serve as cyber defenders. In November 2012, Singapore amended its Computer Misuse Act to help the government counter cyber-attack. The amendment gives the government the ability to order an organisation to act against a cyber-attack before the attack is carried out. The Minister of State for Defence and Education announced in July 2012 that the Ministry of Defence is also setting up a new cyber defence training centre to help build cyber security expertise.

SLOVAKIA

Slovakia has distributed responsibility for cyber security among a number of agencies, including the Ministry of Finance (whose Division of Legislation, Standards, and Security of Information Systems is tasked with protecting critical infrastructure), Ministry of Interior, Ministry of Defence, the Personal Data Protection Office, the Slovak National Accreditation Service, and the National Security Authority. The Authority oversees cyber defence and leads an intersect oral working group established to coordinate cyber defence activities. The 2008 National Strategy for Information

Security defined prevention, readiness, and sustainability as three strategic goals for cyber security. The Defence Strategy of the Slovak Republic, issued in 2005, identifies the cyber domain as a key area in a changing security environment. Slovakia routinely participates in NATO cyber security exercises (under the guidance of the National Security Authority).

SOUTH AFRICA

The South African Cabinet approved a National Cyber Security Policy Framework in March 2012 to fight national security threats in cyberspace. The Framework named the State Security Agency the primary government institution for the development, implementation, and coordination of cyber security initiatives in place of the Department of Communication, which formerly led cyber security efforts.[21] The Agency uses a government owned company, Electronic Communications Security (Pty) Ltd, to provide cyber security for government agencies. South Africa's cybercrime law, the Electronic Communications and Transactions Act, penalizes hacking, electronic fraud and extortion, denial of service attacks, and spam. The Act was modelled on the Convention on Cybercrime, which South Africa has signed.

The Ministry of Defence's cyber responsibilities include support for civilian agencies, defence of military networks, deterrence, and offensive missions to enhance information superiority.

SPAIN

Spain's 2011 Security Strategy identifies cyber threats as one of the eight primary risks the country faces, noting that cyberspace represents a new and unique domain. The Strategy proposes strengthening domestic cyber security laws, creating public–private partnerships, enhancing European and global cyber security cooperation, and developing a cyber-security strategy. The Ministry of Defence oversees cyber security for the military.

The National Intelligence Centre is responsible for the security of government networks and classified national security information and manages the government's CERT. Spain has two specialised cyber police forces within the Ministry of the Interior: the National Police Corps' Technological Investigation Brigade and the Civil Guard's Telematics Crime Group. The National Centre for Critical Infrastructure Protection is the body responsible for coordination and critical infrastructure protection, including cyber security. Spain's CERT was established in 2006. Spain has ratified the Convention on Cybercrime.

Royal Decree 3/2010 adapted the National Security Framework to include prescriptions for cyber security practices for the public sector to ensure access, integrity, and confidentiality of information. It stresses that public networks should adopt multi-layered "defence in depth" strategies, and that security will include measures of prevention, detection, and mitigation. Although it does not lay out principles for pre-emptive or retaliatory action beyond national borders, preventive measures include not only lessening exposure to potential threats but also dissuasion. The Defence Ministry participates in national, European, and NATO cyber security efforts.

SRI LANKA

In February 2011, the Commander of the Sri Lankan Army said that the country faces threats in cyberspace, and that online surveillance and defence against information threats is a priority falling in part on the Ministry of Defence Media Division. The national CERT is the focal point for cyber security, and was established under the Information and Communication Technology Agency; it joined the Asia Pacific CERT in February 2012[22].

SWITZERLAND

The National Strategy for Switzerland's Protection against Cyber Risks, released in June 2012, outlines Switzerland's goals for cyber defence. The Federal Council is pursuing increased resilience of critical infrastructure, and the reduction of risks, crime, espionage, and sabotage in the cyber domain.

The Federal Department of Defence intends to develop cyber defence, exploitation, and attack capabilities. The Defence Minister stated in 2011 that between 5 and 10 percent of the total defence budget was allocated to cyber security.[23] The Centre for Electronic Operations of the Armed Forces Command Support Organisation is creating two cyber war-related units. The first of these is a military CERT, which will be tasked to monitor the systems and networks of the armed forces. It will coordinate with the government CERT. The other is a unit for computer network operations. The Federal Intelligence Service, part of Department of Defence, focuses on the protection of critical information infrastructure.

TURKEY

In November 2012, Turkey established the Cyber Security Board, tasked with determining and implementing cyber security measures. The Information and Communications Authority and the Scientific and Technological Research Council are working to draft a national cyber security strategy, planned for release in 2013. The Authority will play a supervisory and coordinating role. Turkey announced the establishment of its first civilian cyber security organisation, the National Cyber Security Coordination Foundation, in October 2011. The Foundation will hire 200 personnel to provided cyber security assistance to government institutions and private entities. Turkey merged two agencies in 2010 to create a new entity that is tasked to intercept signals and secure Turkey's electronic communications. It will be staffed by researchers to study cryptography, cyber security, electronic warfare, and develop software for the public and private sectors.

Turkey's military strategy, revised in October 2010, added cyber security threats. Turkey plans to establish a Cyber Army

Command to counter cyber-attack against the country, with a special unit within the General Staff to deal with cyber threats, in cooperation with the Defence Ministry, the Scientific and Technological Research Council, and Middle East Technical University. The Command will be subordinated to the General Staff, but have its own budget and an autonomous structure. It will monitor the entire internet in Turkey and offer protection to state institutions.

UKRAINE

Ukraine began emphasizing cyber security in 2002, when the Ministry of the Interior developed units to counter high-tech crime. Around that time, a department was created at the Ministry's Donetsk Law Institute specifically pertaining to information technologies. Ukraine continues to develop its cyber capabilities and plans. During the 2011 NATO–Ukraine Defence Council members briefed attendants on the Draft Strategy of Ukraine on Cyber Defence.

The State Service for Special Communication and Information Protection develops policy on the protection of state information resources and ensures government communications systems function. The Security Service is responsible for protecting the "technical and defence potential of Ukraine". The state's cyber security structure continues to develop. In an April 2012 interview, the head of the Security Service noted that Ukraine is creating a Department of Counter intelligence Protection of State Interests in the Field of Information Security in response to numerous attempts to gain unauthorised access to state resources. Additionally, the Security Service proposed creating a national system to fight cybercrime.

The military's role in dealing with cyber threats is outlined in a white paper. It states that "the Armed Forces and other military formations should be capable to participate in ensuring reliability and safety of the national information system". In June 2012, the National Security and Defence Council approved the new Military Doctrine, which states that

Ukraine considers cyber-attacks on nuclear facilities, the chemical and defence industries, military stores, and economic and information entities as grounds for armed conflict. While its military capabilities remain uncertain, the General Staff includes a Central Directorate for Information Security and Cryptology. Ukraine has ratified the Convention on Cybercrime.

UNITED KINGDOM

The United Kingdom has one of the most advanced national approaches to cyber security. In November 2011, the United Kingdom updated its Cyber Security Strategy. The Strategy characterizes cyber-attack as a national security threat. The Strategy's objectives include addressing cyber-crime and creating a secure business environment, enhancing information infrastructure resiliency, ensuring an open, safe cyberspace for the public, and developing an adequate cyber security workforce. The Strategy says the United Kingdom will work bilaterally and through international forums to establish international norms and develop confidence-building measures.[24]

The government has allocated £650 million through 2015 to implement the National Cyber Security Programme. Two thirds of this funding will be allocated to developing "operational capabilities", and 20 per cent to public and private critical cyber infrastructure. Almost half will be allocated to the Government Communications Headquarters, the national signals intelligence agency. The Office of Cyber Security and Information Assurance, created in 2009, provides strategic direction and coordinates cyber security policy from within the Cabinet Office. It is responsible for implementing the National Cyber Security Programme and managing the £650 million budget. The Centre for the Protection of National Infrastructure provides guidance to critical infrastructure owners on cyber threats and operates information exchanges to facilitate public–private information-sharing on threats and protective measures.

In September 2012, the United Kingdom announced the creation of an academic institute dedicated to researching cyber security. It is backed by the Government Communications Headquarters and will increase resiliency against cyber-attack and better equip the government to defend the country's interests in cyberspace. The United Kingdom will also establish a National Crime Agency, to include a national cybercrime unit to investigate and respond to serious national-level cybercrime and provide support and training to local police forces. This unit will be created by combining the Serious Organised Crime Agency and the Metropolitan Police's e-crime units. In March 2012, the Revenue and Customs Service announced that it would establish a cyber-crime team to investigate cyber-abetted tax fraud.[25]

The 2010 National Security Strategy highlights "hostile attacks upon UK cyber space by other states and large scale cybercrime" as among the highest priorities. The updated 2011 Strategy states that the new Joint Forces Command will lead development and integration of cyber defence capabilities. The Strategy also calls for the creation of two Joint Cyber Units. One will be within the Global Operations and Security Control Centre to "proactively and reactively" defend Ministry of Defence networks against attack. The second unit will be within Government Communications Headquarters, with responsibility to develop "new tactics, techniques, and plans to deliver military effects…through operations in cyberspace".

The 2009 Cyber Security Strategy called for the Ministry of Defence to create a Cyber Security Operations Centre, located in the Government Communications Headquarters, responsible for developing both offensive and defensive cyber capabilities. The 2010 Strategic Defence and Security Review called for the creation of a Defence Cyber Operations Group.

The Group, to be operational by March 2015, will be a "federation of cyber units across defence", to "ensure the coherent integration of cyber activities across the spectrum of defence operations". Within the Ministry of Defence, the

Global Operations and Security Control Centre is responsible for defending the Ministry's network.

UNITED STATES

The United States is undertaking an extensive cyber security programme, both in the civilian and military realm, with a number of significant actions in 2012. The United States completed a Cyberspace Policy Review in May 2009, and in December 2009 appointed a mid-level Cyber security Coordinator to the staff of the National Security Council. Many of the provisions in the Cyberspace Policy Review are also found in the 2010 National Security Strategy. Responsibility for cyber security is divided among the Department of Homeland Security, the Federal Bureau of Investigation, and the Department of Defence, including US Cyber Command (which has the National Security Agency as one of its components), with the Departments of State and Commerce leading international negotiations and the development of cyber security standards The Department of Homeland Security's National Cyber security Division is tasked to "work collaboratively with public, private, and international entities to secure cyberspace and America's cyber interest". The Division has a number of programmes to assist companies in protecting cyber infrastructure from attack. The National Cyber Response Coordination Group is comprised of 13 federal agencies and is responsible for coordinating the federal response in the event of a "nationally significant cyber incident". The Department of Homeland Security also has expanded the work of the National Cyber security and Communications Integration Centre to improve situational awareness and information-sharing. The Department of Defence and the Department of Homeland Security signed a memorandum of agreement in October 2010 to increase interdepartmental collaboration.

In 2012, the Congress twice failed to pass administration-backed legislation that would have given the Department of Homeland Security the authority to secure critical infrastructure networks. The failure of legislation prompted an announcement by the White House that the President would issue an executive order (which has the force of law) establishing some minimal requirements for improving security at critical infrastructures.[26]

It has been reported that, in October 2012, President Obama signed a Presidential Decision Directive governing military activities in cyberspace. The Directive itself is classified but remarks by the Secretary of Defence suggest that the military will play a greater role in defending against cyber-attack from foreign sources. Secretary of Defence Leon Panetta, in a speech on 18 December 2012, said that the Department of Defence had recently developed new rules of engagement in cyberspace that clarified its mission to defend the country, and that will enable it "to more quickly respond to cyber threats". He further stated that the Department of Defence is exploring ways to strengthen the Cyber Command, currently a sub-command of the Strategic Command. The Cyber Command, established in 2010 and originally responsible for dealing with threats to the military cyber infrastructure, will now have broader national cyber defence responsibilities because of the Presidential Directive. The Command is responsible for both defensive and offensive operations. Cyber Command's service elements include Army Forces Cyber Command, the Twenty-fourth Air Force, Fleet Cyber Command and Marine Forces Cyber Command.

In November 2012, the Defence Advanced Research Projects Agency released a document soliciting research into the conduct of cyber war, called Foundational Cyber warfare (Plan X). The document states that, "Plan X will conduct novel research into the nature of cyber warfare and support development of fundamental strategies needed to dominate the cyber battle space. Proposed research should investigate innovative approaches that enable revolutionary advances in science, devices, or systems".

Widespread media reports attributed to US national security officials claim that the 2010 "Stuxnet" cyber-attack against an Iranian nuclear facility was propagated by the United States and Israel.

VIETNAM

Viet Nam's Ministry of Public Security has proposed the establishment of a high command to provide electronic and cyber security for the military, citing the "eventuality of cyber wars" as a key impetus for a cyber-military organisation. The Director of the Department of Information Technology within the Ministry of Public Security has been an advocate for improving operational cyber capabilities. The General Department of Logistics and Technology of the Ministry of Public Security, the national CERT, and the International Data Group continue to draft plans for information security advancements throughout the next decade. Viet Nam is planning to invest $42 million to secure sensitive information and to establish a National Centre for Technology and an Agency for Information Security.

As part of this investment, Viet Nam approved a national master plan to secure domestic cyberspace for the period of 2010–2020 and created the National Network Security Technical Centre to develop a system for monitoring, early warning, and incident response, to be operational within two years. The national CERT, a unit within the Ministry of Information and Communication, was established in 2005. Its tasks include the coordination of cyber incident response and the development of computer network security.

References

1. Cunningham, J. B. (1977). Approaches to the evaluation of organisational effectiveness. Academy of Management Review, 2 (3), 463-474.
2. Day, C., Harris, A., & Hadfield, M. (2001). Grounding knowledge of schools in stakeholder realities: A multi-perspective study of effective school leaders. School Leadership & Management, 21 (1), 19-42.
3. Day G. S. (1994). The capabilities of market-driven organisations. Journal of Marketing 58: 37-52.

4. Delaney J. T. & Huselid M. A. (1996). The impact of human resource management practices on perceptions of organisational performance. Academy of Management Journal 39, 4: 949-969.
5. Delery J. E. and Doty D. H. (1996). Modes of theorizing in strategic human resource management: tests of universalistic, contingency, and configurational performance predictions. Academy of Management Journal 39: 802-835.
6. Fahy J. (2000). The resource-based view of the firm: some stumbling blocks on the road to understanding sustainable competitive advantage. Journal of European Industrial Training 24/2/3/49: 4-104.
7. Fazio R. H., Jackson J. R., Dunton B. C., & Williams C. J. (1996). Variability in automatic activation as an unobtrusive measure of racial attitudes: A bonafide pipeline. Journal of Personality and Social Psychology 69: 1013-1027.
8. Fey C. F., Bjorkman. and Pavlovskaya A. (2000). The effect of human resource management practices on firm performance in Russia. International Journal of Human Resource Management 11, 1: 1-1 8.
9. Framee R. M., Nielsen W. R. and Patel. E. (1989). Creating excellence out of crisis: organisational transformation at the Chicago Tribune. Journal of Applied Behavioural Science 25, 2: 109-122.
10. Gerhart B. and Milkovich G. T. (1990). Organisational differences in managerial compensation and firm performance. Academy of Management Journal 33: 663-691.
11. Ghobadian A- and Aservorth J. (1994). Performance measurement in local government- concept and practice. International Journal of Operations & Production Management 14, 5: 35-51.
12. Gamoran, A., & Dreeben, R. (1986). Coupling and control in educational organisations. Administrative Science Quarterly, 31 (4), 612-632.
13. Golden K. and Ramanujam V. (1985). Between a dream and a nightmare: on the integration of the human resource management and strategic business planning processes. Human Resource Management 24: 429-452.
14. Goddard, R. D., Sweetland, S. R. & Hoy W. K. (2000). Academic emphasis of urban elementary schools and student achievement in reading and mathematics: A multilevel analysis. Educational Administration Quarterly, 36 (5), 683-702.
15. Gray, J., & Wilcox, B. (1995). Good school, bad school: Evaluating performance and encouraging improvement. Buckingham, UK:

Open University Press. Greenfield, W. D. Jr. (1995). Towards a theory of school administration: The centrality of leadership. Educational Administration Quarterly, 3 (1), 61–85.

16. Griffith, J. (2002). Is quality/effectiveness an empirically demonstrable school attribute? Statistical aids for determining appropriate levels of analysis. School Effectiveness and School Improvement, 13 (1), 91–122.
17. Inn K. Rowland and G. Ferris (Eds.), Research in personnel and human resource management, vol. 10: 271-299. JAI Press. Greenwich, CT.
18. Ichniowski C., Shaw K., &Prennushi G. (1997). The effects of human resource management practices on productivity: a case study of steel finishing lines. American Economic Review 87, 3: 291-313.
19. Kane B. and Palmer L . (1995). Strategic HRM or managing the employment relationship? International Journal of Manpower 5, 6: 6-21.
20. Kangis P. and Williams D. G. S. (2000). Organisational climate and corporate Performance: an empirical investigation. Management decision38, 8: 531-540.
21. Katz C., Kochan T. A., & Weber N. R. (1985). Assessing the effects of industrial relations systems and efforts to improve the quality of world go on Organisation effectiveness. Academy o f Management Journal28, 3: 509-526.
22. Lahteenmaki S., Storey J. (1998). HRM and company Performancc-The use of measurement and the influence of economic cycles. Human Resource Management journal 8, 2: 51-65.
23. Kaplan R. S. and Norton D. P . (1996). Using the balanced scorecard as a strategic management system. Harvard Business Review, January-February 75-85.
24. Kearns P. (1994). Human resource-measuring effectiveness inTraining and Development 12, 6: 1 1-14.
25. KERR C. A., GLASS J. C., MCCALLION G. NL and McKILLOP D. G. (1999). Best practice measures of resource utilisation for hospitals: a useful complement in Performance assessment public Administration 77, 3: 639-650.
26. Lengnick-Hall C. A- and Lengnick-Hall M. L. (1988). Strategic human resource management: a review of the literature and a proposed typology. Academy of Management Review 13: 454-470.

Regional Cyber Security: Moving Towards A Resilient ASEAN Cyber-security Regime

Introduction

Cyber threats are causing increasingly serious risks to the economy as well as to national and international security. They are now widely accepted in the international community as a top-tier risk, if not the most pertinent risk, to national and international security. The EU considers cyber threats as a major risk to the security, stability and competitiveness of its Member States and the private sector, while the United States Intelligence Community's Worldwide Threat Assessment for 2013 ranks cyber threats first ahead of terrorism, transnational organised crime, weapons of mass destruction proliferation, counter-intelligence, counter-space, natural resources insecurity and competition, health and pandemic threats and mass atrocities. Furthermore, it should be noted that, for the first time since the 11 September 2001 attacks, international terrorism does not rank first in the U.S. Intelligence Community's assessment of global threats to national security.

A number of international and regional organisations, bodies and fora are working on cyber security issues, albeit to largely varying extents. Inter alia these include the OECD, European Parliament, Committee on Foreign Affairs, [1] Draft

Report on Cyber Security and Cyber Defence (2012/2096(INI), p.4, 22 June 2012 and James R. Clapper, Director of National Intelligence, Worldwide Threat Assessment of the US Intelligence Community – Statement for the Record, Senate Select Committee on Intelligence, 12 March 2013 along with Mark Mazzetti and David E. Sanger, The New York Times, Security Leader Says U.S. Would Retaliate Against Cyber attacks affirmingly states that the concept of cyber security is defined within the Cyber security Strategy of the European Union (07February 2013) as commonly referring to the safeguards and actions that can be used to protect the cyber domain, both in the civilian and military fields, from those threats that are associated with or that may harm its inter-dependent networks and information infrastructure. Cyber security strives to preserve the availability and integrity of the networks and infrastructure and the confidentiality of information contained therein.

The OSCE, the EU, the Council of Europe, BRICS, the OAS, AU, APEC, the Shanghai Cooperation Organisation, the G8/G20, the UN, the Internet Governance Forum, ICANN, NATO, and the World Economic Forum. Since international and regional cooperation on cyber security are required in order to deal effectively with the cross-border nature of cyber related threats, this paper therefore examines regional level efforts in the Association for Southeast Asian Nations (ASEAN) region to counter these threats.

To date, national and regional efforts to adopt comprehensive cyber security strategies have been somewhat slow and fragmented. Similarly, ASEAN Member States' efforts to adopt a regional comprehensive framework for cyber security are so far piecemeal and fragmented (as are national level efforts). An ASEAN-wide comprehensive cyber security framework has not yet been developed, official public documents are vague, the 2013 schedule for official meetings does not include cyber security, and the precise extent of discussions and proposed initiatives is difficult to fully ascertain, and lacks full transparency.

While still a developing area, this lack of region-wide cohesiveness detracts from security of the region and a proper functioning market. This paper finds that it is essential for ASEAN as a region to develop a comprehensive approach to deal with cyber security issues so as to enhance its overall resilience to serious cyber threats. Resilience is taken.

ASEAN, Official Meetings 2013, as of April & July 2013.

Council of the European Union conclusions on the wider EU understanding of resilience were issued on 28 May 2013 (Council of the European Union, Council conclusions on EU approach to resilience, 3241st Foreign Affairs Council Meeting, Brussels, 28 May 2013.)

The study focuses on building a resilient cyber security regime in the ASEAN region. The term "Cyber Resilience" is therefore not incorporated within the document since the focus lies rather on the term "cybersecurity" to mean the ability of the ASEAN region, its Member States and its citizens to be prepared, to be able to adapt, and to make quick progress post-incidents. The following sections outline why ASEAN is important to the global cyber security order, the primary global cyber security challenges of common interest to ASEAN Member States, ASEAN cyber security related official documents and measures as well as how the region currently lacks a resilient cyber security regime, and finally several recommendations relevant to the ASEAN context on a way forward to create a resilient regional cyber security regime.

Why ASEAN ?

ASEAN is a particularly significant region in terms of international cyber security issues.[2]

First, ASEAN's centrality in the regional architecture of the wider Asia Pacific region and its potential role as a neutral broker is significant in terms of international cyber security cooperation. In the context of U.S.-China relations and recent political focus on the impact of state and economic cyber espionage, a 2012 Council on Foreign Relations working paper's references to ASEAN's history of working together with the United States and China and to how ASEAN is seen as a neutral broker by most major powers, is particularly important. Furthermore, ASEAN's potential role as neutral broker is even more pertinent in mitigating possible tensions and misunderstanding between these two state actors if, as a 2013 Centre for Strategic and International Studies report states, China's use of cyberspace to gain military and economic advantage is one of the primary forces shaping a new Asian strategic environment and China's activities have created "an implicit Joshua Kurlantzick, Council on Foreign Relations, ASEAN's Future and Asian Integration, International Institutions and Global Governance Program, November 2012.

James Lewis, CSIS, Hidden Arena: Cyber Competition and Conflict in Indo-Pacific Asia, Prepared for the Lowy Institute Mac Arthur Asia Security Project, 07 March 2013. commonality of interests" among other regional powers. It should also be noted that China is similarly concerned about targeted cyber threats.

Second, while citizens in many areas of the region still do not have access to Information and Communications Technology (ICT), numbers are set to increase. According to the 2013 Impact Assessment report accompanying the European Commission's Proposal for a Directive on network and information security, of the 2.1 billion Internet users worldwide, most are located in Asia (922.2 million). The next most significant region in terms of numbers of Internet users is Europe with 476.2 million users. China alone has 485 million Internet users - more than any other country or region (including Europe and the rest of Asia) - and an Internet penetration of only 36.3 per cent. ASEAN, comprising ten Member States, has a total population of slightly over 600 million. Recent indicators forecast that the population growth rate is higher in most of the ASEAN countries than the Asian average for the period 2010-2015.

James Lewis, CSIS, Hidden Arena: Cyber Competition and Conflict in Indo-Pacific Asia, Prepared for the Lowy Institute Mac Arthur Asia Security Project, 07 March 2013.[3] European Commission, Commission Staff Working Document Impact Assessment Accompanying the document Proposal for a Directive of the European Parliament and of the Council Concerning measures to ensure a high level of network and information security across the Union SWD(2013) 32 final, 07February 2013.

European Commission, Commission Staff Working Document, Impact Assessment Accompanying the document Proposal for a Directive of the European Parliament and of the Council Concerning measures to ensure a high level of network and information security across the Union SWD (2013) 32 final, Annex 12:Internet 2011 in Numbers, 07 February 2013.ASEAN Member States: Brunei Darussalam, Cambodia, Indonesia, Lao PDR, Malaysia, Myanmar, Philippines, Singapore, Thailand and Vietnam.

ASEAN Statistics, Selected basic ASEAN indicators, as of January 2013.Credit Suisse Research and Analytics, ASEAN's positive demographics underpins stable growth, on 31 October raise the probabilities of increased demands for ICT usage. Within the region, Internet users have almost doubled during the period 2008 to 2011 and mobile phone density is close to 967.5 units per 1,000 persons. It is estimated that mobile broad band subscriptions will be close to 70 per cent of the world's total population by 2017. Globally, there are twice as many mobile broadband[4] subscriptions vis-à-vis fixed line broadband subscriptions and furthermore, GSM/EDGE mobile technology will cover more than 90 per cent of the world's population with 85 per cent accessing WCDMA/HSPA mobile technology at speeds of up to 2MB per second by 2017. Region targets for ASEAN are set for "exponential growth" in ICT adoption and a ramping up of infrastructure and human capital development is intended to achieve these targets. It is intended that fixed and mobile broadband access be improved in rural and remote areas, more affordable IT access be provided, and prioritised projects include an ASEAN Broadband Corridor. Furthermore, in order to improve speed as well as to lower interconnectivity costs, the region is currently assessing the feasibility of developing an ASEAN Internet-Exchange Network - a platform to facilitate intra-ASEAN Internet traffic"to facilitate peering among ASEAN Internet access providers". Finally, critical infrastructure protection will be essential, particularly in consideration of plans for the region which include establishing "an integrated and regional connectivity".

The ICT Development Divide: Cyber Security Advantage

As it stands, there are varying levels of ICT development and adoption across the region and efforts are under way to "bridge the digital divide" to promote greater adoption of ICT. The three ASEAN Community blueprints are aligned with the Initiative for ASEAN Integration (IAI) and the Hanoi Declaration on Narrowing the Development Gap for Closer ASEAN Integration, which aim to narrow the development divide and provide assistance to Cambodia, Lao PDR, Myanmar and Vietnam (CLMV) to meet ASEAN-wide targets and commitments to realise the ASEAN Community. Furthermore, according to the 2011Master Plan on ASEAN Connectivity, the extent of the digital divide across the region (highlighted by way of example in the below graph of Internet subscriptions and mobile phone density) and how it can be overcome is regarded as the most important challenge First, in this regard, while developed countries globally have higher levels of Internet access (70 per cent) than developing countries (24 per cent), it should be noted that in fact the absolute number of Internet users in developing countries already far outweighs the number in developed countries, 27 and it seems that "the digital divide is larger when measured in terms of subscribed capacity than in terms of subscriptions".28 In 2011, approximately 62 per cent of all Internet users were in developing countries.[5] Vietnam is a particularly significant case in point since it was globally ranked in June 2012 as 18th in terms of Internet use (eighth in Asia and third in ASEAN behind Indonesia and the Philippines), an estimated 31 million people (35 per cent of the population) are connected to the Internet, and usage is expected to reach 45-50 per cent of the population by 2020.30 In Cambodia for example, in March 2013 there was an increase of 60 per cent in Internet users since 2012 and a figure of 2.7 million citizens were reported as online by December 2012. Furthermore, in analysing the ASEAN Secretariat's March 2013 Community in Figures report for 2012, 32 figures for mobile phone density across the region show that Member UNODC (United Nations Office on Drugs and Crime), Comprehensive Study on Cybercrime, Draft – February 2013.

International Telecommunication Union (ITU) Annual Report, Measuring the Information Society – Executive Summary, 2012. UNODC (United Nations Office on Drugs and Crime), Comprehensive Study on Cybercrime, Draft – February 2013. The Citizen Lab, Southeast Asia Cyber Watch– August 2012, Vietnam ranks among the top 20 nations by Internet use, https://citizenlab.org/2012/08/southeast-asia-cyberwatch-august-2012/#vietnam, last accessed 20 August 2013.The Citizen Lab, Southeast Asia Cyber Watch – March 2013, Cambodia reports increased Internet penetration, March 2013.ASEAN Secretariat, ASEAN Community in Figures 2012, March 2013.States are close to saturation in terms of number of units per 1,000 persons marking a narrowing digital divide. The average mobile phone density for the region is close to 967.5 units per 1,000 persons – as compared to an average of 232.8 Internet subscribers/Users per 1,000 persons. There is a marked contrast in the lower variance of mobile phone density as between ASEAN Member States across the region compared to the higher gaps in numbers of Internet users/subscriptions. Vietnam, for instance, now ranks next to Singapore in terms of cellular/ mobile phone density with 1,434 units per 1,000 persons compared to the highest regional average of 1,495 in Singapore. Myanmar is the exception with by far the lowest mobile phone density of 25.7 units per 1,000 persons, although these figures are set to change with the awarding of two telecommunications licences in June 2013. In liberalising communications networks, Myanmar intends to increase mobile penetration by 50 per cent (from one million users for a population of 60 million) by 2015 to increase Internet access. Indonesia has nearly 63 million Internet users of which the majority accesses the Internet through mobile devices.

Second, such digital divides and differing levels of ICT development and adoption should not necessarily impinge upon prospects of regional cyber security cooperation nor should they deter efforts in seriously tackling cross-border cyber related threats, in ASEAN or elsewhere. Rather, regional cooperation efforts can stimulate progress, fuelling collective security and the further enhancement of national cyber security measures no matter where a state is on the spectrum of ICT development. In fact, such disparity in ICT development can advantage countries with a less developed ICT infrastructure and less connected critical infrastructure. As less digitally developed countries become more connected, lessons may be applied from other states' experiences in countering cyber related threats, best practice policies and measures may be implemented, and both security and data privacy by design may be incorporated from inception in the development of ICT and connected critical infrastructures. Furthermore, higher levels of ICT development and adoption as well as connected critical infrastructures have not necessarily been synonymous in the past with equally high levels of development and implementation of cyber security measures. Rather, more often than not, it has instead meant higher exposure to vulnerabilities and possible cyber threats. This has been described as "the combination of a blessing and a curse" so that while the previous technology cycle has been lost and the new technology cycle needs to be built, it means that in doing so it is free of legacy and lessons may be learned from the mistakes of others.

Therefore, where countries are developing (or further developing) their ICT and critical infrastructure, and are in the process of awarding contracts for example (as in the case of Myanmar's issuance of licences for telecommunications in 2013), terms and conditions requiring the implementation of at least minimum standards and best practice measures can now be negotiated. It is contended that "baking in cyber security"[6] from the beginning is perhaps easier for developing countries rather than developed countries where there is less ability to affect things such as basic "cyber hygiene" and "hardening" and the private sector is already more independent. If market incentives are leveraged and if more can be done from the beginning to build a market standard of care (without being too directive so that the private sector can still develop more efficient ways of mitigating threats), it is felt that this could be more effective and more efficient in the long run.[7] In the United States, for example, sectors vary quite a bit in their levels of cyber security capabilities and there is no base-line standard of care so that the U.S. is now challenged with recreating or even breaking some paradigms in order to come up with that base line. Furthermore, it is argued that no matter how wealthy the country, it cannot protect against everything, and therefore, developing countries with lower budgets and less resources or manpower for cyber activities, and developed countries alike, should look for efficiencies where they can by pursuing a risk-based approach. In other words, with a finite amount of resources, a decision must be made regarding the highest risks for which these resources should be used based on data and a constant reviewing of the risks and how they evolve.

It is in the interest of ASEAN states as well as the international community that measures be put in place to mitigate possible "weak links" and havens of vulnerable architectures.In particular, measures should be incorporated from the outset if the CLMV grouping is to participate in the

ASEAN energy schemes delineated under the Initiative for ASEAN Integration Strategic Framework and Work Plan 2, such as the ASEAN Power Grid, segments of the Singapore-Kunming Rail Link, and possible CLMV ICT manufacturing bases/clusters (with expected connection to other IT parks in ASEAN).

From the outset, agreements may be entered for technical assistance as well as training and expertise (both technical and non-technical) in order to assist in building a resilient cyber security architecture. Such assistance could be provided by another ASEAN member or grouping thereof with established expertise, by bilateral engagements with non-ASEAN states, or by third parties such as the ITU-IMPACT alliance and the EU. ITU-IMPACT, for instance, completed a Computer Incident Response Team (CIRT) readiness assessment and cyber drill simulation for the CLMV grouping in December 2011 and the EU proposes in its February 2013 Cyber security Strategy of the European Union to work towards.

It is worth noting that in the EU, previous efforts by the European Commission and EU Member States have also been too fragmented to deal effectively with the growing challenges of cyber issues.

In June 2012, States, divisions within Member States, an aversion to intervening in the affairs of other Member States, and little capability in handling traditional or non-traditional security challenges, and little capacity has developed to combat drug-trafficking, human trafficking, terrorism and other high priority non-traditional security threats. The aforementioned CFR Working Paper outlines how, until now, ASEAN has been more successful in promoting trade integration and creating regional forums for discussing security issues than it has been in promoting more concrete security or economic integration.

III. Primary Global Cyber Security Challenges of Common Interest to ASEAN Members:

Recent Status & Emerging Trends

In dealing with cyber threats, some of the most significant global challenges of common interest to ASEAN Member States include:

- The increasing volume and complexity of threats
- The dilemma of accurate attribution
- An increasing number of state and non-state actors
- The lack of harmonised definitions and understanding of "cyber" terminology
- Achieving effective public-private sector cooperation
- Insufficient levels of R&D
- The inadequacy and unavailability of expertise
- Insufficient public awareness, and

Increasing Volume and Complexity of Cyber Threats

First, the alarming and continually increasing volume and complexity of threats is a serious global challenge common to the wider international community including ASEAN Member States. The increased frequency at which attacks are occurring is becoming unwieldy and posing a serious challenge to effective and timely implementation of policy and legislation. In some instances, according to James R. Clapper, the United States Director of National Intelligence, these technologies are being applied faster than the policy community's ability to understand the security implications and mitigate the potential risks. In addition, the time between an attack and systems compromise can take a matter of minutes yet it can often take months for the breach to be discovered. Multi-national computer security firms assessing the global threat landscape continually highlight changes in the frequency and complexity of evolving or new threats by way of quarterly and annual reports. In 2012 at least two new viruses were discovered every second and one in fourteen Internet downloads contained malware. Mobile malware samples discovered by McAfee Labs were 44 times that discovered in 2011, and it is estimated that 150,000 computer viruses are in circulation daily with 148, 000 computers compromised per day. Furthermore, according to the World Economic Forum, there is a APTs: Advanced Persistent Threats: Targeted compromises that occur largely without public disclosures. They present a far greater threat to government and to companies, as the adversary is tenaciously persistent in achieving their objectives. The key to these intrusions is that the adversary is motivated by a massive hunger for secrets and IP – this is different to the immediate financial gratification that drives much of cybercrime first ransom ware "kits", which enable criminals without programming skills to extort financial payments, were introduced for sale on the black market.

According to McAfee's Threats Report for 2012, 60 predictive assessments suggest that a variant of a new APT development called Operation High Roller designed to target financial services infrastructure and attack the Automated Transfer Systems in Europe and new High Roller-based attacks aimed at manufacturing and import/export firms will target the Automated Clearing House infrastructure which processes much of the world's e-commerce transactions. Threat predictions for 201361 expect an increase in or introduction of threats such as mobile phone ransom ware kits. The marked increase in the number of mobile-enabled threats is particularly relevant for the ASEAN region when "Ransom ware attacks tend to come in two forms. In the first form of attack the cybercriminal expropriates confidential information either from the user system or enterprise IT infrastructure and then demands payment for not releasing the data into the public domain. In the second form of attack the cybercriminal establishes control of a user system (or mobile device), encrypts user data, and demands payment in exchange for this encryption key. Users who agree to the ransom demand may have no way of knowing if they will ever receive the promised encryption key."

An increase in or introduction of "hacking as a service", where anonymous buyers and sellers exchange malware kits and development services in underground forums, and"large-scale attacks like Stuxnet"[8] that will attempt to destroy infrastructure rather than focus on financial gain are also to be expected. Hacking as a service is a particularly concerning development since cybercriminals and organised cybercrime gangs, seeking financial gain by selling or leasing kits and services anonymously, may cause unintended or unexpected consequences if their customers are either criminals without programming skills or more malicious non-state or state actors.

Stuxnet is regarded as the first known "cyber missile" identified with the capability to destroy hardware and cause kinetic damage. These new advanced cyber capabilities have the ability to cause physical damage and can manipulate the behaviour of a target in a way that could destroy the target. Once released, they can be reverse-engineered, tampered with, and manipulated for new targets (including against the authors) by a multitude of actors. There is therefore an increasing concern over the evolution and See also McAfeeLabs, McAfee Threats Report: Fourth Quarter 2012–ExecutiveSummary, http://www.mcafee.com/us/resources/reports/rp-quarterly-threat-q4-2012-summary.pdf, last accessed 04 April 2013 escalation of these attacks and their possible "transition from disruptive to destructive" as compared to Distributed Denial of Service (DDoS) attacks and theft of government data as well as intellectual property theft which can cause virtual destruction.

Dilemma of Accurate Attribution

Second, the accurate attribution and identification of those responsible for a cyber-attack is not easily achieved. Varying techniques may be employed to avoid detection such as the more recently discovered trend of building out of a "super domain" of infected websites, which allows hundreds or thousands of websites to be placed behind one IP address, and frequently changing the address in order to avoid detection. A report of the Institute for Information

Infrastructure Protection further argues that without accurate appropriation of blame it is difficult to take action against a perpetrator and hold those responsible to account. It states that creating a system of deterrence is therefore difficult and that legal and policy frameworks for responding to cyber-attacks cannot work unless there is adequate attribution since these frameworks remain incomplete if there is no basis to actually use them, in other words, "sufficient attribution". Finally, insofar as states may be concerned, misappropriation can lead to misunderstandings, misinter-pretations, or possible escalation in tensions or conflict.

Increasing Number of State and Non-State Actors

The third issue is the recent increase in the involvement of state and non-state actors in cyber issues. The fundamental shift in challenges facing national security is particularly evident with cyber related threats where a wide range of varying threats are not coming American Forces Press Service, NSA Chief: Cyber World Presents Opportunities, Challenges, http://www.defense.gov/News/NewsArticle.aspx?ID=117060, 10 July 2012, last accessed 02 January2013 solely from state actors but from a range of non-state actors such as cyber-criminals, terrorists, hackers, hack ativists, and individuals (as well as natural disasters or mistakes). Solutions will therefore require cooperation between public authorities, the private sector and civil society. Finally, according to General Keith B. Alexander, Director of the National Security Agency in the United States, since such non-state actors must now also be considered, cyber-attack deterrence is even more difficult than nuclear deterrence.

Regarding non-state actors, some of the following reports comprise predictive components and are therefore worthy of consideration by ASEAN Member States.[9] There is an increasing concern in the European Union over the possibility of politically motivated attacks and cyber threats from organised criminals and terrorist groups against the critical information systems and infrastructures of the EU and its

Member States. In March2013, the U.S. Intelligence Community confirmed indications of "heightened interest" from terrorist organisations to develop offensive cyber capabilities, although it estimates that these groups will probably be constrained by resource and organisational limitations as well as competing priorities. McAfee Labs considers that today, fears of a terrorist group moving to the next step and launching a "cyber-physical attack", in other words, an online attack in conjunction with a physical attack by remotely disrupting critical infrastructure such as a defence or communications system and easily causing more damage are "not just fantasy". Like the European Union, the U.S. Intelligence Community confirms76 government concern that a more radical group of hack activists could form "to inflict more system impacts" or perhaps even "accidentally trigger unintended consequences that could be misinterpreted as a state-sponsored attack". Equally, McAfee Labs researchers foresee a decline in online hack activists such as Anonymous to be replaced by more politically committed or extremist groups in their wake. The U.S. Intelligence Report judges that "there is a remote chance of major cyber-attack against US critical infrastructure systems during the next two years that would result in a long-term, wide-scale disruption of services, such as a regional power outage." While it estimates that the level of technical expertise and operational sophistication (including the ability to cause physical damage or overcome manual overrides) will be out of reach for most actors within this time, the concern is that isolated state or non-state actors might use less sophisticated cyber-attacks to access poorly protected networks that control core functions and these less sophisticated attacks could cause unforeseen significant outcomes due to mistake.

Regarding the role of state actors in the cyber domain, which has also markedly increased, threat predictions for 2013 foresee that states and armies will now become "more frequent sources and victims of cyber threats". A significant increase in state actors' useof cyber capabilities, which could possibly lead to an increase in the chances of miscalculations, misunderstandings, and unintended escalations is reported by the U.S. security community, although aside from a military conflict or crisis threatening vital interests, it suggests that it is unlikely that other advanced cyber state actors will launch a "devastating attack".

According to a 2013 CSIS report based on findings produced for the UNIDIR, while states are slow to admit possessing offensive cyber capabilities, ten Asian countries are developing cyber capabilities and "all are wrestling with how to adjust their policies and practices to new technology". Eight are developing military capabilities and doctrine – Australia, China, North Korea, India, Malaysia, Myanmar, Japan and South Korea; Brunei and Singapore are developing defensive capabilities; and capabilities of other Asian nations range from "nominal to relatively sophisticated". According to this report, cyber conflict has a "large Asian dimension" – in Asia it includes "planning for military competition and asymmetric warfare, engagement in economic espionage to gain long-term economic and trade advantages, as well as a new kind of transnational mass political action". It concludes that Asia has become the locus of cyber conflict, and that malicious activity in cyberspace, which could possibly inflame existing tensions or increase misperceptions or miscalculations among governments of the intent and risk of cyber actions, poses the greatest cyber risk to security in Asia.

Lack of Harmonised Definitions and Understanding of "Cyber" Terminology

This leads to the fourth issue for the global community, which is the lack of shared norms for responsible state behaviour at international level and agreement on the applicability of international law. There is no international or regional agreement on clear and harmonised definitions for what constitutes "cyber security", "cyber-attack" or "cyber defence", and the lines between cyber-crime, cyber espionage and cyber-attack are considered difficult to distinguish.

Furthermore, the very understanding of cyber security and other key terminologies vary significantly between jurisdictions.

Achieving Effective Public-Private Sector Cooperation

Finally, since critical infrastructure and critical information infrastructure are mostly either owned or operated by the private sector and the design and manufacturing of most software and hardware mainly conducted by it, close cooperation and information sharing with the public sector is essential to allow for real time response and the identification of threats.

Trust and confidence issues arise and many known incidents often remain unreported on account of the sensitive nature of information, fear of negative corporate publicity and possible damage to brand reputation.

The most suitable approach for cooperation between the public and private sector is contentious and an increasingly heated issue of concern across the international community. Aspects of current debate surround whether cooperation should be regulated and if so, whether it should be through voluntary or mandatory means. Some governments have chosen to regulate critical infrastructure providers by imposing minimum standards, while other governments have chosen to incentivise the private sector to encourage industry cooperation.

Overview of ASEAN Cyber Security Related Measures: How the Region Currently Lacks a Resilient Cyber Security Regime

In light of the principles of the ASEAN Charter and Member States' aims to establish the ASEAN Community (comprising the ASEAN Political-Security Community, the ASEAN Economic Community, and the ASEAN Socio-Cultural Community) by 2015, in other words, a region that is "politically cohesive, economically integrated and socially responsible in order to take advantage of current and future opportunities, and effectively respond to regional and international challenges", cohesive efforts to comprehensively tackle cyber security issues are crucial to these aims and in the shared interests of ASEAN's Members.

In this respect, ASEAN's intentions to contribute to and "be part of the solution" to global challenges as part of the international community are particularly noteworthy. At the April 2013 ASEAN Summit, Member States reconfirmed their commitment to facilitate the region in addressing global issues of common interest, thereby assisting in strengthening regional and international collaboration, and confirmed their determination to strengthen cooperation in addressing terrorism and transnational crime as well as to effectively tackle increasing non-traditional security threats in the region.

The shared responsibility of the region for comprehensive security is delineated in the ASEAN Political-Security Blueprint (Appendix 2 provides an overview of ASEAN cyber security related official documents). It envisages a cohesive, peaceful, stable, and resilient region with shared responsibility for comprehensive security. Under the principles of comprehensive security, a key purpose of ASEAN is to respond effectively to non-traditional security issues - trans-boundary challenges, trans-national crimes and all forms of threats. ICT, important for social development, is promoted under the ASEAN Socio-Cultural Community Blueprint. In accordance with the Economic Community Blueprint, it is intended that by 2015 ASEAN will become a single market and production base, a highly competitive economic region, and one that is fully integrated into the global economy. Its capacity as a global production centre or as a part of the global supply chain is to be enhanced and regional sourcing promoted by integrating industries across the region. Furthermore, its competitiveness in attracting foreign direct investment (FDI) and intra-ASEAN investment is to be further enhanced. Improving and ensuring the region's attractiveness as a single production and investment destination is a key ambition and FDI figures for the region, which is regarded as a "USD2.2 trillion engine of global economic growth", show increases of 23 per cent from USD92 billion in 2010 to a "record" USD114 billion in 2011.

In order to sustain such regional economic growth and competitiveness, the Economic Community Blueprint identifies the importance of creating a secure and connected information infrastructure, and areas of cooperation include enhanced infrastructure and communications connectivity. The higher probabilities of cross-border challenges mobile, and satellite communication networks and the Internet as well as the software supporting the development and operation of these communication networks. And transnational crime resultant from such closer connectivity are recognised by the 2011 Master Plan on ASEAN Connectivity (as well as the ASEAN ICT Master plan 2015 (AIM2015)) in its underscoring of the premise that enhanced ASEAN connectivity is essential to achieve the ASEAN Community. However, although ASEAN and other regional organisations[10] are undertaking efforts to fight cyber crime by improving legal structures.

Of note, the Master Plan on ASEAN Connectivity requests a feasibility study on the possibility of developing an ASEAN Single Telecommunications Market post-2015 in the context of free flow of products, investments and skilled human resources.

AIM 2015 charts the approach for ICT to 2015 in line with the ASEAN Community and underlines that ASEAN can achieve greater competitiveness and attract global investments if it leverages ICT collectively.

Please consult: ASEAN Ministerial Meeting on Transnational Crime (AMMTC); ASEAN Senior Officials Meeting on Transnational Crime (SOMTC); ASEAN Declaration on Transnational Crime, 20 December 2007; ASEAN Plan of Action to Combat Transnational Crime, 23 June 1999; Work

Programme and enhancing law enforcement cooperation and while INTERPOL is setting up its Global Complex for Innovation in Singapore in 2014, contemporary cyber incidents and cyber related threats are still a relatively new and emerging common global threat which requires further solutions.

AIM2015 calls for the development of a common framework for network security, the establishment of common minimum standards for network security to ensure a high level of preparedness and integrity of networks across ASEAN, a network security "health screening" programme for ASEAN to be implemented at regular intervals, the development of best practice models for business continuity and disaster recovery for all sectors, and the establishment of a multi-stakeholder ASEAN Network Security Action Council (ANSAC) to promote Computer Emergency Response Team (CERT) cooperation and sharing of expertise.

In line with AIM2015 and in acknowledging the increased frequency of information and network security activities,[11] the ASEAN Ministers responsible for Telecommunications and Implement the ASEAN Plan of Action to Combat Transnational Crime.

ASEAN Regional Forum

In this respect, although the ARF has no authority beyond that of ASEAN's, the opportunity that this forum provides for an environment of open dialogue for three of the most advanced global cyber actors as ARF participants - the United States, Russia and China – is particularly noteworthy. The ARF's objectives, which include fostering constructive dialogue and consultation on political and security issues of common interest and concern, more recently include cyber security issues of common interest and concern.

Furthermore, the forum promotes the role of ASEAN in the centrality of the regional architecture, contributes to future regional security architecture, and serves as a platform for countries in the region to deal with challenges in the security environment. At the 19th ASEAN Regional Forum of 12 July 2012, the Foreign Ministers of the ARF participants underscored the need to foster coordination to ensure security for the use of ICT, an ARF Statement on Cooperation in Ensuring Cyber Security was adopted, and agreement made to develop an ARF Work Plan relating to cyber security. In addition, the forum has hosted a number of workshops on cyber security matters such as proxy actors, cyber incident responses, and confidence-building measures in cyberspace.

Moving Towards a Resilient Cyber Security Regiment ASEAN: Several Recommendations for Consideration

In order to achieve a more resilient architecture for ASEAN-wide cyber security, Member States should develop and implement as soon as possible a comprehensive forward-looking cyber security framework (plus plan of action) to coordinate cohesive regional cooperation and collectively tackle common global cyber security challenges.

Such a framework should be published openly for purposes of transparency and provision should be made for regular review and updating of agreed measures and plans toASEAN Regional Forum, Chairman's Statement of the 19thASEAN Regional Forum, Cambodia, 12 July 2012 incorporate the principles of flexibility, adaptability, timely implementation, and strategic foresight. Since the nature of the threat environment is in constant flux, an inflexible framework with fixed work plans and work programmes might not be sufficiently effective.

A Comprehensive, Multi-pronged Cyber Security Framework: Several Measures and Tools for Consideration.

A non-exhaustive set of possible measures are proposed as elements of the wider comprehensive framework in order to address common global cyber security challenges and fill several gaps identified in the preceding sections. These include:

- Establish a Permanent Coordinating Mechanism: Regional Coordination & Information Sharing
- Establish a Robust ASEAN-CERT: Further Enhancing and Strengthening National CERTs' Operational Cooperation & Information Sharing
- Ensure Adequate Security of the ASEAN Secretariat
- Create a Cyber Security Hub of Excellence in the Region: Training & Capacity Building
- Ensure a Secure Supply Chain & Regional Harmonisation of International Standards: A "Cyber-Secured Zone"
- Increase Public Awareness & Civil Liberties' Protection: Engaging Citizens
- Enhance Defence Cooperation & Law Enforcement Authorities' Coordination for Cyber Related Threats
- Agree a Common Position on Responsible State Behaviour and Applicability of International Law
- Further Strengthen International Cooperation

Although ultimately the wider purpose of a comprehensive framework including its proposed measures is the creation of a more resilient regional architecture for cyber security, given the inherent limitations of ASEAN it is worth considering that those measures which complement the aims of the ASEAN Economic Community and ASEAN Socio-Cultural Community are perhaps more likely to be attained in the shorter term vis-à-vis the more politically sensitive measures.

Establish a Permanent Coordinating Mechanism: Regional Coordination & Information Sharing at a minimum and in the shorter term, a rotating coordinator could be appointed to support a network of national points of contact established to ensure the timely and proper implementation of agreed action plans and work programmes as well as to prevent possible cyber related misunderstandings. The feasibility of establishing a permanent coordinating mechanism such as a committee or network to ensure functional coordination and cooperation in enhancing cyber security (possibly constituting Member State representatives from each of the ten members to abate concerns that control might be ceded) should be explored. This mechanism could possibly function as a stand-alone mechanism, either within the ASEAN Secretariat or a more robust regional CERT. It could serve to assist cooperative work on cyber security, to serve as a network for agencies and bodies within the region to exchange policy experience, to assist in information sharing outside of traditional CERT operational cooperation, to provide training and research to Member States when requested, and to coordinate pan-ASEAN and international cyber security exercises as well as table top exercises. Such a mechanism can support ASEAN Member States in possibly establishing a regional high-level working group in line with the multi-stakeholder model. This working group should include foreign affairs, defence, justice, trade, science / technology, ICT, transport, and energy government officials as well as industry, academia, civil society, and law enforcement authorities (Track 1.5 ARF Experts and Eminent Persons (EEPS) Meetings and the CSCAP working group on cyber security can assist by producing further recommendations).

It should be noted that although ANSAC's inaugural meeting was held on 05 June 2012 and a second meeting in June 2013, its activities are not yet sufficient nor do they seem to be developing at a fast enough pace to seriously tackle cross-border cyber threats.

Establish a Robust ASEAN-CERT: Further Enhancing and Strengthening NationalCERTs' Operational Cooperation & Information SharingUnder the Singapore Declaration, it was decided that all ASEAN Member States develop and operationalize national CERTs by 2005, in line with mutually agreed minimum performance criteria. The Lao Computer Emergency Response Team (LaoCERT).

Ensure Adequate Security of the ASEAN Secretariat

The ASEAN Secretariat has been victim to intrusions such as the infamous Operation Shady RAT, which began in October 2006, a month before the ASEAN summit in Singapore and continued for another ten months. A more recent emerging trend, which should concern the Secretariat, the ARF Unit at the Secretariat and ASEAN Members, is the use of organisations as "watering holes". Symantec's Internet Security.

Threat Report for 2013111 identifies the watering hole attack as one of the most important trends in 2012.

It explains how an organisation, irrespective of whether it might hold significant classified and sensitive information since it is not the real target, can be used in a targeted attack – a "watering hole" - where the website (such as the ASEAN website) is hijacked and used to infect the real target (such as Member State organs or specifically targeted individuals) when visiting the site in order to leverage the weaker security of one entity to defeat the stronger security of another. In December 2012.

As have the Vietnamese government and victims in Singapore.mitriAlperovitch, Vice-President, Threat Research, McAfee, Revealed: Operation Shady RAT, White Paper, 2011.Operation Shady RAT (RAT is an acronym for Remote Access Tool): The compromises were standard procedure for these types of targeted intrusions: a spear phishing email containing an exploit is sent to an individual with the right level of access at the company, and the exploit, when opened, on an unpatched system will trigger a download of the implant malware. That malware will execute and initiate a backdoor communication channel to the C&C web server and interpret the instructions encoded in the hidden comments embedded in the webpage code. This will quickly be followed by live intruders jumping on to the infected machine and proceeding to quickly escalate privileges and move laterally within the organisation to establish new persistent footholds via additional compromised machines running implant malware, as well as targeting for quick exfiltration the key data for which they came.

Foreign Relations and Capstone Turbine Corporation were targeted in this fashion using a zero-day vulnerability in Microsoft's Internet Explorer web browser to compromise the computers of individuals visiting their websites.

Member States should therefore ensure that the ASEAN Secretariat (and the ARF Unit) determine the level of attacks against their systems, ensure cyber security resilience, and train its staffon cyber security.

Member States should encourage and stimulate the creation of a global cyber security hub of excellence in tandem with and in support of AIM2015 visions to create a global ICT hub in the region and ASEAN's intentions to distinguish itself as a region of high quality ICT infrastructure, skilled manpower and technological innovation. In doing so, not only will Member States increase the attractiveness of the region for FDI and enhance competitiveness in line with aims for the ASEAN Economic Community (ICT is regarded as a growth industry sector for the region, employing more than 11.7 million and contributing more than USD32 billion to ASEAN's GDP with figures due to increase by 2015114), but they will also reduce the crucial skills gap which is of serious concern to most states across the international community in their countering of cyber incidents and enhancing of cyber security. Furthermore, in accordance with the social development

Ensure a Secure Supply Chain & Regional Harmonisation of International Standards: A "Cyber-Secured Zone"

In the interests of ASEAN-wide cyber security and aims for a single market and production base as well as the enhancing of ASEAN intentions to become a global production centre or part of the global supply chain, it is essential that quality assurance and guarantee be provided that the supply chain (from design to production to delivery) is secure and standards harmonised in line with international cyber security standards. ASEAN Member States could therefore consider creating a cyber-secured zone for the supply chain of products signed and manufactured within the region in order to ensure regional cyber security, to promote trade, to enhance the region's competitiveness, and to increase its attractiveness for intra-ASEAN investment and FDI as a single investment destination. In addition, Members could consider developing a regional guideline by adopting guidelines on international standards and best practices in accordance with the intentions of the ASEAN Economic Community (i.e. extra-ASEAN rules and regulations should be taken into account when developing policies to facilitate its competing internationally, support its aims to make the region a strong segment of the global supply chain, and ensure that the single market is attractive to FDI in the region). Finally, it is equally essential that a mechanism be established to ensure that hardware and software imported from outside the region is secure.

It is also worth considering that it is highly likely that consumers will in future expect, if not demand, an assurance of such high-level security. Certification, or similar mechanism, should therefore be created for products and companies which adhere to the region's cyber security regulations and standards.

In this regard it is worth noting the European Commission has made a proposal to examine how providers of hardware and software could inform national authorities of detected vulnerabilities that could have significant security implications. Increase Public Awareness & Civil Liberties' Protection: Engaging Citizens First, while recommended actions under AIM2015 include an outreach[12] campaign to promote public awareness of cyber security through education about online security, further measures need to be employed in order to increase awareness among end-users. For instance,

ASEAN could consider synchronising a region-wide "cyber security month" like that proposed for the EU from 2013 onwards and the EU-US Cyber security Month which will be organised from 2014.

Second, a balance between security initiatives and civil liberties must be ensured. Citizens' buy-in and loyalty as well as cooperation with the public sector are essential for fully functioning cyber security strategies. While the ASEAN Charter and more recent commitments under the Bali Concord III to respect and protect human rights and fundamental freedoms go some way to protecting civil liberties, if fundamental rights such as the rights to freedom of expression and association, the rights to data privacy and data protection (AIM2015 specifically calls for ensuring personal data protection), and the right of access to Internet are not responsibly managed by public authorities it could lead to a potential and possibly very serious flashpoint. Government transgression, including received wrongdoing, could be construed negatively and sometimes in the extreme, and could possibly cause backlash whether by physical protest, disruptive cyber incidents by personally empowered citizens or a combination of both. Such disruptive cyber incidents can either emanate from within the state held to be responsible or from outside its own European Commission and the High Representative of the European Union for Foreign Affairs and Security Policy, Joint Communication to the European Parliament, the Council, the European Economic and Social Committee and the Committee of the Regions, Cyber security Strategy of the European Union: An Open, Safe and Secure Cyberspace (JOIN(2013) 1 final), 07 February 2013 borders. Mission creep should therefore be avoided and clear assurance provided to the public that it is not going to occur.

Enhance Defence Cooperation & Law Enforcement Authorities' Coordination for Cyber Related Threats

Coordination and cooperation among law enforcement authorities across the region and with third countries as well as Europol and INTERPOL should be strengthened. Given the unique nature of cyber threats, civil-military coordination should also be considered. At the 6th ASEAN Defence Ministers' Meeting (ADMM) in May 2012, the Minister of Defence for Malaysia, Datum Seri Dr Ahmad Zahid Hamidi, reportedly said that it is crucial for the Defence Ministers to work together to restrain cyber threats for the sake of peace and stability of the region, and in June 2012 he argued that with the increasing sophistication of cyber threats, national efforts to protect their networks might be left wanting. Whether this might therefore be the right time to signal stronger collaboration in cyber defence among ASEAN members was discussed at the ADMM in May 2012 and the possible development of an "ASEAN master plan of security connectivity" was suggested. However, these issues have not been fully discussed and a Defence White Paper on offensive cyber capabilities and techniques should at a minimum be published.

References

1. Lewin A. Y. and Minton L. W. (1986). Determining organisational effectiveness: another look at an agenda for research Management Science 32, 5: 514-538.
2. Lewis D. S. (1994). Organisational change: relationship between reactions, behaviour and organisational performance. Journal of Organisational Change Management, 5: 41-55.
3. Lord F. M. (1953). On the statistical treatment of football numbers. American Psychologist 8: 750-751.
4. Huselid M. (1995). The impact of human resource management practices on turnover, productivity, and corporate financial performance. Academy of Management Journal 38, 3: 63 5-672.
5. Mahoney J. T. & Pandian J. R (1992). The resource-based view within the conversation of strategic management. Strategic Management Journal 13: 3 63-380.
6. Maxwell S. E. (1980). Pair-Wise multiple comparison in repeated measures designs. Journal of Educational Statistics 5: 2 69-287.
7. Mawaide H. S., Hayajneh Y. and Al-Qutob R. (1997). The effect of type of Hospital and health insurance on hospital length of stay in Irbid, North Jordan. Health Policy and Planning 12, 2: 166-172.

8. McAfee Labs, McAfee Threats Report: Fourth Quarter 2012– Executive Summary, http://www.mcafee.com/us/resources/reports/rp-quarterly-threat-q4-2012-summary.pdf, p.4, last accessed 04 April 2013.

9. Arthur J. B. (1992). The link between business strategy and industrial relations systems in American Steel Minimi. Industrial and Labour Relations Review45: 488- 506.

10. Gupta, . M. A &Vohra, N. (2010). Measuring Effectiveness of Schools in India: A Multiple Stakeholder Framework. e-Journal of Organisational Learning and Leadership. Volume 8, No. 2.

11. ARF Workshop on Proxy Actors in Cyberspace, 14-15 March 2012; ARF Workshop on Cyber Incident Response, 6-7 September 2012; ARF Seminar on Confidence-building Measures in Cyberspace, 11-12 September 2012.

12. Hendry C., Woodward S., and BRADLEY P. (2000). Performance and rewards: out the stables. Human Resource Management Journal 10, 3: 46-62.

Conclusion

It is clear that the issue of cyber security, and how international and regional security may be impacted by cyber activities, is coming to the forefront of multilateral debate. However, it is also clear that there remain among states competing threat assessments and concepts for potential responses. There is lack of agreement about the role multilateral bodies and instruments should play. Further, the technical communities and the political/military communities remain blocked in an unhelpful way, given the complex, interrelated problems facing the cyber sphere. At the same time, the international community is beginning to grasp that securing the cyber sphere and preventing conflict, either in the cyber domain or sparked by cyber-attacks, will require multilateral approaches.

The overall goal of developing and implementing future norms, rules, and regulations, such as international guidelines or principles of appropriate state behaviour, is to maintain and further develop a peaceful, safe, stable, and predictable cyberspace. This will require more focused multilateral cooperation and a multi-stakeholder process. The debate is at an early stage; much work remains to be done.

With the growth and expansion of the Internet and related information and communications technologies (ICTs) there is an emerging international concern regarding the potential use of cyberattack during conflict and war. While a pure cyberwar is highly unlikely, future armed conflicts or skirmishes might be increasingly accompanied by the disruption of digital networks and services. Additionally, massive attacks on the Internet and/or critical infrastructure of states potentially could trigger conventional counter attacks. Despite the fact that many key questions about terminology, feasibility, rationale, and motivation of potential cyber attacks are not yet answered sufficiently, the international debate about the future challenges and possible legal, technical, and political reactions of the international community to those challenges has begun. In 2010, a United Nations Group of Governmental Experts, including diplomats from China, the Russian Federation, and the United States, stated in its consensus report, "Existing and potential threats in the sphere of information securityare among the most serious challenges of the twenty-first century".

Many states are now developing national strategies to implement safer and more secure digital infrastructures. Some argue that humankind is entering "a new era of warfare"; others believe that militarisation of the cyber sphere is looming, including new kinds of cyber weapons.1 It is often argued by military thinkers that cyberspace is becoming the "5th battlefield", after land, sea, air, and space. Others take a more subtle view: that while cyber weapons might be new sorts of weapons, there is little difference2 between cyber weapons and other types of weaponry.

In any event, militaries around the world seem to be rushing to incorporate both defensive and offensive cyber options as part of their operational tool kits for war fighting. Thus, strategies to prevent the misuse of the cyber sphere are now being considered in many national, regional, and international forums. Although debate about cyber and national/international security remains at an early stage, different stakeholders can already been seen to be favouring different strategies. The most direct measures for governments to take include the improvement of security standards of national critical information infrastructures through cooperation with the public and private sectors.

Another national approach would be to improve civil preparedness for contingency planning, as well as to implement best practices and training of operators, and raise the awareness of individual citizens. However, national strategies are not enough. Given the global access to digital technology and the worldwide structure of the Internet, international cooperation will be a key factor in preventing future cyber conflict. Governments, the private sector, and civil society must work together to coordinate national efforts, legal and regulatory approaches, and international responses to prevent future cyber threats.

International conferences and meetings on cyberspace sponsored by governments and international organisations3 are taking place frequently to bring together a wide range of stakeholders to discuss political, technical, educational, and legal responses to cyber challenges. The spread of ICTs and networking technologies is also a cross-dimensional issue, which—beyond technical development—has human, political, cultural, and legal dimensions that affect many societies. Also, several aspects of the problem overlap significantly: cybercrime and cyber terrorism, the protection of critical information infrastructure and information networks, the preservation of fundamental human rights, and the emergence of "cyber weapons" as part of the military arsenal. Various obstacles also have to be overcome in addressing these aspects, for example the dual-use character of modern ICTs, the open nature and the fast-growing use of the Internet, different cultures of communication, competing interests among stakeholders, and national differences regarding threat perceptions.

Review of Literature

1. India and ASEAN as a comprehensive and cooperative security regime, the security notion was first coined in Japan in the 1970s. The Japanese interpretation of 'comprehensive' or 'overall security' (*sogo anzen bosbo*) was developed as an alternative[4] to the concept

of 'national security' based on Japan's military policy in the period of wartime expansionism and aggression. Following a series of government studies on comprehensive security under such circumstance, the 'Report on Comprehensive National Security' was submitted to Prime Minister, Masayoshi Ito, in July 1980.

2. Humanitarian aid, Cyber security[5] and economic cooperation with developing countries have been more salient than other policies that India, Soviet Russia and Japanese government has used to respond to the multidimensional nature of threats.
3. Singapore has pursued a comprehensive approach through the concept of 'Total Defence' which has five constitutive elements: "psychological defence", "social defence", "economic defence", "civil defence", and "military defence". Singapore's interpretation of comprehensive security was largely internally focused and there were no explicit terms like 'national resilience' and 'comprehensive security'; Thai scholars have also offered their own interpretation of a comprehensive security concept.
4. Malaysia's concept of comprehensive security placed a similar priority on economic development and non-military threats, although the concept was perceived that internal security concerns were more immediate and urgent. The origins of Malaysia's interpretation of comprehensive security dated back to war against the banned Communist Part of Malaysia (CPM) during 1948-60.
5. Indonesia's National Defence Board between 1968 and 1972 and was formally accepted as a national doctrine in 1973 in the 'Guidelines of State Policy.' In addition, Indonesia's interpretation of comprehensive security was influenced by the struggle against Dutch colonialism and the subsequent desire to build a united Indonesian state, which linked the participation of the military (ABRI, or Angkatan Bersenjata

Republik Indonesia)[6] and its dual functions in Indonesia's political system. Therefore, the emphasis of comprehensive security was "on maintaining internal security and stability to deny opportunities for infiltration and subversion.

6. However, the changing security environment in the post Cold War era has raised ASEAN leaders' awareness that bilateral security arrangements were insufficient to maintain stability in Asia-Pacific. The US strategic withdrawal from military bases in the Philippines in 1992, the highlighted territorial disputes in the South China Sea along with the regional consequence of a powerful China, and potential conflicts on the Korean

Peninsula as well as the expansion of ASEAN membership all became the major focus of ASEAN's security outlook in the early 1990s. Meanwhile, the Canadian government in 1991 envisaged the cooperative security concept in the North Pacific Cooperative Security Dialogue (NPCSD), which inspired ASEAN to develop multilateral models on security issues. Acharya argues that "the NPCSD, being the first government-backed multilateral security consultations to take place within the Asia-Pacific region, added a sense of urgency to ASEAN's own ideas about regional security consultations. Certainly, it impressed on ASEAN the need to respond to the growing number of proposals from 'outsiders', which, if pursued, would deeply affect security management in its own geostrategic environment".

Testing of Hypothesis

H-1. United Nations is the main international body to coordinate and mobilise assistance in the event of any disaster anywhere in the world. This aspect is looked after by two main agencies the UN Dept of Humanitarian Affairs agency and OCHA. UN-HABITAT activities contribute to the overall objective to reduce poverty and promote sustainable development. The DMP operates under the Urban Development

Branch, of UN-HABITAT. A UN Disaster Management Team is formed in the event of a disaster and normally comprises of country level representatives of FAO, UNDP, UNICEF, WFP, WHO and UNHCR ....

H-2. A good DM plan primarily stands on four pillars, i.e., strategic thinking, sound organisation structure, quick response and coordinated relief operations; therefore, formulating an integrated policy at the national level is of vital importance. To highlight some positive recommendations on this subject, The Key Strategic Issues are:-

- Responsibility.
- Doctrine.
- Organisation.

DM is primarily a state function. But unlike, the Union War Book, there is no statute book as yet, that comes into act when a disaster strikes. On the issue of organisation, we are moving forward and in the process of setting up a comprehensive body.

H-3. Despite of all these strengths, there were some glaring weaknesses too..

(a) Lack of a Disaster Management Authority at each level.

(b) Role and response of Armed Forces during a national disaster is not clearly defined.

(c) Inadequacy in coordinating immediate relief and lack of effective Search & Rescue capability, and finally,

(d) Inadequate plans for disaster mitigation.

However there are certain threats that plague the system.

H-4. In the aftermath of the Tsunami, major changes are already in the pipeline. Quite recently, the Disaster mgt bill has been passed by the parliament. How it unfolds on ground is yet to be seen. But let me tell, how I feel this organisation needs to be structured:

(a) At the apex we have the NDMA with the PM as the chairman. As recently, General NC Vij an Ex COAS has been appointed the Dy chairman. An executive committee, comprising of secretaries from all relevant ministries should in conjunction with the NDMA. During emergencies a crisis mgt gp should also become operational.

(b) To ensure adequate integration of the armed forces a DEFENCE CRISIS MGT GROUP should be set up. And of course, most importantly as we need a state of the art national emergency operations centre. This should have facilities like communications, conferencing and media briefing rooms and adequate emergency Support Function work stations.

Research Methodology

(a) Conceptual Frame Work. The research will take into consideration the prevalent preparedness with respect to disaster management in the Indian National/ ASEAN arena, carrying out a realistic assessment of role required to be executed in each type of disaster (Natural as well as man made and suggest measures towards capacity building).

(b) Coverage. The research will attempt to cover the various types of disasters and responses required envisaged, role and task of various agencies, role played by different nationality Armed Forces played traditionally in disaster management in coordination of response, and employment in various disasters in the past.

(c) Data Collection. The research will strive to collect available data of unclassified nature on the subject and draw inference from data of sensitive nature having a bearing on international security issues[7].

(d) Analysis of Researched Material. The researched material would be analyzed to arrive at measures to be suggested at National and International levels both organisational and military for capacity building of the armed forces to meet the challenges of natural and man made disasters in view of changing risk environment and to safeguard urban security.

ROLE OF INTERNATIONAL ORGANIZATIONS

Some studies have already been undertaken to address the function, role, and activities of international organisations in the cyber spacefield. International efforts to address cyber threats are, in comparison to national strategies, more limited in terms of resources. Most international organisations now active in the cyber domain are intergovernmental, founded and influenced by governments, and based on multilateral-treaties. The most prominent example is certainly the United Nations, which has near global state participation and outreach. The International Telecommunication Union (ITU) is another key international body.

Regional organisations such as the Organisation of American States (OAS), the Association of Southeast Asian Nations (ASEAN) Regional Forum (ARF), the Asia–Pacific Economic Cooperation Organisation, and the Organisation for Security and Co-operation in Europe (OSCE) also play important roles.

While most of the concrete work on cyber defence is organised by states, international organisations can discuss, coordinate, and develop proposals to enhance global strategies for the creation of appropriate regional and international structures, institutions, and policies. This spectrum of work ranges from establishing/strengthening norms and principles to prevent the malicious use of new cyber technologies, to brokering of agreements about the application of the law of armed conflict, to promoting national prevention of, preparation for, response to, and recovery from cyber incidents be incidents. For these purposes, international organisations have the power to bring together the most relevant actors in the cyber security domain—governments, the private sector, civil society, and individual citizens.

UNITED NATIONS: The United Nations General Assembly has approved a number of resolutions relevant to ICTs and cyber security that have served to draw the attention of United Nations Member States to future cyber challenges. A recent study underlined the emerging norm-building process within the United Nations system.500 Several specialised United Nations agencies are dealing with cyber security on different levels. The United Nations Office on Drugs and Crime supports the United Nations by addressing illicit drug control and crime prevention, including through the cyber domain. The World Customs Organisation, which facilitates global supply chain security, is active in promoting strategies for critical infrastructure protection. The United Nations Economic and Social Council is focusing on improved information exchange, best practices, and training to fight the criminal misuse of information technology.

The issue of telecommunication and information security has been on the United Nations agenda since the Russian Federation in 1998 first introduced a draft resolution (A/35/576, 18 November 1998) in the First Committee of the General Assembly, which[8] was adopted as resolution53/70 in January 1999 without a vote.

INTERNATIONAL TELECOMMUNICATION UNION: The ITU is a specialised United Nations agency for regulating telecommunications and use of the radio frequency-spectrum. The ITU has been seeking to expand its remit to include cyber security, not without some tensions among its member states about what the limits should be to its involvement, particularly in political questions of international peace and security. It has 193 members from the public and private sectors, including ICT regulators, academic insti-tutions, and some 700 companies.

Since its founding in 1865, the ITU has played a major role in setting standards in telecommunication security. The ITU consists of three sectors: the Radio communication Sector, the Standardisation Sector, and the Telecommunication

Development Sector. It is the only inter governmental organisation within the United Nations system embracing all actors in the ICT domain. The ITU is currently working on cyber security issues through a range of activities related to standardisation and technical assistance, as well as to developing technical guides for critical infrastructure protection, botnet mitigation, and training development for developing countries.

An ITU High-Level Expert Group on Cyber security was founded in2007 as a consultation platform for information security experts from various domains and regions. On 17 May 2007, the ITU launched the Global Cyber security Agenda "to provide a framework within which all stakeholders can coordinate an international response to the growing challenges in cyber security" and "to build confidence and security in the information society". The Agenda is built on five pillars: legal measures, technical procedures, organisational structures, capacity-building, and international cooperation. The ITU also collaborates with the International Multilateral Partnership Against Cyber Threats, which focuses on early warning systems and a secure electronic collaboration platform for coordination of incident response measures,[9] and the Forum for Incident Response and Security Teams, which is an international confederation of trusted computer incident response teams (CIRTs) that cooperatively handle computer security incidents and promote incident prevention programmes. The Forum also accredits computer emergency response teams (CERTs) worldwide. The Agenda continues to form partnerships for different stakeholders and seeks to enable states to implement concrete measures for cyber security.

INTERNET GOVERNANCE ORGANIZATIONS: The Internet as a new global infrastructure for communication and business was created as an open "bottom up" medium for free speech and the exchange of information. From the beginning, internet governance groups have played an important role by self-regulating and promoting new internet applications. According to a 2011 European Union study, organisations can be divided into the technical and the political domains.

Governments, which are "latecomers" in the dynamic and volatile internet world, are supportive but not central in these "bottom up" institutions. Thus, these groups have a significant role to play in technical questions of cyber security, but they have not as yet been directly influential on questions of international security and military use. On the other hand, the political debate among governments[10] about the extent of national sovereignty in the cyber sphere in recent years has started to spill over to these venues.

Technical groups such as the Internet Engineering Task Force or the Institute for Electrical and Electronics Engineers are developing and discussing software protocols, connectivity, and electronic standards. The non-profit, private Internet Corporation for Assigned Names and Numbers (ICANN) oversees vital internet-related tasks such as assigning names and internet addresses, ensuring its stable and secure operation.

The United States government, which helped to establish ICANN in 1998, still has significant influence on the Government Advisory[11] Council that gives advice to ICANN on issues of public policy, especially where there may be an interaction between ICANN's activities or policies and national laws or international agreements.

Approximately 50 governments and distinct economies, global organisations (such as the ITU and the United Nations Educational, Scientific and Cultural Organisation), and regional organisations (such as the Organisation for Economic Co-operation and Development, the Asia Pacific Forum, and the Council of Europe)attend three meetings a year. In the cyber security field, informal internet governance initiatives also exist, such as the Meridian Forum for Global Critical Infrastructure Protection, which is an important trust-building and consultation forum.

Slightly afield from these technical organisations but concerned with the same issues is the Internet Governance Forum, a multi-stakeholder forum for facilitating dialogue. It was created by the United Nations Secretary-General in 2006, and first convened in Athens the same year. The group holds annual meetings, as well as workshops and consultations, to help articulate issues such as internet development of resources, ensuring access for all, and maintaining security.

CONVENTION ON CYBERCRIME: The 2004 Budapest Convention on Cybercrime of the Council of Europe is the only international binding treaty on cybercrime. It serves as a guide for states to develop national legislation on cybercrime and as a framework for international cooperation.[12] The Convention laid out general principles for international cooperation on cybercrime, especially between internet service providers and law enforcement agencies. Cybercrimes such as hacking and data interception are specifically addressed in the Convention.[13] It states that cyber attacks are illegal, regardless of their motivation. It does not focus on other cyber attacks such as espionage or sabotage, although there is an overlap between cybercrime, cyber terrorism, and cyber war, both from a technological view point and with regard to actors. The Convention requires signatories to establish a basic legal framework to address cybercrime. It also forms a basis for cooperation in the case of a severe cyber incident. However, only 37 states have ratified the treaty. While most European states have ratified the Convention, the Czech Republic, Greece, Ireland, Luxembourg, Poland, Sweden, and Turkey have not. Outside of Europe, only Japan and the United States have ratified.[14] The Council of Europe holds annual conferences in Strasbourg and supports states in implementing the Convention, as it is considered "a useful tool for 'exporting' European norms on the issue". The Council and the private sector have launched the Global Project on Cybercrime to promote broad implementation of the Convention and related international standards.

GROUP OF EIGHT: The Group of Eight is an international forum of the governments of Canada, France, Germany, Italy, Japan, the Russian Federation, the United Kingdom, and the United States. In 2011 in Deauville, France, these states for the first time discussed and agreed on a number of principles the must be upheld in order to underpin a stable and flourishing Internet, such as freedom, respect, privacy, protection of intellectual property, multi-stakeholder governance, cyber security, and prosecution of crime.

In addition, the Group maintained that "non-discrimination and fair competition", as well as "flexibility and transparency", are key aspects of the multi-stakeholder approach required to protect the Internet in the future. The Deauville Declaration underlines that "Governments have a role to play, informed by a full range of stakeholders,[15] in helping to develop norms of behaviour and common approaches in the use of cyberspace". The main goal of the Group of Eight is to establish a sharing mechanism among leading industrialised nations to prevent, investigate, and prosecute cyber crimes. To this end a special forum was held in Paris on 24–25 May 2011. A subgroup worked on the protection of critical information infrastructure and cybercrime, and created a network for points of contact in more than 50 countries. This work could be expanded by follow-up discussions in the Group of 20 framework.

TRANSPARENCY & CONFIDENCE-BUILDING MEASURES: APPLICABILITY TO THE CYBER SPHERE?TRANSPARENCY & CONFIDENCE-BUILDING MEASURES: APPLICABILITY TO THE CYBER SPHERE?

In contemplating multilateral approaches to reducing risks of conflict in the cyber sphere, policymakers confront a number of complex problems. Unlike in traditional arms control and confidence-building, the focus cannot be on "weapons", military forces, or government/military-controlled assets and facilities, due to the dual-use, and largely civilian owned, infrastructure of the domain. In addition, the integration of the global economy into the cyber domain makes state-based regulatory control somewhat difficult. None the less, as cyberspace becomes increasingly a tool for militaries and for state-sponsored activities such as espionage and the dissemination of propaganda, there is widespread agreement that boundaries on some activities, and measures to reduce the risk of conflict, must be found at the multilateral level. However, the debate at this stage remains undeveloped, as states continue to hold competing and often contradictory views about legal obligations, threats, what constitutes an attack, and appropriate/responsible responses to threats or attacks. For example, most Western states16 believe that freedom of access to the cyber sphere is a basic human right, which must be protected by law and regulations. Other states, in contrast, favour the concept of "information security", and thus are seeking the right to limit the access of their citizens to the public cyber sphere if the stability or survival of the regime is deemed to be at stake. Obviously, these two ideological approaches are in direct conflict, and complicate the effort to find multilateral solutions to the problems that face all states.

Nonetheless, a spectrum of preventive and crisis-management strategies to secure the cyber sphere for different stakeholders already can be envisioned. At the sub state level, strategies should obviously include raising awareness, and the improvement of security standards for individual computers, servers, and networks. Making national critical information infrastructure more robust and resilient can only be achieved in cooperation between the public and private sectors. Governments and industry can strengthen civil preparedness for contingency planning as well as offering best practices and training for operators. Early warning and quick reaction is of upmost importance should a massive cyber attack occur. Just as obviously, given the interconnected nature of the cyber sphere, states will need to work together to ensure cyber security, as many threats, such as cyber crime or cyber terrorism, know no boundaries.[17] However, there is a lack of a central international mechanism for discussing strategies—rather there isa plethora of potential forums all, with different focuses. This is proving another obstacle for state-based efforts to establish norms, common security standards, and ways to adapt or strengthen existing regulations, law enforcement, and information-sharing.

Due to the growing concerns about the potential for the use of cyber tools to spark conflict and even traditional warfare, there are nascent[18] efforts within the United Nations and the Organisation for Security and Cooperation in Europe (OSCE), and among like-minded states, to identify practical transparency and confidence-building measures to avoid miscalculations or misperceptions regarding the use of the cyber domain.

As noted, in 2010, a United Nations Group of Governmental Experts reached agreement on five general recommendations for future actions, among them "Further dialogue among States to discuss norms pertaining to State use of ICTs [information and communications technologies], to reduce collective risk and protect critical national and international infrastructure", and, in particular, "Confidence-building, stability and risk reduction measures to address the implications of State use of ICTs, including exchanges of national views on the use of ICTs in conflict". The first chapter explores the dimensions of the problem, including the challenges to and opportunities for a secure and stable cyber space. The second chapter refers to classical concepts19 of confidence-building developed during the Cold War and applied to different weapon systems, including nuclear, conventional, and space weapons, as well as in nonmilitary fields such as disaster relief. The third chapter compares how traditional types of trust and confidence-building measures (TCBMs) could or could not be applied in the cyber domain.

CIVILIAN AND MILITARY CYBERTHREATS: SHIFTING IDENTITIES AND ATTRIBUTION

The characteristics of the global cyber domain include low barriers of technological entry, minimal technical skills required of the individual user, and rapid dissemination, replication, and exchange of all forms of data all over the world, which has lead to an unprecedented global connectedness. In his seminal report, Joseph Nye described the key characteristics of cyberspace and the implications for foreign policy: "The low price of entry, anonymity, and asymmetries in vulnerability means that smaller actors have more capacity to exercise hard and soft power in cyberspace than in many more traditional domains of world politics". A closer look at current cyber incidents reveals that different forms of cyber-conflict with changing motivations and actor categories are emerging.

Increasingly, organised global cybercrime using sophisticated cyber technology (for example, bot nets) is a concern for states. Terrorist organisations have so far only used the cyber sphere to recruit followers and to organize fundraising, but there is no guarantee that will remain the limits of their activities. "Hacktivist" groups such as Anonymous and Lulz Sec are challenging corporations, institutions, and governmental agencies whose policies or actions the hackers dislike.

In the West, there are constant rumours that "cyber warriors" supported by state entities are systematically attacking governments. Following revelations about Stux net, worms and trojans such as Flame, Duqu, and Gauss have been discovered, revealing that sophisticated espionage programmes using cyber tools are being actively applied, especially in the Middle East. In most cases the origin of such malware is unclear: are these efforts state-sponsored or private activities? What are the motivations and resources behind these incidents? Are states preparing for cyber war?

Types of actors also vary widely. “White Hat” hackers, or “ethical” hackers, exploit computer systems for enjoyment or—when employed by an organisation—to reveal security gaps. “Black Hat” hackers, however, break into computer systems for personal gain. Cybercriminals include thieves who steal personal data or charge bank accounts illegally, but also those who threaten to do so to extort money from the private sector. The differentiation among these categories is thin and fluctuating, but very often the tools being used are the same. A 2011 study sponsored by the European Parliament concluded that, “Most cyber threats involve elements of loosely connected networks and actors with rapidly shifting identities, whereas government responses tend to take place within preexisting institutional settings”.

STATES AS ACTORS: PREPARING FOR CYBERWAR?

Strong assertions have been made by security companies and academics about future cyber threats that could be caused by, and directed against, states. For some, cyber war is already real, and is capable of devastating modern countries. Former National Coordinator for Security, Infrastructure Protection, and Counter-Terrorism for the United States Richard A. Clarke wrote that cyber war “has already begun as nations prepare the battlefield...[by] hacking into each other’s networks and infrastructure”. The internet security company McAfee warned in 2012 that a “cyber arms race” is developing based on a survey of 250 leading authorities worldwide. It said that 57 per cent of global experts believe that an arms race is taking place in cyberspace. On the other hand, a 2011 Organisation for Economic Co-operation and Development (OECD) study dismissed such doomsday visions because in order to effect massive disruption or damage to national infrastructures, highly orchestrated attacks would be required, based on unprecedented levels of preparatory work, coordination, and resources.

Nonetheless, governments increasingly perceive cyber threats to be rapidly on the rise and that future cyber conflict between states might become a reality. If cyber attacks cause massive damage, the conflict might escalate, leading to a full-fledged armed conflict. Without doubt, many states are now implementing military cybercapabilities.550 As noted earlier, this study has identified six states with explicit military cyber strategies, two more with pending military cyber strategies, and 30 which identify cyber security as a military priority. James Lewis has explained that already military doctrines of some states include "the use of cyber capabilities for reconnaissance, information operations, the disruption of critical networks and services, for cyber attacks, and as a complement to electronic warfare and information operations". His analysis concludes that "only a few major 'Cyber Powers' have the capability to use software commands sent over the Internet to cause physical destruction". However, he points out that a number of states are developing military capabilities, and that" non-state actors will gain this capability as techniques and tools are commoditized".[20] Obviously, militaries around the world must protect their own critical infrastructure against attack from the outside. It is thus completely understand able that national militaries are seeking strategies to defend assets and networks; what is unclear is how those strategies can be crafted so as not to imperil[21] international security and stability. What is even less clear is how the advent of offensive cyber tools for use in warfare will affect international stability, crisis escalation, war fighting, civilian infrastructure, and the global economy.

CLASSICAL CONFIDENCE-BUILDING IN THE MILITARYAND NON-MILITARY DOMAINS

As noted earlier, the United Nations and the Organisation for Security and Co-operation in Europe (OSCE) have a lot of experience in developing and promoting CBMs. Other regional organisations, such as the Association of Southeast Asian Nations (ASEAN) Regional Forum (ARF) and the

Organisation of American States (OAS), also discuss and consult on regional issues including the function and implementation of regional CBMs. The United Nations Disarmament Commission[22] developed guidelines for CBMs, which were presented at a session of the General Assembly on 28 May1988.559 The major objective cited for the development of CBMs was "to reduce and even eliminate the causes of mistrust, fear, misunderstanding and miscalculations with regard to relevant military activities and intentions of other States". A central aim was "to help to prevent military confrontation as well as covert preparations for the commencement of a war, to reduce the risk of surprise attacks and of the outbreak of war by accident".

Spurred during the Cold War because of the concern about nuclear war, the modern "arms control school" proposed and developed a number of different measures for crisis stability, damage limitation, and war prevention. A variety of arms control treaties and measures were introduced over time" to place political or legal constraints on the deployment and/or disposition of national military means".561 Confidence- and security-building measures(CSBMs) are an integral part of the arms control agenda. During the early days of the Cold War, "nuclear confidence-building measures" were introduced as an initial step to increase transparency by the two military blocs. After the 1962 Cuban Missile Crisis, both superpowers established direct and effective communication hotlines to prevent the outbreak of a nuclear war caused by unauthorised or accidental use of nuclear weapons. In 1971, the superpowers signed the Agreement on Measures to Reduce the Risk of Outbreak of Nuclear War.

In 1977, the Soviet Union and the United States broadened cooperation by signing the Agreement to Establish Nuclear Risk Reduction Centres, aimed at avoiding accidental nuclear war. Bilateral hotline agreements were also signed between the Soviet Union and France in 1976, and the Soviet Union and the United Kingdom in 1977.

After the end of the Cold War, proposals were made to reduce the high alert level of deployed, nuclear-equipped intercontinental ballistic missiles—de-alerting measures, that included removing the warheads from the missiles and storing them separately. In September 1998, US President Clinton and Russian President Yeltsin released a statement on the establishment of a Joint Data Exchange Center in Moscow for the exchange of information derived from each state's warning systems for the launch of ballistic missiles or space vehicles. Unfortunately, a Center was never realised, but risk reduction measures[23] such as early warning were imperative in the nuclear standoff between the superpowers.

The most important multilateral nuclear agreement is the 1968 Treaty on the Non-Proliferation of Nuclear Weapons (NPT),[24] which was extended indefinitely in 1995.562 It aims to prevent the spread of nuclear weapons and weapons technology (articles 1–3), to promote cooperation in the peaceful use of nuclear energy (article 4), and to further the goal of achieving nuclear disarmament (article 6). An autonomous organisation, the International Atomic Energy Agency (IAEA), helps to check compliance with the NPT, and has additional tasks in the area of nuclear safety.

The NPT was opened for signature in 1968, entered into force on 5 March1970, and as of April 2013 had 189 states parties, including the five nuclear weapon states. Four threshold nuclear-weapon states (the Democratic People's Republic of Korea, India, Pakistan, and Israel) are not members.

Safeguards, and promoting the peaceful use of nuclear energy. Building confidence in the safe running of nuclear facilities and the non-diversion of nuclear material to underline peaceful use under article 4 is a key objective of the NPT regime.

An interesting regional approach has been the establishment in 1991 of the Brazilian–Argentine Agency for Accounting and Control of Nuclear Materials (ABACC), which was created after the rapprochement between both states after 1986. ABACC is a bilateral "safeguard agency" run by both states to guarantee that all nuclear material is exclusively used for peaceful purposes.

These agreements all include inspections, consultations, workshops, and concrete practical CSBMs and CBMs, which have helped to decrease mistrust between states, to reduce the dangers of armed conflict from misunderstandings and miscalculations in the nuclear weapons arena, and to build up additional insurance against an "outbreak" by a state. Traditional arms control also can include bans on development, stockpiling, and use of certain types of weapons. The 1972 Convention on the Prohibition of the Development, Production and Stockpiling of Bacteriological (Biological) and Toxin Weapons and on Their Destruction(BTWC) prohibited the development, production, stockpiling, or acquisition of biological agents or toxins for non-peaceful purposes, as well as any related delivery means. The BTWC has no verification mechanism, but the states parties have agreed to use voluntary measures to declare high-security facilities or unusual outbreaks of diseases. The1993 Convention on the Prohibition of the Development, Production, Stockpiling and Use of Chemical Weapons and on Their Destruction(CWC) outlaws the production, stockpiling, retention, transfer, and use of chemical weapons and is administered by its own verification body, the Organisation for the Prohibition of Chemical Weapons (OPCW).563 Both conventions are restrictive in nature and are aimed at eliminating weapons based on dual-use substances—biological and chemical agents—that play an important role in daily life. Although specified lists of prohibited chemical or biological agents exist, both conventions also address future types of agents in a comprehensive way. The "general purpose criterion" that is enshrined in both conventions allows the development of a flexible list of prohibited agents. Complex technical and legal issues regarding definitions, access to industrial facilities, verification of precursors, and so forth were successfully negotiated despite difficulties.

While arms control of nuclear, biological, and chemical weapons is mainly based on the control of precursor agents and materials[25], another approach is to restrict or regulate weapons delivery systems, such as missiles or aircraft. Missiles are the most ubiquitous delivery systems, but remain in sufficiently restricted by arms control accords. Supply-side arms export regulations, such as the 1987 Missile Technology Control Regime, have helped to delay regional missile programmes and impede technological cooperation with non-member states. Many missile-related CBMs have been proposed, but never implemented universally. One reasonably successful accord is the Hague Code of Conduct against Ballistic Missile Proliferation, which aims to enable more transparency concerning the spread of ballistic missiles. The politically binding Code was first signed on November 2002 and its signatories have increased to 134 states. Members have to provide pre-launch notification of ballistic missile and space launch vehicle launches and test flights, as well as to submit annual declarations of policy on ballistic missiles and space launch vehicles, including annual information on the number and generic class of ballistic missiles and space launch vehicles launched during the preceding year. Although the Code raised the level of awareness and transparency of the proliferation of ballistic missiles, key regions were left out, and cruise missiles, which can also carry weapons of mass destruction, are not covered by the agreement.

TRANSPARENCY AND CONFIDENCE-BUILDING FOR CYBER ANDOUTER SPACE ACTIVITIES

Cyberspace is dominated by dual-use technologies that can have military as well as commercial and civilian applications. It is also a technical domain[26] in which private sector actors control most of the assets. In both these ways, cyberspace is quite similar to the space domain. Missile and rocket technologies are vectors for military payloads such as nuclear weapons, but can also serve as space launch vehicles for civil or commercial payloads. Outer space, like cyberspace, is an important strategic asset for national and international security—despite its highly commercial infrastructure. Thus, there is some value in reviewing the specific TCBMs that have been proposed for outer space with an eye to future solutions for cyberspace. The overarching international framework for outer space, including the concepts of "peaceful use" and "free access", are codified in the 1967.

Treaty on Principles Governing the Activities of States in the Exploration and Use of Outer Space, Including the Moon and Other Celestial Bodies, known as the Outer Space Treaty (OST). Although the deployment of weapons of mass destruction in orbit is prohibited under article 4 of the OST, the deployment and use of conventional space weapons is not excluded explicitly[27]. Over the decades since the OST, a number of initiatives have been launched by states and non-governmental organisations to prevent the weaponisation of space and to keep the space environment free from potential armed conflict—including the 2008 proposal by China and the Russian Federation for the Conference on Disarmament to negotiate a treaty to ban weapons placed in space, the Draft Treaty on the Prevention of Weapons in Outer Space and of the Threat or Use of Force against Outer Space Objects. The Conference on Disarmament has not succeeded, however, to negotiate any multilateral agreement regarding military space activities since it began work on the subject in the mid-1990s. Indeed, as most efforts to develop bilateral or multilateral space arms control measures have come to naught, recent efforts to protect the space domain have centred on the development of CBMs and norms of conduct. In December 2008, the European Union published the Draft Code of Conduct for Outer Space Activities, subsequently revised in 2010. This effort is aimed at establishing non-legally binding norms of behaviour in space. The proposed international code is intended to enhance "the safety, security and predictability of outer space", and includes both civilian and military provisions. For example, the proposal seeks to minimize "the possibility of accidents in space, collisions between space objects or any form of harmful interference" (article 4.1).

The United Nations began studying the question of TCBMs for outer space in 1991. A General Assembly resolution in 2006, spearheaded by the Russian Federation, asked United Nations Member States for concrete proposals on such measures; the Russian Federation in 2009 put forward a detailed set of potential measures that ranged from basic transparency measures to "rules of the road" for space activities.575 In 2010, the General Assembly mandated a Group of Governmental Experts to explore TCBMs; the group began its work in July 2012 and will wrap up in July 2013. The goal is to reach agreement on a series of recommendations for TCBMs to the Secretary-General. Concepts widely discussed have included the notification of launches, orbital changes, and high-risk re-entries of satellites into the atmosphere. In addition, the United Nations Committee for the Peaceful Uses of Outer Space (COPUOS), comprising 69 Member States, is studying new multilateral, voluntary measures for ensuring "the long-term sustainability" of the space environment. While this effort is highly technical and focused on "best practice guidelines", many of the measures required for ensuring safe and secure space operations, such as exchange of data regarding objects on orbit, are also functional TCBMs.

References

1. R.A. Clarke, *Cyber war: The Next Threat to National Security and What to Do About It*, 2010, p. 30–31.
2. *Ibid.*, pp. 51–52.
3. B. Baseley-Walker, "Transparency and confidence-building measures in cyberspace: towards norms of behavior", *Disarmament Forum*, no. 4, 2011, p. 32.
4. Chapman, et al., 1983, pp. xiii-xviii.
5. (2004), 'How Ideas Spread: Whose Norms Matter? Norm Localisation and Institutional Change in Asian Regionalism', *International Organisation* (Spring), Vol. 58, pp. 239-275.

6. (Leifer, 1996, pp. 16-19; Morada, 2010, pp. 14-15)
7. Bray, John (1992), 'Burma: Resisting the international community', *The Pacific Review*, Vol. 5, No. 3, pp. 291-296.
8. H. Lin, "Some modest steps toward greater cyber security", *Bulletin of the Atomic Scientists*, vol. 68, no. 5, 2012.
9. J.A. Lewis, "Confidence-building and international agreement in cyber security", *Disarmament Forum*, no. 4, 2011, p. 57.
10. Deauville G8 Declaration, *Renewed Commitment for Freedom and Democracy*, 2011, p. 6.
11. *Ibid.,* p. 38.
12. Deauville G8 Declaration, *Renewed Commitment for Freedom and Democracy*, 2012, p. 96.
13. H. Lin, "Some modest steps toward greater cyber security", *Bulletin of the Atomic Scientists*, vol. 69, no. 5, 2012.
14. *Ibid.,* p. 89.
15. *Ibid.,* p. 119.
16. General Assembly, *Group of Governmental Experts on Developments in the Field of Information and Telecommunications in the Context of International Security*, UN Document A/65/201, 30 July 2010, para. 18.
17. *Ibid.,* para. 2.2.6.
18. D.J. Betz and T. Stevens, *Cyberspace and the State. Toward a Strategy for Cyber-Power*, International Institute for Security Studies, 2011, pp. 16–34.
19. *Ibid.,* p. 8.
20. H. Lin, "Some modest steps toward greater cyber security", *Bulletin of the Atomic Scientists*, vol. 72, no. 5, 2013.
21. *Ibid.,* p. 80.
22. 559 General Assembly, *Special Report of the Disarmament Commission to the General Assembly at its Third Special Session Devoted to Disarmament*, UN document A/S-15/3*, 28 May 1988, paras. 1.3–2.4.
23. S. Tulliu and T. Schmalberger, *Coming to Terms with Security: A Lexicon for Arms Control, Disarmament and Confidence-Building*, UNIDIR, 2003, p. 7.
24. *Ibid.,* p. 229.
25. General Assembly, *Group of Governmental Experts on Developments in the Field of Information and Telecommunications in the Context of International Security*, UN Document A/65/201, 30 July 2010, p. 6.

26. OSCE Conflict Prevention Centre, *OSCE Guide on Non-Military Confidence Building Measures (CBMs)*, 2012, p. 9.
27. S. Tulliu and T. Schmalberger, *Coming to Terms with Security: A Lexicon for Arms Control, Disarmament and Confidence-Building*, UNIDIR, 2003, p. 157.

Bibliography and References

1. Adsit D. J., London M., Crom S. and Jones D. (1996). Relationships between employee attitudes, customer satisfaction and departmental performance. Journal of Management Development 15, 1: 62-75.
2. Agarwal S. & Ramaswami S. N. (1993). Affective organisational commitment of salespeople: an expanded model. Journal of Personal Selling and Sales Management13, 2: 49-70.
3. Agarwal, Pawan. 2006. 'Higher Education in India: The Need for Change'. Working Paper no. 108, Indian Council for Research on International Economic Relations, June.
4. All India Council for Technical Education (AICTE). 2005. 'Regulations for Entry and Operation of Foreign Universities/Institutions Imparting Technical Education in India'. Notification, All India Council for Technical Education, 16 May.
5. 'Approval Process Handbook 2012–2013'. All India Council for Technical Education.
6. Al-Ansari (1995). In-service education and training of teachers in Saudi Arabia: A study of current provision and future needs. Unpublished doctoral thesis. University of Southampton. Southampton, UK.
7. Al-Dogether A. H. (1988). Analysis of expatriate employee turnover using the Mobley Model: nurses

in King Khalid University Hospital. Master Thesis, Sangamon State University. USA.

8. Alimo-Metcalfe B. (1993). Women in management: organisational socialisation and assessment practices that prevent career advancement. International Journal of Selection and Assessment 1, 2: 68-83.
9. Al- Amri H. S. (2001). Human Resource Management Practices and Performance Indicxators in Hospitals. PhD Thesis. University of Birmingham.
10. Amit R., Schoemakerp . J. (1993). Strategic assets and organisational rent. Strategic Management Journal 14: 3, 346.
11. Anastos A. and Seaman B. (1980). The development of modern management practices in Saudi Arabia. Columbia Journal of World Business, Summer8:1-92.
12. Andersong and Hussey P. (2001). Comparing health system performance in OECD. Health Affairs, May/ june: 219-232.
13. Argyris C. (1977). Double loop learning in organisations. H arvard Business Review, September-October 5: 9-72.
14. Armstrong M . (1998). A handbook of personnel management practice. Kogan Page Limited. London.
15. Armstrong M. and Baron A (1998). Performance management handbook. IPM. London.
16. Arthur J. B. (1992). The link between business strategy and industrial relations systems in American Steel Minimi. Industrial and Labour Relations Review45: 488- 506.
17. Arthur J. B- (1994). Effects of human resource systems on manufacturing Performance and turnover. Academy of Management Journal 37, 3: 670-687.
18. Atkinson A. A., Waterhouse J. H., and Wells R. B. (1997). A stakeholder approach to strategic performance measurement. Sloan Management Review, Spring: 25-37.

19. Alutto, J. A. & Belasco, J. A. (1972). A typology of participation in organisational decision making. Administrative Science Quarterly, 17 (1), 117-125.

20. Bauch, P. A. (2000). Do school markets serve the public interest? More lessons from England. Educational Administration Quarterly, 36 (2), 309-323.

21. Blasé, J. J. (1988). The politics of favoritism: A qualitative analysis of the teachers' perspective. Educational Administration Quarterly, 24 (2), 152-177.

22. Blasé, J. & Blasé, J. (2002). The micro politics of instructional supervision: A call for research. Educational Administration Quarterly, 38 (1), 6-44.

23. Blasé, J. & Blasé, J. (1999). Principal' instructional leadership and teachers' development: Teachers perspectives. Educational Administration Quarterly, 35 (3), 349-378.

24. Boyle, P. (1997). Educational Quality Assurance in Universities: an enhanced model, Assessment & Evaluation in Higher Education, Volume 22, Issue 2.

25. Bredeson, P. V. (1985). An analysis of the metaphorical perspectives of the school principals. Educational Administration Quarterly, 21 (1). 29 – 50.

26. Bacharach S. (1989). Organisational theories: some criteria for evaluation.

27. Academy of Management Review 14: 496-515.

28. Bae J., Chen S., and Lawler J. (1998). Variations in human resource management in Asia countries: MNC home-country and host-country effects. The International Journal of Human Resource Management 9, 4: 653-670.

29. Baines A. (1997). Productivity improvement. Work Study 46, 2: 49-5 1.

30. Baird L. and Meshoulan 1. (1988). Managing two fits of strategic human resource management. Academy of Management Review 13, 1: 116-128.

31. Balnaves M. and Caputi P. (2001). Quantitative: introduction to quantitative research methods- an investigation approach. Sage. London.

32. Banker R., Datar S., and Kaplan R. S. (1989). Productivity measurement and management accounting. Journal of Accounting, Auditing, and Finance 4, 4: 528-554.

33. Barney J. (199 1). Firm resources and the theory of competitive advantage. Journal of Management 17: 99-120.

34. Baruch Y. (1996). Evaluating quality and reputation of human resource management. Personnel Review 26, 5: 377-394.

35. Baruch Y. (1998). Walking the tightrope: strategic strategic issues for human resources. Long Range Planning 31: 467-475.

36. Bass B. M. (1981). Stogdill's handbook of leadership (rev. ed.). The Free Press. New York.

37. Beaumont (1993). Human resource management: key concepts and skills. Sage. London.

38. Becker B. &Gerhart B. (1996). The impact of human resource management on organisational performance: progress and prospects. Academy of Management Journal 39: 779-801.

39. Becker G. (1964). Human capital. National Bureau of Economic Research. New York.

40. Beer M., Spector B., Lawrence P. R., Mills D., & Walton R. E. (1984). Managing human assets. The Free Press. New York.

41. Best I W. (1970). Research in education. Prentice-Hall. Englewood Cliffs, NJ.

42. Blaug M. (1976). The empirical status of human capital theory: a slightly jaundiced survey. Journal of Economic Literature 14: 827-855.

43. Bloor K. and Maynard A. (2001). Workforce productivity and incentive structures in the UK National

Health Service. Journal of Health Research and Policy 6, 2: 105-73.

44. Blyton P. and Turnbull P. (1996). Reassessing human resource management. Sage Publications. London.
45. Borg M. (1989). Stress and job satisfaction among primary school teachers in Malta. Educational Review 41, 3: 271-279.
46. Borg W. R- & Gall M. D. (1996). Educational research: an introduction. Longman.
47. New York. Intellectual capital: a human capital Perspective. Journal of Intellectual capital 2, 2: 127-135.
48. Basu, Kaushik. 2009. 'Report of the Committee to Advise on Renovation and Rejuvenation of Higher Education in India: A Note of Dissent'. Retreived from http: //prayatna. typepad. com/. Assessed on: 6 July 2014.
49. Business Standard. . 'Raj Govt to Issue Ordinance on Fee Regulatory Commission', 30 May 2012.
50. Boudreau J. W. (199 1). Utility analysis in human resource management decisions. In M. D. Dunnette and L. M. Hough (Eds.), Handbook of industrial and organisational psychology (2d ed.), vol. 2: 621-745. Consulting Psychologists Press. Palo Alto, CA.
51. Bovaird T. & Davis P. (1999). Learning to manage with limited resources: coping strategies and learning breakthroughs in UK local government. International Journal of Public Sector Management 12, 3: 293-313.
52. Boxall P. (1992). Strategic HRM: a beginning, a new theoretical direction. Human Resource Management Journal 2, 3: 61-79.
53. Boxall P. (1996). The strategic HRM debate and the resource-based view of the firm. Human Resource Management Journal 6, 3: 59-75.
54. Boyle S. and Harrison A. J. (1995). Provider competition: Wheel and deal. Health Service Journal, 30 March: 24-26.

55. Bradley J. V. (1968). Distribution-free statistical tests. Prentice-Hall. Englewood Cliffs, NJ.
56. Brayfield A. H. & Rothe H. F. (195 1). An index of job satisfaction. Journal of Applied Psychology35: 307-31 1.
57. Brignall T. J. (1993). Performance measurement and change in local government: a general case and childcare application. Public Money and Management, October-December: 23-30.
58. Brignall T. J. (1994b) Performance measurement and change in local government: a postscript, in Terry F. (Ed.), The Dimensions of Change in Local Government. Public Finance Foundation: 41-50. butler J, E., Ferris G. R., and Napier N. K. (1991). Strategy and human resource management. South-West. Cincinnati, Ohio.
59. Carmer S. G. & Swanson M. R_ (1973). An evaluation of ten multiple comparison procedures by Monte Carlo methods. Journal of the American Statistical Association 68: 66-74.
60. Carter N. (199 1). Learning to measure performance: the use of indicators in organisations. Public Administration 69: 85-101.
61. Carver R. P. (1978). The case against significance testing. Harvard Educational Review 48, 3: 378-399.
62. Chamberlin E. H. (1933). The theory of monopolistic competition. Harvard University Press. Cambridge. MA.
63. Chambers R-J. (1965). Measurement in accounting. Journal of Accounting Research 3, 1: 32-62.
64. Charnes A., Cooper W., and RHOADES E. (1978). Measuring the efficiency of decision making units. European Journal of Operation Research 2: 429-444.
65. Chen T. (1997). An evaluation of the relative performance of university libraries in Taipei. Asian Libraries 6, V23: 9-50.

66. Churcibaan C. (1971). On the facility, felicity, and morality of measuring social change. Accounting Review XLVI, 1: 30-35.
67. Clark-Carter D. (2001). Doing quantitative psychological research: from design to report. Psychology Press Ltd. East Sussex, UK.
68. Clarke A- and Rosen R- (2001). Length of stay: how short should hospital care be? European Journal of Public Health 11: 166-170.
69. Cleverly W. 0. (1993). The 1993 Almanac of Hospital Financial & Operating Indicators. Columbus, Ohio: The Center for Healthcare Industry Performance Studies.
70. Coh. C., Patuwo B. E., & Hu M. Y. (1998). The human factor in advanced manufacturing technology adoption: an empirical analysis. International Journal of Operations & Production Management 18, 1: 87-106.
71. Cohen J. (1988). Statistical power analysis for the behavioural sciences (2nd Ed.). Lawrence Erlbaum Associates. Hillsdale, NJ.
72. Cohen L. & Holliday M. (1982). Statistics for social sciences. Harper & Row. London.
73. Cohen L., Manion L. and Morrison K. (2000). Research methods in education. Routledge Falmer. London.
74. Cohen S., Lichtenstein E., Prochaska J. O., Rossi J. S., Gritz E. R, Carr C. R., Prleans C. T., SChoenbach V. J., Beiner L., Abrams D., Diclementi C., & Curry C. R (1989). Debunking myths about self-quitting: evidence from 10 prospective studies of persons who attempted to quit smoking by themselves. American Psychologist 44: 1355-1365.
75. Conner K. R. (1991). A historical comparison of resource-based theory and five schools of thought within industrial organisation economies: do we have a new theory of the firm? Journal of Management 17: 121-154.

76. Cooper C. A. & Rhodes W. W. (1978). Measuring the efficiency of decision makingunits. European Journal of Operational Research 2, 6: 429-444.
77. Cornelius N. and Gooch L. (2001). Performance management: strater, systems and rewards. In Human resource management: a managerial perspective, 2nd ed., edited by Nelarine Cornelius, pp: 141-177. Thomson Learning. London.
78. Corston R. & Colman A- M. (1996). Gender and social facilitation effects on computer competence and attitudes toward computers. Journal of Educational Computing Research 14: 171-183.
79. Cox T. and Blake S. (1991). Managing cultural diversity: implications for organisation a competitiveness T. h e Executive5: 4 5-56.
80. Cronbach L. J. (195 1). Coefficient alpha and the internal structure of tests. Psychometrica 16: 2, 97-334.
81. Central Advisory Board of Education (CABE). 2005. 'Universalisation of Secondary Education'. Report of the Central Advisory Board of Education Committee.
82. Chakrabarty, K. C. 2011. 'Indian Education System: Issues and Challenges'. JRE.
83. Caldas, S. J. & Bankston III, C. (1998). The inequality of separation: Racial composition of schools and academic achievement. Educational Administration Quarterly, 34 (4), 533-557.
84. Carpenter, H. H. (1971). Formal organisational structural factors and perceived job satisfaction of classroom teachers. Administrative Science Quarterly, 16 (4), 460-465.
85. Chapman, J. & Boyd, W. L. (1986). Decentralisation, devolution and the school principal: Australian lessons on statewide education reforms. Educational administration Quarterly, 22 (4), 28-58.
86. Connolly, T., Conlon, E. J. & Deutsch, S. J. (1980). Organisational effectiveness: A multiple constituency

approach. Academy of Management Review, 5 (2), 211-217.

87. Conway, J. A. (1976). Test of linearity between teacher's participation in decision making and their perceptions of their schools as organisations. Administrative Science Quarterly, 21 (1), 130-139.
88. Crow, G. M. & Pounder, D. G. (2000). Interdisciplinary teacher teams: Context, design and process. Educational Administration Quarterly, 36 (2), 216-254.
89. Cunningham, J. B. (1977). Approaches to the evaluation of organisational effectiveness. Academy of Management Review, 2 (3), 463-474.
90. Day, C., Harris, A., & Hadfield, M. (2001). Grounding knowledge of schools in stakeholder realities: A multi-perspective study of effective school leaders. School Leadership & Management, 21 (1), 19-42.
91. Department of School Education and Literacy, Ministry of Human Resource Development, Government of India. 'Working Group Report on Secondary and Vocational Education: 12th Five Year Plan (2012–2017) '.
92. Daniels S. (1997). Back to basic with productivity techniques. Work Study 46, 2: 52-57.
93. Day G. S. (1994). The capabilities of market-driven organisations. Journal of Marketing 58: 37-52.
94. De Cenzo D. & Robbins S. (1994). Human resource management: concepts and practices. Wiley. New York.
95. Delaney J. T, Lew in D., & Ichniowski C. (1989). Human resource policies and practices in American firms. Washington, DC: U. S. Government Printing Office.
96. Delaney J. T. & Huselid M. A. (1996). The impact of human resource management practices on perceptions of organisational performance. Academy of Management Journal 39, 4: 949-969.

97. Delery J. E. and Doty D. H. (1996). Modes of theorizing in strategic human resource management: tests of universalistic, contingency, and configurational performance predictions. Academy of Management Journal 39: 802-835.

98. Deming W. E. (1986). Out of the crisis: quality, productivity, and competitive position. Cambridge University Press. Cambridge.

99. Devanna M. A, Fombrum C. J. and Tichy N. M. (1984). A framework for strategic human resource management. Wiley. New York.

100. Evans J. R. and Lindsay M. W. (1999). The management and control of quality. South Western College Publishing. Cincinnati. Ohio. Journal of Operations & Production Management, Vol. 14 No. 5, pp. 35-51.

101. Fahy J. (2000). The resource-based view of the firm: some stumbling blocks on the road to understanding sustainable competitive advantage. Journal of European Industrial Training 24/2/3/49: 4-104.

102. Farer & Grosskopf S. (1994). Measuring productivity: a comment. International Journal of Operations and Production Management 14, 9: 8 3-88.

103. Fazio R. H., Jackson J. R., Dunton B. C., & Williams C. J. (1996). Variability in automatic activation as an unobtrusive measure of racial attitudes: A bonafide pipeline. Journal of Personality and Social Psychology 69: 1013-1027.

104. Fey C. F., Bjorkman. and Pavlovskaya A. (2000). The effect of human resource management practices on firm performance in Russia. International Journal of Human Resource Management 11, 1: 1-18.

105. Fitzgerald L., Johnston R., Brignal T. J., Selvistro R. and Voss C. (1991). Performance measurement in service business. CIMA, London.

106. Fitzgerald L., Johnston R., Brignall S., Silvestro R. and Voss, C. (1991). Performance measurement in Service Businesses. CIMA. Black Bear Press Ltd. King's Hedges Road, Cambridge.

107. Flamholtz E. & Lacey J. (1981). Personnel management: human capital theory and human resource accounting. Institute of Industrial Relations. Los Angeles. CA.

108. Fombrum C., Tichy N. M., & Devanna M. A. (1984). Strategic human resource management. Wiley. New York.

109. Foster J. J. (2001). Data analysis using SPSS for Windows. Sage. London.

110. Framee R. M., Nielsen W. R. and Patel. E. (1989). Creating excellence out of crisis: organisational transformation at the Chicago Tribune. Journal of Applied Behavioural Science 25, 2: 109-122.

111. Gerhart B. and Milkovich G. T. (1990). Organisational differences in managerial compensation and firm performance. Academy of Management Journal 33: 663-691.

112. Ghobadian A- and Aservorth J. (1994). Performance measurement in local government- concept and practice. International Journal of Operations & Production Management 14, 5: 35-51.

113. Ghobadian, A and Ashworth, J (1994), Performance Measurement in Local Government – Concept and Practice, International.

114. Golden K. and Ramanujam V. (1985). Between a dream and a nightmare: on the integration of the human resource management and strategic business planning processes. Human Resource Management 24: 429-452.

115. Gamoran, A., & Dreeben, R. (1986). Coupling and control in educational organisations. Administrative Science Quarterly, 31 (4), 612-632.

116. Goddard, R. D., Sweetland, S. R. & Hoy W. K. (2000). Academic emphasis of urban elementary schools and student achievement in reading and mathematics: A multilevel analysis. Educational Administration Quarterly, 36 (5), 683-702.

117. Gray, J., & Wilcox, B. (1995). Good school, bad school: Evaluating performance and encouraging improvement. Buckingham, UK: Open University Press. Greenfield, W. D. Jr. (1995). Towards a theory of school administration: The centrality of leadership. Educational Administration Quarterly, 3 (1), 61–85.

118. Griffith, J. (2002). Is quality/effectiveness an empirically demonstrable school attribute? Statistical aids for determining appropriate levels of analysis. School Effectiveness and School Improvement, 13 (1), 91–122.

119. Gupta,. M. A & Vohra, N. (2010). Measuring Effectiveness of Schools in India: A Multiple Stakeholder Framework. e-Journal of Organisational Learning and Leadership. Volume 8, No. 2.

120. Guest D. & Hoque K. (1994). The good, the bad, and the ugly: human resource management in new non-union establishments. The International Journal of Human Resource Management 5, 1: 1-14.

121. Guest D. (1987). Human resource management and industrial relations. Journal of Management Science 24, 5: 503-521.

122. Guest D. (1989b). Personnel and HRM: can you tell the difference? Personnel Management, January: 48-51.

123. Guest D. (1995). Human resource management, trade unions and industrial relations.

124. GUEST D. E. (1997). Human resource management and performance: a review and Research agenda. International Journal of Human Resource Management, 83: 263- 276.

125. Guest D. E. (2001). Human resource management: when research confronts theory.

126. International Journal of Human resource Management, November: 920-1106.

127. Gupta M. and Zbender D. (1994). Outsourcing and its impact on operations strategy. Production and Inventory Management Journal 35, 3: 70-75.

128. Government of India (GoI). 'Sarva Shiksha Abhiyan. Education for All'. Retreived from: http: //india. gov. in/spotlight/spotlight_archive. php?id=31. Accessed 12 October 2013.

129. Government of India (GoI). 2011. '237th Report on the Foreign Educational Institutions Regulation of Entry and Operations Bill, 2010', Department-Related Parliamentary Standing Committee on Human Resource Development.

130. Hall R. (1992). The strategic analysis of intangible resources. Strategic Management Journal 13: 135-144.

131. Hall, J. W. (1972). A comparison of Halpin and Croft's organisational climates and Likert and Likert's organisational systems. Administrative Science Quarterly, 17 (4), 586-590

132. Hall R. (1993). A framework linking intangible resources and capabilities to outstanding competitive advantage. Strategic Management Journal 14: 607-618.

133. Hendry C. & Petrigrew A. (1990). Human resource management: an agenda for the 1990s. International Journal of Human Resource Management, 1: 17-44.

134. Hendry C., Woodward S., and BRADLEY P. (2000). Performance and rewards: out the stables. Human Resource Management Journal 10, 3: 46-62.

135. Hinkle E. D., Wires W., & Jurs G. S. (1979). Applied statistics for behavioural sciences. Rand McNally Publishing Company. Chicago, IL.

136. Holland W. W. (1983). Evaluation of health care. Oxford University Press. Oxford.

137. Hoppock R. (1935). Job satisfaction. Amo Press. New York.

138. Hunt S. D., Chonko L. B., & Wood V. R. (1985). Organisational commitment and marketing. Journal of Marketing 49: 112-126.

139. Huselid M. (1995). The impact of human resource management practices on turnover, productivity, and corporate financial performance. Academy of Management Journal 38, 3: 63 5-672.

140. Huselid M. A. and Becker B. E. (1996).Methodological issues in cross-sectional and panel estimates of the human resource-firm performance link. Industrial Relations 35, 3: 400-422.

141. Huselid M. A., Jackson S. E. & Schuler R. S. (1997). Technical and strategic human resource management effectiveness as determinants of firm performance. Academy of Management Journal 40: 171-188.

142. India Country Report 2013 by Ministry of Statistics and Program Implementation, Government of India

143. Ichniowski C., Shaw K., & Prennushi G. (1997). The effects of human resource management practices on productivity: a case study of steel finishing lines. American Economic Review 87, 3: 291-313.

144. Institute of Personnel and Development (1992). Performance management. London.

145. Indian Express 16 March 2010. 'Top Educational Institutions Hail Foreign Varsity Bill', .

146. Institute of Chartered Accountants of India (ICAI). 2010. Technical Guide on Internal Audit of Educational Institutions. New Delhi: Institute of Chartered Accountants of India.

147. Inn K. Rowland and G. Ferris (Eds.), Research in personnel and human resource management, vol. 10: 271-299. JAI Press. Greenwich, CT.

148. Johnson M. (1997). Outsourcing in brief, butter worth-Heinemann. Oxford.

149. Jones G. R and Wright P.M. (1992). An economic approach to conceptualizing the utility of human resource management practices.

150. Juneja Nalini (2003). 'Constitutional Amendment to Make Education a Fundamental Right: Issues for a Follow-up Legislation'. National Institute of Education Planning and Administration.

151. Jones G. T. (2000). Indicator-based systems of performance management in the National Health Service: a comparison of the perceptions of local- and national-level managers. Health Services Management Research 13: 16. 26.

152. Kane B. and Palmer L. (1995). Strategic HRM or managing the employment relationship? International Journal of Manpower 5, 6: 6-21.

153. Kangis P. and Williams D. G. S. (2000). Organisational climate and corporate Performance: an empirical investigation. Management decision38, 8: 531-540.

154. Kaplan R. S. (1983). Measuring manufacturing performance: a new challenge for managerial accounting research. The Accounting Review, October 686-705.

155. Kaplan R. S. and Norton D .P. (1992). The balanced scorecard- measures that drive performance. Harvard Business Review, January-February 71-7 9.

156. Kaplan R. S .and Norton D. P. (1993). Putting the balanced scorecard to work. Harvard Business Review, September-October. 134-142.

157. Kaplan R. S. and Norton D. P . (1996). Using the balanced scorecard as a strategic management system. Harvard Business Review, January-February 75-85.

158. Katz C., Kochan T. A., & Weber N. R. (1985). Assessing the effects of industrial relations systems and efforts to improve the quality of world go on Organisation ffectiveness. Academy o f Management Journal28, 3: 509-526.

159. Kazmier L. J (1974). Principles of management: a programd-instructional approach. McGraw-Hill Inc. New York.

160. Kearns P. (1994). Human resource-measuring effectiveness inTraining and Development 12, 6: 1 1-14.

161. KERR C. A., GLASS J. C., MCCALLION G. NL and McKILLOP D.G. (1999). Best practice measures of resource utilisation for hospitals: a useful complement in Performance assessment public Administration 77, 3: 639-650.

162. Keppel G. (199 1). Design and analysis: a researcher's handbook (Yd Ed.) . Prentice-Hall.Englewood Cliffs. NJ.

163. Kerlinger F. N. (1973).Foundations of behavioural research. Holt, Rinehart and Winston, Inc. New York.

164. King D. A & Daniel L. G. (1996). Psychometric integrity of the self-esteem index: a comparison of normative and field study results. Educational and Psychological Measurement 56: 537-550.

165. Kline P. (1992). The handbook of psychological testing. Routlege. London.

166. Kline P. (1997). An easy guide to factor analysis. Routlege. London

167. Kloot L. (1999). Performance measurement and accountability in Victorian local government. The International Journal of Public Sector Management 12, 7: 565-583

168. Kociian T., Katz, and Wkersie R. (1986). The transformation of American industrial relations. Basic Books. New York.

169. Krejcie R. V. and Morgan D. W. (1970). Determining sample size for research activities. Educational and Psychological Measurements 30: 6 07-610.

170. Kapur, Devesh and Mehta (2004). 'Indian Higher Education Reform: From Half-Baked Socialism to

Half-Baked Capitalism'. Working Paper no.108, Center for International Development, Harvard University, September.

171. Kuntz L (1996). Sensitivity of efficient technologies in data envelopment analysis. Judge Institute of Management Studies. Cambridge. UK.

172. Lahteenmaki S., Storey J. (1998). HRM and company Performancc-The use of measurement and the influence of economic cycles. Human Resource Management journal 8, 2: 51-65.

173. Lazear E. P. (1995).Personnel economics.MIT Press. Boston, MA.

174. Legge V, (I 995b). Human resource management: Rhetorics and realities. M acmillan.

175. Basingstoke.

176. Lengnick-Hall C. A- and Lengnick-Hall M.L. (1988). Strategic human resource management: a review of the literature and a proposed typology. Academy of Management Review 13: 454-470.

177. Levene (1960). Robust tests for equality of variances. In Olkin 1. (ed.), Contributions to probability and statistics. Stanford University Press. Stanford. CA.

178. Lewin A. Y. and Minton L. W. (1986). Determining organisational effectiveness: another look at an agenda for research Management Science 32, 5: 514-538.

179. Lewis D. S. (1994). Organisational change: relationship between reactions, behaviour and organisational performance. Journal of Organisational Change Management 5: 41-55

180. Longo D.R. and Bohr D. B. (199 1). Quantitative methods in quality management: A guide for practitioners. American Hospital Publishing, Inc. Chicago.

181. Loomba N. P. (1978). Management: a quantitative perspective. Collier Macmillan Publisher. London.

182. Lord F. M. (1953).On the statistical treatment of football numbers. American Psychologist 8: 750-751.

183. Lynch R-L and Cross KF. (1991). Measuring Up Yardsticks for continuous improvement. Basil Blackwell, Oxford.

184. Macduffie J. P. (1995). Human resource bundles and manufacturing performance: Organisational logic and flexible production systems in the world auto industry. Industrial and Labour Relations Review 48, 2: 197-220.

185. Mahoney J. T. & Pandian J. R (1992). The resource-based view within the conversation of strategic management. Strategic Management Journal 13: 3 63-380.

186. Mawaide H. S., Hayajneh Y. and Al-Qutob R. (1997). The effect of type of Hospital and health insurance on hospital length of stay in Irbid, North Jordan. Health Policy and Planning 12, 2: 166-172.

187. Maxwell S. E. (1980). Pair-Wise multiple comparison in repeated measures designs. Journal of Educational Statistics 5: 2 69-287.

188. Mayo I. (1946). The human problems of an industrial civilisation. H arvard University Graduate School of Business Administration. Cambridge M. A.

189. Meyer A. D., Tsui A. S., and Hinings C . R. (1993). Configurational approaches to Organisational analysis. Academy of Management Journal. 36: 1, 175-79.

190. Meyer E. N. L. & Jones C.A. (1976).A statistical analysis of behaviour. Wods worth Publishing Company. Belmont, California.

191. Ministry of Human Resource Development (MHRD). 'Institutions of National Importance'. Retreived from: http: //mhrd. gov. in/instiutions_imp . Assessed on: 12 October 2013.

192. Meyer J. P. & Allen N. J. (199 1).A three-component conceptualisation of organisational commitment. Human Resource Management Review 1: 64-98.

193. Miles R. and Snow C. (1984). Designing strategic human resource systerns.

194. Organisational Dynamics, Summer 3: 6-52.

195. Miller D. C. & Salkind N. J. (2002).Handbook of research design & social measurement. Sage. London.

196. Miller P. (1987). Strategic industrial relations and human resource management: distinction, definition, and recognition. Journal of Management Studies 24, 4: 347-3 6 1.

197. Miller P. (199 1). Strategic human resource management: an assessment of progress. Human Resource Management Journal 1: 23-39.

198. Morrison K. R. B. (1993). Planning and accomplishing School-centerd Evaluation. Peter Francis Publishers. Norfolk.

199. Mowday R. T. .Steers R.M., and Potter L. W. (1979). The measurement of organisational commitment. Journal of Vocational Behaviour 14: 224-247.

200. Ministry of Human Resource Development, Government of India, 'Report to the People on Education 2010–11'.

201. Ministry of Labour and Employment. 2011. 'Report of the Working Group on Skill Development and Training: 12th Five Year Plan (2012–2017) '. Ministry of Labour and Employment, Government of India.

202. National Bureau of Statistics (NBS) of China. 2007. China Statistical Yearbook 2007. Beijing: China Statistics Press.

203. National Knowledge Commission (NKC). 2007. Recommendations on School Education. New Delhi: National Knowledge Commission, Government of India.

204. National University of Educational Planning and Administration (NUEPA). 2009. 'Elementary Education in India: Progress towards UEE — Flash Statistics 2007–08'. District Information System for Education, National University of Educational Planning and Administration.

205. Nanni A. J, Dixon JAL and Vollnlann T. E. (1990). Strategic control and Performance measurement. Journal of Cost Management, Summer 3: 342.

206. Nanni AJ, Dixon J. R. and Mann T. E. (1992). Integrated performance measurement: Management accounting to support the new realities. Journal of Management Accounting Research. Fall: 1-1 9.

207. Nerdrum L., Erikson T. (2001). Intellectual capital: a human capital Perspective. Journal of Intellectual capital 2, 2: 127-135.

208. Newman J. (1977). Development of a measure of perceived work environment. Academy of Management Journal 20: 520-534.

209. Ngo H., Turban D., Lau C., & Yun S. (1998). Human resource practices and firm performance of multinational corporations: influences of country origin. The International Journal of Human Resource Management, 94: 633-651 .

210. Official Website: Department of Higher Education-Ministry of Human Resource Department, Government of India - Retreived from: http: //mhrd. gov. in/ overview_uni_higher_english. Assessed on: 11 August, 2014.

211. Official Website: CBSE, Retreived from: http: //cbse. nic.in/affili~1/aff. pdf. Assessed on: 13th September, 2014.

212. Official Website: NUEPA. Retreived from: http: //www. nuepa. org/Download/Publications/NUEPAR-2009-10-Eng. pdf. Assessed on: 10 August 2015.

213. Official Website: MHRD. Retreived from: http: //mhrd. gov. in/node/16. Assessed on: 5 January 2015.

214. Official Website: National Center for Education Statistics (NCES). 2010. The Condition of Education 2010. Washington, DC: National Center for Education Statistics, Institute for Education Sciences, US Department of Education. Retreived from: http: //nces. ed. gov/pubs2010/20100 28. pdf .Accessed 16 July 2014.

215. Official Website: The Hindu. Retreived from: http: // www. thehindu. com/todays-paper/tp-national/tp-kerala/directive-to-cbseicse-boards-on-teachers-salary/article3899741. ece. Assessed on: 2 January 2015. Official Website: Planning Commission of India. Retreived from: http: //planningcommission. nic.in/ plans/stateplan/Presentations12_13/jharkhand12_13. pdf. Assessed on: 15 February 2014.

216. Official Website: CIPD, Retreived from: http: //www. cipd. co. uk/NR/rdonlyres/64B9C9FD-8168-4EDC-9B71- DD3D8B5C2B90/0/performance_management_ discussion_paper. pdf. Assessed on: 15 February 2014.

218. Official Website: World Bank. Retreived from: http: / /data. worldbank. org/indicator/SE. XPD. SECO.PC. ZS/countries/IN-8S-XN?display=default. Assessed on: 1 March 2014.

219. Official Website: PWC. Retreived from https: //www. pwc. in/assets/pdfs/industries/education/publication/ pwcreportredefininghighereducation. pdf. Assessed on: 18 November 2015.

220. Official Website: Department of School Education and Literacy. 'Vocational Education'. Department of School Education and Literacy, Ministry of Human Resource Development, Government of India. Retreived from: http: //mhrd. gov. in/voc_eduu Accessed on: 11 October 2012.

221. Official website: Ministry of Human Resource Development. '172nd Report on University and Higher

Education', Department-Related Parliamentary Standing Committee on Human Resource Development.Retreived from: http: //164. 100. 47. 5/newcommittee/reports/EnglishCommittees/Committee%20on%20HRD/172ndreport.htm. Accessed on: 10 October 2014.

222. Official Website: Ministry of Human Resource Development, Government of India 'Report of the Committee for Review of Existing Institutions Deemed to be Universities (2009) '. Retereived from:

223. http: //mhrd. gov. in/sites/upload_files/mhrd/fi les/RepoRevCom-DmdUniv. pdf. Assessed 18 October 2015.

224. Official Website: UGC. Retreived from: http: //www. ugc. ac. in/oldpdf/xplanpdf/academisstaffcollege. pdf. Assessed on: 2 January 2015.

225. Official Website: UNICEF. Retreived from: http: // www. unicef. org/india/education. html. Assessed on: 2 January 2015.

226. Official Website: U. S. Department of Commerce. Retreived from: https: //www. census. gov/population/international/files/ib-9701. pdf. Assessed on: 2 January 2015.

227. OskampS . (1977). Attitudes and opinions. Prentice Hall, Englewood Cliffs, NJ.

228. Osters .A (1996). Non-profit organisations and their local affiliates: a study in organisational forms. Journal of Economic Behaviour and Organisation 30, 1: 83-95.

229. Palmer A. J. (1993). Performance measurement local government. Public Money and management, October-December 31-36.

230. ParasuramanA-. Zeithanil V. A., &Sherryl L. (1985). A conceptual model of service quality and its implications for future research. Journal of Marketing 49: 41-55.

231. Parker C. (2000). Performance measurements Work Study 49, 2: 63- 66.

232. Parkin D. & Hollingsworth B. (1997). Measuring production efficiency of acute hospitals in Scotland, 1991-1994: validity issues in data envelopment analysis. Applied Economy 29: 1425-1433.

233. Patterson M. G., West M. A., Laytitiom R-, & NickelL S. (1997). Impact of people management practices on business performance. Institute of Personnel and Development. London.

234. Peck S. R. (1994). Explaining the link between organisational strategy and the employment relationship: the role of human resources policies. Journal of Management Studies 31: 715-736.

235. Penrose E. (1959). The theory of growth of the firm. Blackwell. Oxford.

236. Pfeffer J. (1994). Competitive advantage through people. Harvard Business School Press. Boston.

237. Pfeffer J. (1998). The human equation. Harvard Business School. Boston, MA.

238. Pitt L. F., Foreman S. K., & Bromfield D. (1995). Organisational commitment and service delivery: evidence from an industrial setting in the UK. The International Journal of Human Resource Management 6, 1: 369-389.

239. Porter L. W., Steers R. M., Mowday R. T. and Boulian P. V. (1974). Organisational commitment, job satisfaction and turnover among psychiatric technicians. Journal of Applied Psychology 59, 5: 603-609.

240. Prior D. (1996). Technical efficiency and scope economies in hospitals. Applied Economics 28: 1295-1301.

241. Quick J. C. (1992). Crafting an organisational culture: Herb's hand at Southwest Airlines. Organisational Dynamics 21, 2: 45-56.

242. Quinn J. B., Anderson P., & Finkelstein S. (1996). Leveraging intellect. Management Executive 10: 7-27.

243. Robinsonj. (1933). The economics of imperfect competition. Macmillan Press. London.
244. Rondeau K. V. & Wagar T. H. (2001). The impact of human resource management practices on nursing home performance. Health Services Management Research 14: 1-12.
245. Rudestam K. E. Newton R- R- (2001). Surviving your dissertation: a comprehensive guide to content and process (2 nd Edition). Sage Publications Inc. London.
246. Russell J., Ter13org J., and Power S M. (1985). organisational performance and organisational level training and support. Personnel Psychology 38: 849-863.
247. Ryan A- M., Schmit M. J. and Johnson R_ (1996). Attitudes and effectiveness: examining relations at an organisational level. Personnel Psychology 49: 853-882.
248. Schneider B., Parkington J. and Buxton V. (1980) Employment and customer perceptions of service in banks. Administrative Science Quarterly 25: 252-267.
249. Schuler K S. and Jachson S. (1987a). Linking competitive strategies with human resource management practices. Academy of Management Executive 1, 3: 207-219.
250. Schuler R_ S- and Jachson S. (1999). Strategic human resource management. Blackwell. London.
251. Schuler R_ S., Dowling P. J., and De cieri H. (1993). An integrative framework of strategic international human resource management. Journal of Management 19, 2: 419-459.
252. Shian L. L. (1990). A study of the relationship of quality circles to job satisfaction, absenteeism and turnover of nurses and patients' satisfaction with nursing care in Taiwan, Ph. D. dissertation. George Mason University.
253. Sicotte C. and Btland F. (2001). The effect of medical work groups on hospital resource use. Health Services Management Research 14: 165-180.

254. Siegel S. & Castellan N.J. (1988). Non-parametric statistics for the behavioural sciences (2nd Ed.). McGraw-Hill. New York.

255. Smith A. (1776). An inquiry into the nature and causes of the wealth of nations. In Campbell, Skinner, and Todd (Ed.). Clarendon Press. Oxford.

256. Smith A- and Hayton G. (1998). What drives enterprise training? Evidence from Australia. Routledge. London.

257. Smith P. andMayston (1987). Measuring efficiency in the public sector. OMEGA 15, 3: 181-189.

258. Sparrow P. and Hiltrop J. (1994). European human resource management in transition. Prentice Hall. London.

259. Stevens J. (1996). Applied multivariate statistics for the social sciences (3 rd Ed.). Lawrence Erlbaum. I-Ellsdale, NJ.

260. Stinchfied R_ D. Burlingame G.M. (199 1). Development and use of the directive rating system in group therapy. Journal of Counselling Psychology 38, 3: 253.

261. Stogdill R_ M. (1974). Handbook of leadership: a survey of theory and research. Free Press. New York.

262. Storey I (1992). Development in the management of human resources. Blackwell. Oxford.

263. The Times of India, Ranchi. 3 December 2012. "Education takes a backseat in Jharkhand".

264. Thompson B. & Daniel L. (1996). Factor analyticevidence for the construct validity of scores: a historical overview and some guidelines. Educational and Psychological measurement 56, 2: 197-208.

265. Thompson B. (1998). In praise of brilliance: where that praise really belongs. American Psychologist 53: 799-800.

266. Thompson B .and Snyder P. A. (1997).Statistical significance testing practices. Journal of Experimental education 66: 75-83.

267. Truss C., Gratton L., Hope-Hailey V., McGoverN P., & StileS P. (1997). Soft and hard models of human resource management: a reappraisal. Journal of Management Studies 34, 1: 53-73.

268. Tyson S. (1995). Human resource strategy. Pitman. London.

269. UdvarbelY I., Goldman L., Komaro F. A., and Lee T. (1992). Determinants of resource utilisation for patients admitted for evaluation of acute chest pain. Journal of General Internal Medicine 7, 1: 1-10.

270. Ulrich D. (1998). Intellectual capital = competence x commitment. Sloan Management Review 39: 15-30.

271. Van De Ven A. & Ferry D. (1979). Measuring and assessing organisations. Wiley. New York.

272. Venkatraman N. andRamanujan V. (1987). Measurement of business economic performance: an examination of method convergence. Journal of Management 13, 1: 109-123.

273. Vroom V. H. (1964). Work and motivation. John Wiley. New York.

274. Walker J. (1992). Human resource strategy. McGraw-Hill. New York.

275. Wallach E. (1983). Individuals and organisation: the cultural match. Training and Development Journal 12: 28-36.

276. Walton R. E. (1985). From control to commitment in the workplace. Harvard Business Review 63, 2: 76-84.

277. Ware J. E., Brook R. H., Davies A. R, andLohr K. N. (198 1). Choosing measures of health status for individuals in general populations. American Journal of Public Health 71, 6: 620-625.

278. Warner M. (2000). Regional encyclopaedia of business and management: Management in Asia-Pacific. Business Press-Thomas Learning. New York.

279. Warner, W. Keith (1967). Problems in measuring the goal attainment of voluntary organisations. Journal of Adult education, 19: 3-14.

280. Weis D. (1992). Uninsured maternity clients: a concern for quality. Applied NursingResearch 5, 2: 74-82.

281. Weiss D.J., Davis R. S., England G. W., & Lofquist L. H. (1970). Manual for the Minnesota Satisfaction Questionnaire, Industrial Relations Center, University of Minnesota.

282. Weiss D. J., Davis R. S., England G. W., and Lofquist L. H. (1967). Manual for the Minnesota satisfaction questionnaire. Minnesota Studies in Vocational Rehabilitation, p. xxii.

283. Welch J. R- &Kleiner B. H. (1995). New development in hospital management.

284. Health Manpower Management 21, 5: 32-3 5.

285. Wiley J. W. (1990). Customer satisfaction: a supportive work environment and its fmancial cost. Human Resource Planning 14: 117-127.

286. Wilson C. L., Wilson J. L., &wilson K. B. (1996). Meaningful measures. Silver Spring, MD: Clark Wilson Group, Inc.

287. Wisner J. D. and Fawcett S. E. (199 1) Linking firm strategy to operating decisionsthrough performance measurement. International Journal of Operations & ProductionManagement 16, 3: 4246.

288. Wright D. B. (1998). Understanding statistics: an introduction for the social sciences. Sage Publications. London.

289. Wright P. and Snell S. (1998). Towards a unifying framework for exploring fit and flexibility in strategic human resource management. Academy of Management Review 23: 756-772.

290. Wright P. M. & McMahan G. C. (1992). Theoretical perspectives for strategic human resource management. Journal of Management 18: 295-320.

291. Wright P. M., McMahan G. C. and McWilliams A. (1994). Human resources and sustained competitive advantage: a resource-based perspective. International Journal of Human Resource Management 5, 2: 301-326.

292. 'All India Survey on Higher Education: Pilot Report'. Planning, Monitoring & Statistics Bureau, Department of Higher Education, Ministry of Human Resource Development, Government of India.

293. Annual Report 2010–11. New Delhi: Department of School Education & Literacy and Department of Higher Education, Ministry of Human Resource Development, Government of India.

294. 'Consolidated Working Group Report of the Department of Higher Education for XII Five Year Plan on Higher Education, Technical Education and Private Sector participation including PPP in Higher Education'. Department of Higher Education, Ministry of Human Resource Development, Government of India.

295. 'Statistics of School Education, 2009–10 (Provisional)'. Bureau of Planning, Monitoring and Statistics, Mini-stry of Human Resource Development, Government of India.

ABBREVIATIONS

APCERT	–	Asia Pacific Computer Emergency Response Team
ARF	–	ASEAN Regional Forum
ASEAN	–	Association of Southeast Asian Nations
BTWC	–	Convention on the Prohibition of the Development, Production and Stockpiling of Bacteriological (Biological) and Toxin Weapons and on their Destruction.
CBM	–	Confidence-Building Measure
CCBM	–	Civil Confidence-Building Measure
CCDCOE NATO	–	Cooperative Cyber Defence Centre of Excellence
CERT	–	Computer Emergency Eesponse Team
CFE	–	Treaty on Conventional Armed Forces in Europe
CFSP European	–	Common Foreign and Security Policy
CICTE OAS	–	Inter-American Committee Against Terrorism
CIRT	–	computer incident response team
CSBM	–	confidence- and security-building measure
CSIRT	–	computer security incident response team
CWC	–	Convention on the Prohibition of the Development, Production, Stockpiling and Use of Chemical Weapons and on Their Destruction
GGE	–	group of governmental experts
IAEA	–	International Atomic Energy Agency
ICT	–	information and communications technology
ITU	–	International Telecommunication Union
NATO	–	North Atlantic Treaty Organisation

NPT	–	Treaty on the Non-Proliferation of Nuclear Weapons
OAS	–	Organisation of American States
OECD	–	Organisation for Economic Co-operation and Development
OPCW	–	Organisation for the Prohibition of Chemical Weapons
OSCE	–	Organisation for Security and Co-operation in Europe
OST	–	Treaty on Principles Governing the Activities of States in the Exploration and Use of Outer Space, Including the Moon and Other Celestial Bodies
SCO	–	Shanghai Cooperation Organisation
TCBM	–	transparency and confidence-building measure

INDEX

A

B

C

D

E

F

J

K

L

M

N

O

T

U